The Story of My Life

The Story of My Life

Dosebai Cowasjee Jessawalla

SPEAKING TIGER

SPEAKING TIGER BOOKS LLP
125A, Ground Floor, Shahpur Jat, near Asiad Village,
New Delhi 110049

First published in 1911
This edition published by Speaking Tiger Books in 2023

ISBN: 978-93-5447-043-1
eISBN: 978-93-5447-051-6

10 9 8 7 6 5 4 3 2 1

Typeset in Minion Regular by SÜRYA, New Delhi
Printed at Chaman Enterprises, New Delhi

To the memory of my beloved mother Meheribai who, by giving me the privilege of being the first Indian girl to receive the benefits of English education, laid the foundation in the middle of the nineteenth century of the noble movement for the dissemination of higher culture among the women of His Majesty's Indian Empire, and who inspired me with that public spirit and self-sacrificing zeal which led me to pioneer many social reforms among my Indian sisters, this record of my life and work is most gratefully and affectionately dedicated.

CONTENTS

INTRODUCTION

Packing for Balloons

There are many reasons to read *The Story of My Life*, the magisterial autobiography of Dosebai Cowasjee Jessawalla (24 August 1832–11 January 1911).

You could read it for nostalgia, which may be the crudest, simplest reason to read any hundred-and-more-year-old autobiography. I have no time for nostalgia myself because it always seems to me to be a feeling that comes over a class of people when they consider a time when they had power, which time and circumstance has stripped from them.

And yet, I am among those who used her book for that very reason, selecting scenes out of it to fit into an anthology of writings on Bombay that Ravi Singh commissioned when he was at Penguin and which Naresh Fernandes and I edited: *Bombay, Meri Jaan: Writings on Mumbai*. What could be more Bombay than a piece by Khada Parsi's granddaughter? On my way to my grandmother's home in Byculla, I had passed the statue of this venerable Parsi philanthropist who stared bleakly out over a rising tide of cement. Fernandes and I placed the piece between a poem by Kipling—Dosebai and Rudyard shared an enthusiasm for the Raj—and an excerpt from Daya Pawar's seminal autobiography *Baluta*. We liked the characters standing next to each other: the boy who was born in Bombay and was frightened by the hens of Mahim, the affluent upper-class Parsi lady in the white English satin sari she had embroidered herself, the Dalit poet whose grandmother cleaned the veterinary clinic. There was a rhythm here too, Kipling with his ships, Pawar's grandmother talking of horse-drawn trams, and Dosebai going up in balloons. And all this turning on that same corner on which Set Cursetjee Manekjee would become a landmark. ('Turn left at Khada Parsi...')

But this is an important book because it is written by an interesting woman. I believe that if Dosebai were alive today, she would have been a feminist. She may speak often of the weaker sex but in all the things that matter, she knows her rights, and she will have them. (And as we see, she also knows the rights she doesn't have.) She believes in education for women. Her bravery and her feminism run in the family, I believe. Her mother Meheribai Guzdar made the life-changing decision of getting her daughter a British education.

It sounds like a sensible decision. Which parent does not want to give their child a good start in life? But that wasn't how it was seen then. Meheribai had to face criticism from the community and sarcastic remarks in the popular press for putting her daughter in Mrs Ward's Seminary. However, she did not let that deter her and the result was that Dosebai could move easily in both Indian and Western society. No wonder Dosebai works hard at correcting the record when female education in the Parsi community is attributed to the doings of men.

You could also read this book as a way of looking at the cultural evolution of the Parsi community. The current stereotype of the Parsi is that s/he is a Raj enthusiast who talks of *aapri Rani* (Our Queen) in hushed and dulcet tones. However this is not the Parsi of the 1830s. Dosebai tells us that the Parsi would cross the street rather than talk to the Briton. And as for the Parsi women:

> The Parsee ladies could not speak or understand a word of English nor often of Hindustanee and their servants could not command courage enough to ask or answer a question and excused themselves by saying they feared the females would all swoon away in affright.

Needless to say Meheribai was not one of these. She was not going to swoon for she had many British friends. She may have taken Dosebai out of school at the age of thirteen but she did not get her engaged until she turned eighteen and she was twenty when she finally got married.

We all know the arguments for child marriage. Life expectancy was low and so it was best to get things going as quickly as possible. Dosebai was born in 1832. I thought it might be interesting to know what life expectancy might be at the time so I turned to my friend, the historian Chinmay Tumbe. He told me that we did not have figures for that kind of thing until the 1880s rolled around. He sent me a chapter by demographer P N Mari Bhat from Tim Dyson (ed): *India's Historical Demography*. This tells us that in the 1880s, men's life expectancy at birth was 26.3 years and women's was 27.2 years.

Of course, Dosebai was born in a wealthy family and would have been given every advantage—if people *only knew what the advantages were*. Think again about the 1830s. You could cough in the morning and be dead before dinner. This happens often in Dosebai's life. Her daughter dies of diphtheria, an illness that takes the baby in a day. Her youngest brother survives an attack of cholera but is taken by a fever. The plague takes another family member. Death stalks these pages for this isn't just the time before penicillin—that's more than a hundred years in the future. This is before germ theory has been proved. It will only be in 1863 that Louis Pasteur shows what bacteria can do to wine and only in the late 1870s that he will discover vaccination.

Dosebai gets married in 1852. Her husband has been married before and has children from the marriage. He is much older but thankfully for the young and Westernised Dosebai, he is not set in his ways. She tells us what he says:

> He further went on to say: "My family is a large one and quite of the old school; you, however, blessed with an English education as well as trained up in Parsee usages, will wisely discern how to maintain the family concord, without depriving yourself of anything to which you have from infancy been accustomed." These kind words of confidence in me soothed my anxieties, and I offered fervent praise and thanksgiving to Almighty God for the happy lot he had ordained me. It would be out of my power to describe the thrill of ecstasy which the love of my husband excited in my hitherto virgin breast—what could I do, but strive to live in harmony with all the members of his family and act a mother's part to my step-children?

But try as she will, it doesn't work. Dosebai wears stockings; none of the women of his family do. This doesn't seem like much of a muchness but since she mentions it, there must have been some comment. Eventually, she and her husband move out of the family home and set up an independent household. This must have been quite revolutionary too but Dosebai goes over it swiftly. And though her husband is indulgent, it is a claustrophobic world that they live in. When they acquire a carriage, she tells us:

> We would not go the length of taking a drive together, as the parents of my husband would not have approved of such a step, and although he was regardless of public opinion he was always obedient to the will of his father and mother.

Husband and wife taking a drive together? What next, eh?

The marriage, for all its longevity, does not seem to have been a match made in heaven; although Dosebai would never say so. Throughout the book, she expresses nothing but the most commonplace of Victorian wifely affections and yet you can see the scars of the relationship. Her husband gets into business and starts a factory at Oomrawuttee which is never completed. Dosebai weathers this storm and the considerable loss of face. She curtails her expenditure and her socialising. She gets her husband a job in a British firm and slowly they come about. But the entrepreneur is not dead in Mr Jessawalla and at one point in her story, Dosebai recounts the Case of the Runaway Husband. Without notice, Mr Jessawalla ups and vanishes. He is spotted in Rawalpindi where he is set on trying his hand at business again. Dosebai gives chase and collars the errant husband and brings him back to the city. Nothing more is said about this event; nothing more need be said.

This is a woman who was born before Lytton Strachey and was writing before his *Eminent Victorians* (1918), which we are told reinvented biography. Therefore, she need not have said anything about that rather strange moment in her life. But when there is a court case in her family, she says, 'I feel it uncouth to introduce such dark, uninteresting episodes in my smooth and happy career and nothing but a desire to paint me as I am, induces me to do so.' This is a modern sentiment and gives us cause to trust her account of herself.

When her husband dies and her court cases have been won, Dosebai is situated comfortably enough to be able to set off on a voyage around the world. This could not have been cheap since Dosebai will spend most of her time in England and the United States of America. She does not stay with friends and relatives, except on certain occasions and when she returns to her native city, after being away for fourteen months. No doubt she must have been wealthy in the first place but wealth has a way of making its way out of certain hands. At the beginning of their marriage, her fond husband, some years her senior, tells his wife that she should make a good present to her brother Heerjeebhoy because she has married into an affluent family and so a handsome gift would be expected. Towards the end of her life, it is clear that her husband has run through his money and the best she can hope for is for him to find steady work in a British firm while she controls expenditures and clears his debts.

The men in her life do not do well by Dosebai. The first time I read the book I remember wondering why a clear-headed woman like her should have put her money in her brother's name. Surely there must have been some reason for this, some reason that would be so obvious to the readers she anticipated for her book that she did not feel she had to explain it.

I turned to Bina Agarwal for help. Agarwal is a professor of development economics and environment at the University of Manchester and is the author of the award-winning book, *A Field of One's Own: Gender and Land Rights in South Asia* (Cambridge University Press, 1994). She came through splendidly with an emailed explanation:

> 'For Parsis, the Married Women's Property Act of 1874 applied. This was an extension of the Law of Coverture that existed in the United Kingdom (and in fact across Europe and the United States of America). Under this, the husband had full control of his wife's property. The Act did not apply to Hindus/Sikhs/Jains and Muslims however.
>
> Your heroine must have given the money to her brother to keep some control over it and to prevent her husband from frittering it away.'

But, as Juvenal remarked, *'Quis custodiet ipsos custodies?'* (Who will guard the guards themselves?), both Meheribai and Dosebai had to go to court against their own blood in order to secure their rights. They won their cases eventually but not without some cost.

And so Dosebai must have been a tough woman. Perhaps she was not an easy mother either. If you are reading carefully, you will see that her souring relationship with her daughter is prefigured when she says the daughter in question lacked her taste. It is not something you would say about a beloved daughter. Her daughter, she says, begins to be influenced by other people and treats her mother badly. There is a rift and it is never repaired.

Her sons were loyal though, and it is through their good offices that the book was published.

Finally, there is Dosebai the traveller. She is not the kind of traveller we are accustomed to. Her eye is not trained to look beyond the surface and if the surface is beautiful, she can be happy. But there is something rather charming about the decisive way she makes sure that everyone goes on an early morning walk during a Delhi winter. She deploys a diligent pin on the slugabeds.

Dosebai works her way through the Delhi Durbar, only focussing on the spectacle and the pomp, the way the jewels on the rajas and maharajas blinded the eye. (Enough jewels and a famine may be eclipsed.)

And then she ventures to go abroad. She has no fear of crossing the black waters. After all, all her ancestors did just that, they say, when they sought refuge in India. So she takes a steamer and she goes off to England. Perhaps it is time someone studied the Parsi traveller in detail. Here, for instance, is an excerpt from *Rambles and Reflections* by Rustom N. Vatchagandhy who was the editor and proprietor of *Sanj Vartaman*. The book bears no date but internal evidence suggests that it was published before 1931. On 8th May 1926, Mr Vatchagandhy set off to Europe on the *Rajputana* of the P&O Line. His advice is simple: pack an overcoat.

> "...an overcoat is indispensable. It is wonderful to what uses an overcoat can be put to [sic]. As its name implies, it is a coat meant to be worn over a coat and as such it is meant to hide many a sin underneath. When one's coat and trousers have seen a long service or have been knocked out of shape by constant use, or when these useful articles have given way at certain awkward corners, a good long overcoat will decently hide all the wreckage and give one the appearance of gentility."

Dosebai would have no need of such advice. Wherever she went, her costume was remarked upon and she was at pains to explain who she was, what her community was, what her faith was. She was an ambassador at large for the Parsis and her calling card was her costume, which must have been the Parsi gara.

Before you begin to judge her as a clothes horse, you should consider that even here, Dosebai was forging her own way. The past she lived in was truly a different place. She tells us:

> Shopping being in those days unknown, all purchases were made by the men of the family from pedlars and artisans plying the streets, the women and children wearing without word or comment what they were given.

Thus for her to be designing her own clothes, embroidering them to suit her own styles, was to break with tradition, to take charge of herself in a way that we can only approve of. She tells us early on that she had a length of white English satin made up into a sari and embroidered it over its entire length. Now anyone who knows anything about embroidered saris knows that you don't have to embroider the entire length; you only do the bits that are on display. In fact, the Chinese embroiderers who worked for the Parsi community often ignored even a few centimetres of cloth because these would be tucked into the waistline. And here was Dosebai covering the whole sari with her handiwork.

I think it must have been a sari in Rome that caught the eye of a cardinal and convinced him to secure a meeting for Dosebai with the Pope. Dosebai is delighted but regrets that she is not wearing a good enough sari; she has sent her best clothes off to Brindisi. They bless each other which is rather nice; after all it was the Magi who came with gifts to the stable in Bethlehem.

But that isn't all. On her next trip abroad, her world tour, she acquires a car and learns to drive. She's come a long way from the woman who would not sit in the same carriage as her husband. Here she is now, tootling down from London with her son in tow, on her way to see the King and Queen. The car breaks down but she will not take a lift. She gets it repaired and arrives, a little late, a little breathless but she has gifts for their Majesties, her own embroidery again, embellished with seed pearls and portraits.

Now here is Dosebai preparing to get into a balloon and ascend into the heavens, armed with some wine and a piece of iron.

Why would she need a piece of iron? Well, what if she needed to send a missive down to the people on terra firma? You'd have to attach it to something, wouldn't you?

There's something in the idea of carrying a piece of iron into a balloon as a way of sending down a last message in case something happens. What would you write about? What do you want to say?

Perhaps that is what an autobiography is, in a way, a message from the past, written not in case something happens, but because death *will* happen. The glories of our blood and state are shadows, not substantial things, as James Shirley reminds us. But words? Words can live forever but sometimes they need a little help.

And so Mrs Dosebai Cowasjee Jessawalla's words get a new lease of life because Ravi Singh thought a series of city anthologies would be interesting; because Adil Jussawalla had a copy of this book; because Cyrus Guzdar's father, the charming Jimmy Guzdar, helped a Parsi woman who thought she was indigent after the death of her husband in Hong Kong. He got her on her feet again and helped her sort out her things. In the course of doing so, a few old share certificates turned the tide for her; she discovered she was wealthy. When she died she left some money in trust for causes such as these. There are many different ways in which that piece of iron manifests itself.

And so a hundred and more years after her death, ladies and gentlemen, *here's* Dosebai.

—Jerry Pinto
2021

Preface

Every human life plays its God-assigned part in the unwritten history of the world. But there are some lives that are privileged to participate in movements destined to be recorded in the annals of the country whose future they are designed to influence. From the very dawn of my life, my dear departed mother Meheribai, with a rare foresight and judgment, prepared me for an active part in the history of Indian women. She made me the instrument of pioneering the noble cause of higher education among millions and millions of the gentler sex in India.

The story of that movement is told in these pages with an earnest solicitude for the cause of History, which is the cause of truth. That which is historical within us is higher, nobler, greater and stronger than ourselves, and I have spoken because the voice of Truth within me has bidden me speak. Even now I may be misunderstood, misinterpreted and misrepresented, as I have been in the past. Indian society is still so backward because it is still so much exposed to the canker of jealousy. But I have faith in the Divine within the human. I believe that whilst there may be many who may not appreciate the value of my work, yielded as it has been in the service of my fellow countrywomen, there must yet be a few who would scan these pages with an open mind and a liberal heart, and may read there the lesson which God may have intended to impart through my humble deeds to those around me.

It would have rejoiced me immeasurably had my dear husband, whose enlightened support and encouragement had helped me so much in achieving what my career will stand for in the eyes of future generations, been alive to see this record published. But the life of a woman is as full of vicissitudes, if not more, than that of a man; and I obey God's will with a resigned heart.

But there are many friends, yet happily spared to me, who will be glad to receive this work in printed form and who have given cordial encouragement from time to time to my intention to give a permanent form to a truthful record of the events of my life. Such encouragement has flowed spontaneously from every European friend who was acquainted with my desire in this behalf. My special thanks are due to my most beloved friend, Mrs Ahlers, for the invaluable help she has extended to me in compiling the autobiography. But for her guidance, advice and co-operation this work would not have seen the light of day, and to her I pour forth the deepest gratitude of my heart. I must not fail to acknowledge, too, the sympathetic advice and suggestions given to me by my venerable friend, Sir George Birdwood. I may also be permitted to record the loyal assistance afforded to me by my dear sons, Dadabhoy and Jamsetjee, in keeping careful notes of my movements especially during my first voyage to Europe and my tour round the world.

I let this book go forth in the evening of my life, to tell the story of progress and reform—of the victory of self-sacrificing courage over narrow-minded opposition—of the march of advancement in the face of obloquy—of the final triumph of that which is noble and virtuous and beautiful in human life.

—Dosebai Cowasjee Jessawalla

Cumballa Hill,

Bombay, 1 January 1911.

I

Influences of British Rule in India

His late Imperial Majesty, King Edward VII, in his gracious message to the Princes and People of India, gave expression to a just sense of satisfaction in surveying the great work which British Rule has achieved in his Majesty's vast Indian Empire since the Crown of England took over the direct administration of that important Dependency. As the late American President Theodore Roosevelt observed on a recent memorable occasion, England's achievement in India during the past half century may be truthfully regarded as the greatest accomplishment of any human race since the days of the Roman Empire.

The most salient feature of British rule in India has been the perfectly equal distribution of justice—to high and low, to rich and poor alike. Another and no less important feature is the universal spread of education, the happy influence of which, like the air we breathe, is diffused throughout the length and breadth of the Indian Empire. By Education and the Arts, two main pillars of human greatness, man acquires a gauge of his power to improve his general condition. It would be moreover beyond my power to state here the various beneficent measures which the British administration has introduced and which all tend towards the amelioration of the condition of the masses, without looking to individual interests. But of all the multifarious benefits conferred by it, there are none which raise us so high as Western art and education, and he whose enterprising spirit leads him into such new and untrodden channels will not fail to gain for himself wealth and glory.

This affords a fresh impetus to us, Hindoos and Moslems and Parsees, to take the lead in adopting the various means designed for our advancement by our kind and paternal government. It will be my humble effort in this work to bring to notice those who, notwithstanding caste prejudice, have had the courage to introduce several salutary reforms amongst their communities.

The steadily increasing spread of education amongst both the male and female population of the Empire lies faithfully recorded in various educational reports, the endorsement of which we find in the fact that our people are beginning to shun the tortuous paths of evil customs and are betaking themselves to those which lead to peace and happiness. Notwithstanding this evident reformation and the prosperity ensuing therefrom, it has been customary for ignorance to decry it. But carping critics should compare India as it was with what it is now. I cannot do better than quote the following rhetorical description of the India of pre-British times given by Macaulay in the memorable speech he delivered in the House of Commons on the 10th of July 1833:

"In what state, then, did we find India? And what have we made India? We found society through that vast country in a state to which history scarcely furnishes a parallel. The nearest parallel would, perhaps, be the state of Europe during the fifth century. The Mogul Empire in the time of the successors of Aurangzeb, like the Roman Empire in the time of the successors of Theodosius, was sinking under the vices of a bad internal administration, and under the assaults of barbarous invaders. At Delhi, as at Ravenna, there was a mock sovereign immured in a gorgeous state prison. He was adored with servile prostrations. He assumed and bestowed the most magnificent silks. But, in fact, he was a mere puppet in the hands of some ambitious subject.

While the Honorii and Augustuli of the East revelled and dozed without knowing or caring what might pass beyond the walls of their palace gardens, the provinces had ceased to respect a government which could neither punish nor protect them. Society was a chaos. Its restless and shifting elements formed themselves every moment into some new combination, which the next moment dissolved. In the course of a single generation a hundred dynasties grew up, flourished, decayed, were extinguished, were forgotten.

Every adventurer who could muster a troop of horse might aspire to a throne, every palace was every year the scene of conspiracies, treasons, revolutions, parricides.

Meanwhile a rapid succession of Alarics and Attilas passed over the defenceless empire. A Persian invader penetrated to Delhi, and carried back in triumph the most precious treasures of the House of Tamerlane. The Afghan soon followed, by the same track, to glean whatever the Persian had spared. The Jauts established themselves on the Jumna. The Seiks devastated Lahore.

Every part of India, from Tanjore to the Himalayas, was laid under contribution by the Mahrattas. The people were ground down to the dust by the oppressor without and the oppressor within, by the robber from whom the Nabob was unable to protect them, by the Nabob who took whatever the robber had left them. All the evils of despotism, and the evils of anarchy, pressed at once on that miserable race. They knew nothing of government but its exactions. Desolation was in their imperial cities, and famine all along the banks of their broad and redundant rivers. It seemed that a few more years would suffice to efface all traces of the opulence and civilisation of an earlier age."

Whereas in those days we remained stationary, in these we are making such rapid strides towards civilisation as defy description. Only those who have carefully studied the advance of English education can fathom the immense good it has effected. Its blissful influence, though not always acknowledged, is felt by all, and it is nowadays no surprising phenomenon to see those in the lowest ranks raised, by no other means than persevering study, to power and affluence. We have seen schools springing up throughout the length and breadth of the land, raising the poor native from his ignorance and indigence to a knowledge of the learned arts and sciences and an honourable place in the administration of his country. We see natives of every grade of society attaining eminence as schoolmasters, medical men, attorneys and barristers, even to the honour of a judicial chair in our courts of law; others, by taking an active part in municipal affairs and benevolent societies, are enabled to render assistance to their countrymen. The truly statesmanlike policy of reform just inaugurated by Viscount Morley has opened a new era in the history of the people of India.

Amongst the wonderful blessings received by my country with the advent of British rule, is one which to my mind is all-paramount, namely the emancipation of Indian women. For this alone our hearts go out in gratitude to the memory of Victoria the Good. An ornamental statue of her late Majesty, with crown on the head and eyes bent in pitying concern on her humble subjects, occupying a central position on the Esplanade of Bombay, commemorates the beneficent reign of the fair ruler of India who held her peaceful sway under the title of Her Imperial Majesty the Queen-Empress. I deem it my loyal and affectionate duty to give in this work a picture of this beautiful statue and doubt not that my readers will consider the tribute both fitting and appropriate.

The year 1842 may be cited as the dawn of English education amongst Indian women, but much obscurity surrounds the name of the pioneer who first publicly ventured to advocate it, and it shall be our endeavour to elucidate this matter. I, however, take the liberty of mentioning that this important task is undertaken at an advanced stage of my life, after many ups and downs have been trodden and the rugged path seems nearly ended. But I look upon it as a sacred moral obligation to clear away the obscurity and misrepresentation enveloping that benefactress of her people, and hold myself in readiness to refute whatever doubts ignorance or bigotry may throw on my statements.

In a work of this nature, the first of its kind to afford a true picture of the social and domestic life of a Parsee woman, it would be anomalous to presume that everything will be found palatable to the members of my community. My English readers will doubtless give due credence and support to my assertions, and I trust the unprejudiced witness of that time, when education was, like the new-born moon, feebly struggling to spread its enlightening influence upon the ignorance of that period, will also bear us out. From out the darkest cloud, truth, like a star, will ultimately reveal itself, and similarly, he who treads the path of uprightness will at last shine forth. My reader will see this axiom verified as he progresses.

For various reasons it has been thought advisable to introduce into this work a short sketch of my paternal and maternal grandfathers.

Set Cursetjee Manekjee Shroff, my paternal grandfather, was descended from a noble and well-known family, and during his life enjoyed great popularity amongst Parsees, Europeans, Hindoos, in short amongst all castes and creeds. The needy and the poor found in him a staunch supporter and, by being placed at the head of the Parsee Punchayet, he was enabled to expose the foibles and counteract the oppression of the rich and to protect and cherish the suffering and the poor, willingly rendering them assistance to the utmost extent of his purse and power.

During his life, which was a happy and prosperous one, he enjoyed such honours as his high character deserved. At that time, when the grievances of the poor did not transpire before the public, his services and still more his tact in reconciling litigant parties were most admirable. He used to send his own carriage to fetch the parties at variance or he would meet them at some chosen house and by simple and effective argument disarm their animosity and effect a speedy settlement of family feuds.

Ruinous and dilatory proceedings in courts of law were little dreamt of in those days and thus he became the recognised dispenser of justice amongst the Parsees. People then did not see their fortunes melt away under the greedy grasp of attorneys and barristers, as is unfortunately but too often the case now; no wonder, then, if their prosperity remained unblighted by the chilling blasts of adversity.

Under the present deplorable state of affairs, it is no exaggeration to say that the great proportion of the intelligent Parsees cast their mental eyes back longingly to the good old times when Set Cursetjee used, without assumption, to dispense justice. Thus his name is still remembered and honoured by the oldest inhabitants. To the rising generation his name may possibly be forgotten, but a considerable time after his decease, his noble deeds and his exemplary life were chronicled in the leading papers of the day. By virtue of the high authority vested in him, he was enabled to alleviate the sufferings of many of his poorer brethren, and his pious life was commemorated and his memory preserved by a splendid statue, occupying a prominent position at the junction of four roads, just opposite Messrs Treacher & Co.'s shop, at the intersecting point of Bellasis and Duncan Road—a point well-known to every citizen. Typical of his cool disposition, fountains of pellucid water, thrown up by flute-shaped jets and collecting again beneath in stone basins, refresh many a weary wayfarer. Thus, living or dead the poor of every caste and creed rise up and call him blessed. As a tribute of filial affection and gratitude, this monument was erected to his memory by his son, Mr Manekjee, and in spite of diverse difficulties and objections, as futile as they were trivial, on the part of the municipal authorities, he at last succeeded in putting it up on its present site. I introduce here a photograph of this splendid memorial statue.

Nothing short of sterling virtue and disinterested benevolence could have entitled Set Cursetjee to this unique and universal homage. Unlike the "Sethias" (leading members of the community) of today, he never spent his money to gain titles and rewards, but aspired only to divine honours in his charities and efforts on behalf of the countless thousands of the poor. During the latter period of his life, he had the misfortune to lose the greater portion of his wealth, but his sympathy with the poor continued unabated and his remains were escorted to their last resting-place by such an immense concourse of people as has never been seen within the range of our memory. Rich and poor alike honoured him and participated in his funeral obsequies, which lasted three days. Nowadays all bow to the rising and none to the setting sun, but in contradiction of this all but universal maxim, Set Cursetjee was honoured even in his downfall. In confirmation of my several assertions, I beg to refer the reader to a pamphlet issued in May 1845, giving an account of Set Cursetjee's career and throwing additional light on the subject.

When his marriage proved unproductive of issue, his wife with a magnanimity as unparalleled as her self-abnegation, suggested his taking to himself another wife.

In order to celebrate this second marriage with fitting pomp and festivity, the Parsee Punchayet were requested to lend the great utensils in their possession, but this they refused to do, contending that it was objectionable to contract a second marriage during the life-time of the first wife. However, seeing that it was at the express wish and permission of the first wife that the second marriage was to take place that excuse was over-ruled, still the Punchayet persisted in their refusal to lend the public utensils and ultimately similar large-sized utensils had to be made expressly for the occasion. This singular marriage was celebrated amidst the greatest rejoicing, and to the credit of the first wife, it may be mentioned that she (as is customary amongst natives) not only participated in this important ceremony, but with her own hands decorated the bride and escorted her to her new home.

Set Cursetjee's family was soon after blessed by a son of this second marriage. Mr Cursetjee's happiness may now be said to have been complete, as his second wife successively gave birth to four sons and one daughter. The first wife was looked upon as the head of this happy domestic circle and she exercised her power so considerately as never to give the slightest offence to the second wife.

Bai Barozbai, the first wife of Set Cursetjee, by her singularly urbane disposition, won the favour of all around her, and I am very sure that such nobleness of mind as hers would only be met with in one of a thousand. While living she was held in the highest esteem by her husband and all connected with her, and now that her place on earth knows her no more, we may well cherish the belief that she has found a home in the realms of bliss. I have given the leading incidents of this noble woman's life to incite my fair readers to emulate her example of unselfishness and amiability. Before quitting the theme, I may mention that Bai Barozbai was kept in close custody by her bigoted parents who hoped thus to coerce her into withholding her consent to her husband's second marriage, but, as we have seen, she rose superior to all objections and escaping from her parent's roof she fled to her husband.

Through her medium, Providence blessed Set Cursetjee with a host of rosy-cheeked children, and we, who owe indirectly our very existence to her, cannot but regard her as one of the most estimable ladies amongst the Parsees. The four sons by whom Set Cursetjee was blessed were named Eduljee, Dhunjeebhoy, Hormusjee and Manekjee and his daughter Aimai. It only remains to add that, with such a God-sent progeny, together with two wives all living in love and perfect harmony, Set Cursetjee's life may well be styled supremely happy. In the course of time his second wife died.

After this, Set Cursetjee's life presents to our notice a continued series of misfortunes and woes. He lost two children in the prime of life, one of whom, his only daughter, whom he deeply loved, succumbed to a slight indisposition, lasting a single day. She had married into the well-known family of Heerjee Readymoney, her husband being Kaikhasroo, son of Soonabai Readymoney. She left one son. The bereaved father was destined to suffer a more terrible blow in the untimely death, owing to commercial difficulties, of his third son Hormusjee, in 1840, at the age of thirty. Thus rendered woefully miserable, by misfortunes following each other in rapid succession, Set Cursetjee passed the eve of his life in great sorrow, leading a sort of ascetic life.

Notwithstanding this, his zeal to benefit the poor continued unabated. He was much attached to the children of his son Hormusjee, who had left a widow, four sons, and one daughter to mourn his loss. On the twelfth day of the eighth month, 1214 Yerdijardi (Parsee), Set Cursetjee breathed his last, at the patriarchal age of eighty-one, leaving behind him a happy group of children and grandchildren.

Set Jamsetjee Nanabhoy Guzdar alias "Supla" by which cognomen his family was readily known, was the maternal grandfather of the authoress. Being a timber merchant, he was proficient in mensuration, hence his surname of Guzdar (Guz being, in Gujarati, a yard). His other surname seems to have originated in his ingratiating and sweet disposition when in the company of juvenile friends, they calling him "Sipla" (Gujarati for humility) which became corrupted into "Supla," by which name he was universally known. He was charitable and popular, maintained a large family in comfort, and led himself an easy, pleasure-seeking life, but it is not recorded of him, as of Set Cursetjee, that he was ever ready to extend a helping-hand to the needy.

By his first wife (for he had also to contract a second alliance) he had an only child; a son named Ardeshir, who, according to the prevailing custom, was during his boyhood married, with all the pomp and ceremony attendant upon such an event. But the fond hopes and aspirations which the father had centred on the sole heir of his name and fortune were cut off by the death of his son at the age of fourteen.

Soon after this sad blow he made a journey to Surat to transact some business on behalf of Set Hormusjee Bomonjee Wadia, and there he contracted a clandestine marriage, clandestine that is to say, towards his lawful wife, but with the full approval of his revered mother. On his return to Bombay, accompanied by his hopeful partner, his first wife created quite a scene, because he had consoled himself with another wife within a short period after his only son's sad death. Under these trying circumstances, he thought it best to pacify his enraged spouse by allowing her to have her own way in all ordinary matters, at the same time reasoning with her on the purity of motive which alone necessitated this second alliance, he at the same time instructed his new wife how to conduct herself, and by this prudent management created a sort of harmony out of the discordant elements.

Though on the shady side of forty, Providence blessed him with a host of children, two sons and seven daughters, and thus far the eve of his life was supremely happy. The eldest of the group was the well-known Bai Meheribai, held in the highest respect by the rest of the family, and possessed of an interest equal to a son's in the family assets. I doubt not my readers will have perceived a striking analogy in the matrimonial affairs of my two grandfathers. Three years after the said Meheribai's birth, Set Cursetjee's third son, Hormusjee, was born, and it seemed desirable that two families holding such an influential position among the Parsee community should be united. Thus, despite the disparity of age, Meheribai and Hormusjee were destined for each other. This pair, whom I am permitted to call by the endearing name of "parents," owed their being in each case to a second union, and this incident, I trust, will not fail to interest my readers by its tinge of romance.

II

My Mother Meheribai—A Historical Figure

The respected names of our grandfathers are connected with many charitable institutions, the Agiaries (Fire-temples) as well as a Tower of Silence at Gandevi built by them still standing to commemorate them. It is gratifying to record the fact that a daughter of this well-known family was the first to espouse the cause of English education amongst the Parsee women—that a feminine, not, as is generally supposed, a masculine mind conceived the idea and to a great extent gave the first impetus to so pre-eminent an undertaking. I have therefore deemed it by no means unfitting to give this brief sketch of the two families.

With all the honour due to a beloved and revered mother, I would endeavour to present to my readers a bird's-eye view of her chequered life. The eldest child of her wealthy parents, she was as the phrase goes, born with a silver spoon in her mouth, was reared in luxurious ease by her parents and afterwards established in equal comfort and affluence by the side of a doting husband in her father-in-law's house.

She was known in her community for her great ability. Many still living could testify to this. She was very skilful with her needle and used to adorn herself and her children in most tasteful garments, beautifully embroidered by workmen according to her taste. She differed from other Parsee ladies in cultivating a wide field of acquaintances outside her own creed. She possessed an independent spirit and clear sound judgment, and was accustomed to take the lead in every noble enterprise, thus incurring the displeasure of her own people.

At the age of twenty she was overwhelmed by her first grief, the death of her father. By his will, his wealth, which was considerable, was left to be divided in equal shares between Meheribai and his two sons, deducting merely the nominal sum of £8,000 for each of the other daughters. The major portion of his estate, *viz.*, eight lacs of rupees (£53,333) was advanced on interest to Nawab Nizam Ali Khan, known also as Hazat Khan, on the security of his entire property, moveable and sunk, this was eventually discovered to have been much over-estimated and the shock so seriously affected Set Jamsetjee's health that after a short illness he died. In time, a large portion of the invested capital was recovered, though great loss and vexation were thereby incurred. So we see that no one is exempt from the great law of nature—the equal distribution of weal and woe, misfortune, like the scythe in old Father Time's hand, sparing none and often putting the man who is upright and oppressed to such shifts that his only recourse, for the vindication of his rights, is the law, thus exemplifying the adage "Out of the frying-pan into the fire." How true it is, too, that "Money makes or mars the man."

After the death of her father, the widowed mother reasoned thus with Meheribai: "As all the monies are out on loan and as Providence has happily placed you under the protection of an indulgent father-in-law and blessed you with a good loving husband, you will, if you at all honour the word of your mother, sign a release on getting a share equal to that of your sisters."

But to this counsel Meheribai turned a deaf ear and thus estrangement sprung up between her and her own family. Unfortunately no amicable settlement could be come to, so at last Bai Meheribai became involved in the inextricable meshes of the law—the first time in which a Parsee lady figured in this unenviable position. To avoid being too diffuse, I must, however, confine myself to the leading events of her life gleaned from the authentic original manuscripts which she, on the verge of death, that is, in 1878, gave into my charge.

The extensive and ruinous lawsuit dragged its weary length along for ten years and when, through the influence of her husband, it was drawing to a conclusion favourable to Meheribai, it gave rise to an event more unhappy and disastrous in its effects than the case itself. With heartfelt sorrow I record the bitterness and dismay which now crept into a hitherto united and happy home and wrought such cruel suffering upon her who gave me birth.

When all suspense seemed over and her handsome patrimony within her grasp, Hormusjee took it into his head to lay claim to it, and thus money, the prolific source of evil, cast its evil eye upon this blessed pair. Meheribai reasonably contended that her money should be settled on their children, to which, however, her husband would not consent. Subsequently, by his refusal to sign any paper connected with the same, the unfortunate lawsuit was postponed *sine die.* Maternal love at last prevailed over the anger nursed for years, and Meheribai's mother again opened her arms to her unhappy child. To end the conjugal quarrels Meheribai left her husband and took refuge with her mother. This step only widened the breach and Hormusjee, to stifle his feelings, launched forth upon all sorts of commercial enterprises. He alone conducted his father's affairs while speculating largely in opium on his own account; on his father sustaining a heavy loss, the burden of the entire household fell on him, his father remarking that his wife's portion would be more than sufficient for them all. But worse was coming.

Being under her mother's roof and again in the familiar intercourse of close relationship, one day Meheribai was made to listen to the old demand, *viz.*, "the suit will no doubt end in your favour, making your name popular, but your husband's claim will be established and the whole amount will be swallowed up in opium speculations; therefore, be prudent, give your consent in writing to my former proposal and then your husband will come to his senses."

To this Meheribai would only agree, provided that her doing so would meet with her husband's approval and effect a complete reconciliation between them, whereupon she was mercilessly ordered to quit her mother's house and return to her husband. But without sacrificing her children's future, she could not conciliate their father, so she was cast out by each of those bound to succour her.

Through the kind interposition of two families, those of Set

Jehangir Nusserwanjee Wadia and Set Hormusjee Bhicajee Chinoy, she was enabled to hire a top floor in a large block known up to the present date as Byramjee Botliwalla's Chawl (building), the said true friends supplying all the furniture and requisites. She established herself here with three children, two sons remaining with her husband.

All attempts at reconciliation proved fruitless. Hormusjee would not condescend to live in hired lodgings and she would not return to her father-in-law, well knowing that he had encouraged her husband's claim. Thus two months elapsed and then a terrible calamity broke over her head.

Separated from his wife, whom he really loved and honoured, Hormusjee, who naturally possessed a humane disposition, suffered keenly. Sustaining a heavy loss in his opium ventures, with no one to share his anxiety and solace his perturbed spirit, he sought to lay violent hands on himself and unfortunately succeeded but too well. This awful intelligence reached Meheribai in the midst of an altercation with her mother's deputy, the aforenamed Kaikhasroo and, in the intensity of her bitter anguish, she exclaimed, "Take my all, yes, everything, but spare him."

Flying to him she loved, all remedies which human ingenuity could suggest were tried, but alas! in vain. The vital spark had fled. This tragic occurrence spread horror through the entire family and drew down upon poor Meheribai the unmerciful enmity of all.

Returning to her father-in-law's, she passed the first days of her widowhood in deep affliction, aggravated by the undisguised odium of those around her. For two months the bare earth was her only couch and the only words of kindness she heard were uttered by the few friends who came to condole with her; these were the ladies of the Wadia and Chinoy families, Mrs Jehangir Framjee Jessawalla and Mr Cursetjee Cowasjee Banajee, all of whom evinced the liveliest sympathy in her sad circumstances. Of the latter it may be mentioned that he was a man of great intelligence and influence, whose slightest word carried weight with it. After enduring great harshness and many affronts from her relatives, she moved with her five children to a separate abode. The unfortunate lawsuit, the prime cause of all her sufferings, had meantime by the efforts of kind friends, been brought to a settlement, by which she was content to receive the half of her rightful portion, but sufficient to live comfortably upon.

Being now relieved of pecuniary anxiety, Bai Meheribai turned her attention to the wants of others and, extending the scope of her energy, applied herself to the introduction of salutary reforms amongst her own people, incurring thereby the most vehement opposition on the part of the orthodox Parsees, amongst whom were the two families most nearly related to herself. But her indomitable courage, her sound judgment, her inborn spirit of progress, and her aspirations for the good of her country enabled her, alone and unsupported, to brave the torrent of bigoted resistance and ultimately to sow the seeds of that culture of which we are all now thankfully reaping the fruits. It is the most ruthless pruning which produces the noblest harvest.

In 1841 she took up her abode in a small secluded house in Hornby Row, adjoining that of Sir (then Mr) Dinshawjee Manekjee Petit, who in 1855 purchased and added it to his own. On the other side stood the office of the Presidency Engineer and to the back rose the stony rampart surmounted by its guns, with the trench below, which in those days ran round the Fort. In this new home she lived an active, happy life.

Her father-in-law, Set Cursetjee, took a lively interest in her children, and after the death of Hormusjee evinced much affection towards them. But Meheribai, though rejoicing in this change, carefully maintained her control and educated both sons and daughter in conformity with her own enlightened ideas, which in no way clashed with the tenets of her religion, the love of which she early instilled into the breasts of the children. At this time Meheribai did what men shrunk from doing and took the lead in every good innovation, extending her acquaintance to other castes and nationalities, to the consternation of her community, in whose eyes she was rash, unconventional and therefore reprehensible. She had no English education, but was expert in Gujarati, in which language she had a fluent and graceful style.

Through her family Doctor, Mr Baptist, son-in-law of Sir Roger de Faria, she made the acquaintance, which ripened into friendship, of the Faria family, and at their house she first met Mrs Ward, an English school-mistress, and her mother Mrs Mackenzie. In the companionship of these two ladies she acquired a taste for European manners and customs and her circle of friends rapidly extended.

It was then considered so singular, in fact wrong, to form even an acquaintance beyond one's own caste, that her conduct often provoked the remark not unmixed with hatred: "Is it possible for a Parsee female to enter an English house, to mix in such society!" but imbibing the broad and liberal principles introduced by the British rule, she could afford to pass over these silly remarks in silence.

To give one example, the innocent enjoyment of a morning or evening walk, to say nothing of a drive, was at that time quite out of the question for a Parsee female, but Meheribai was not slow to perceive the wholesome influence of air and exercise, and made it a rule to be out with her children enjoying the evening breeze and had her reward in seeing them healthy and happy. But this harmless freedom was an offence to the orthodox Parsees. They, like bullocks in the mill, were content to tread in the beaten track of their forefathers. "Keep the females stationary" was their motto. They were culpably negligent of the wants, physical and moral, of their wives and children, though themselves foremost in every luxury and pleasure. With their fingers in every dish, from a pie to a pudding, they yet denied to their wives and daughters the simple diversion of an evening ramble. The ladies even of the wealthiest families were only allowed to take the air in their own gardens, but a walk by the sounding beach or by the more lively Bandstand was altogether undreamt of; till Bai Meheribai set prejudice at defiance, whereupon contempt and suspicion were poured upon her by her own people but applause and encouragement by the whole English community.

III

Meheribai's Heroic Action—The Ordeals of an Indian Pioneer

We now turn to the domestic life of Bai Meheribai. She was the hopeful mother of six children, of whom one died during her husband's lifetime. The remaining four sons and one daughter were named respectively Dorabjee, Furdoonjee, Heerjeebhoy, Shapoorjee and the writer of these pages—Dosebai. On account of the estrangement between Meheribai and her mother, she had to betake herself, as the expected birth of each child approached, to the house of her aunt (father's sister), and on all but the last occasion, the kind offices of this dear relative had been gratefully accepted.

In consequence of the sale of her aunt's house, as the time of delivery for the sixth time drew near, Meheribai proposed going to one of the bungalows owned by her father-in-law, situated by the sea-side, at Chowpatty, and usually tenanted by Europeans. Hormusjee readily gained his father's consent to his temporary occupation of this house, and accordingly removed thither with wife and children. When this came to be known, the female members of the family, actuated by their usual jealousy, represented Meheribai's sojourn at Chowpatty as so unseemly that Set Cursetjee was persuaded to recall his son, informing him that it was ill advised to take his wife at such a critical time to so secluded a spot; those who permanently lived in that quarter thought it imperative to move into the Fort for these events, whereas his wife acted contrary to established custom in going there then. It was, therefore, his will that they should return at once. But meanwhile Bai Meheribai had been happily delivered of a daughter—need we say how the parents' hearts were filled with joy!

As Meheribai had gone some distance away from her relatives and this was, in their eyes, a very blameworthy and uncommon proceeding, so contrary to the established rule among Parsee woman, the female members of her family did not assemble round her to render every possible assistance, and to soothe and enliven her during the long days of confinement.

For our religion demands that for forty days after delivery, the mother and child and their attendants must be kept entirely separated and aloof from the outer world; therefore there are chambers reserved and railed off for their use, iron cots are provided for such occasions and all furniture, clothing, eating utensils, etc., must be kept scrupulously separate. The dresses, mattresses, and everything used or even touched by any of them during this period, save the bedsteads which are therefore of iron, are deemed permanently polluted and are either buried or given away to sweepers or such low caste people.

For the first forty days of its life, the child is carefully wrapped up in old worn-out clothes kept for the purpose. Thus debarred from society and occupation, the young mother is naturally very dependent upon the friendly assistance and encouragement of relatives, but Meheribai had to rest content with the services and company of servants hired for the occasion.

It was in the Muktad* days in the course of which falls the Pateti or New Year's Day, that Meheribai's daughter first saw the light, and for this twice-blessed season she had previously prepared and carefully wrapped up costly silken dresses, embroidered in gold of an old-fashioned and uniform pattern, for her four sons. These treasures were folded away in the top shelf of the wardrobe, and on a lower one were

*An annual festival, lasting from twelve to eighteen days, in commemoration of the dead, the belief being that the spirits of the departed are released for a short time every year.

laid the old stuffs for the baby—the servant was sent to fetch the latter, but unfortunately laid hold of the bundle of valuable suits, and handed them over to Meheribai. As already stated, they were now rendered unfit for the use for which they were intended, but the fond mother consoled herself, as she tore the beautiful garments for swaddling clothes, that the child who could command such luxuries from her birth, was destined to be always one of fortune's favourites.

Our readers may find this a very trivial incident, but perhaps it has its own interest. A confinement is a trying ordeal, and the absence of matronly friends would be a bitter trial, and such it was felt to be by Meheribai. After the period of retirement was over, she returned with her children to the old family residence, where she was viewed with disfavour and envy by the entire circle, save her husband whose tender love for her was unabated. Her youth was as blissful and happy as her after-life was sad and embittered.

The year 1842 saw the beginning of English education amongst Indian women and I again venture to assert that it was Meheribai's bold act, which effected this. In consequence of her friendship with Mrs Ward and other English ladies, she resolved to place her only daughter (the present authoress) under the tuition of the former, in an English seminary of which she was the mistress. This was at a time when fathers entertained not the remotest idea of educating their daughters. Already amongst the different people of India, Parsees, Jews, Hindoos, Mahomedans, there was some knowledge of the English language, but that was quite one-sided. No one ever thought of disseminating it amongst the women of his caste. A slight smattering of the Vernacular was the extent of a young Indian lady's attainment; indeed, there was a general desire to keep the fair sex in ignorance.

Amid so much that was discouraging, Meheribai took the first step towards better things by introducing English education into her own family, under the benign rule of her late Majesty, Queen Victoria, and by slow degrees others have followed her example. How multifarious are the changes of the last half century wrought by means of education amongst our Indian women!

Previous to 1840 what little nominal education our Indian girl could get was imparted in an antiquated and clumsy fashion. A ground-floor verandah in some prominent locality, with boys and girls squatting on a hard mattress, formed the school, where the young were taught according to the whims and capability of their native teachers. Too often the very appearance and habits of these male teachers—or *Mehetajees* as they were popularly called—were not such as to command respect. They squatted on a mat, their uncovered grimy feet stretched out at ease, their dhotar* half drawn up, without either turban or shirt. Like the Moollah (Mahomedan priest) calling the faithful to prayer, these teachers were wont to recite, at a bawling pitch of voice and in a state of dreamy sluggishness, the multiplication table, which was then caught up, and repeated in a united roar by the pupils.

Amid this unmeaning jargon, in such adverse surroundings, the girls of those days picked up a few crumbs of learning which fell to their lot and even this was the portion of but a fortunate (?) minority, as will be apparent when one hears that only two such schools existed at that time—one conducted by Heerjibhoy and Purbhoodas, the other by Gowrishankar *alias* "the Humpbacked."

The native opinion was: "Of what avail is education to our females, it would not bring wealth?" They were at the same time debarred from intercourse beyond that of their own immediate circle. Thus without education and without elevating example, they were content to run in the same channel from one generation to another. They passed the one-half of their time in the routine work of the household, and the other half in sluggish idleness or gossip. A noble or even useful career was undreamt of for a woman, the weaker sex being considered by the Indians vastly the inferior, and woman's rights and wants in those days very limited. Hence it can well be conceived how the action of one, and that one a woman, stirred up the wrath of the entire male portion of the whole native community, for Meheribai's independent spirit waged war upon the custom of centuries. The man or woman who stands foremost in a reformation needs to draw strength and support mainly and mostly from an approving conscience. Meheribai had to bear the brunt of the ignorance and prejudice of her whole family and community, by placing her only daughter in Mrs Ward's school.

The school was situated in that part of the Fort exclusively

---

*An article of masculine attire worn around the waist, passing under and tucked in behind.

inhabited by Europeans, and known by the name of the English Ward, a quarter scrupulously avoided by native ladies. Meheribai's young daughter going thither every morning with her servant created a great scandal amongst the Parsees, some of whom went so far as to send threatening letters to the family. Her very father-in-law expressed his high displeasure and all were unanimous in declaiming against the vices which English education would assuredly bring with it. In the teeth of this united opposition, the brave mother faltered not in her pursuit of what she deemed right for her child, and replied in calm and dignified terms to indignant slanderers.

Two Gujarati journals of the day, the *Jam-e-Jamshid* and the *Chabook*, the former being the organ of the Parsee aristocracy, passed comments on Meheribai's conduct. Some of these Parsee lordlings had unanimously resolved to excommunicate Bai Meheribai and her house. This news coming to her ears impelled her to write to the instigator, begging him to make his decision public, in order that she might claim her right to provide herself and her family with a separate Tower of Silence for the reception of their bodies after death. No written reply was received to this request, but a well-known Mobed (priest) named Shapoordaroo, came with a verbal message from the worthy Sethias, in which the threat of excommunication was ignored, and merely their disapproval of her daughter's training expressed, thus avoiding an allegation which they could not sustain in public. Noticing this fact Mr Navrojee Dorabjee *alias* "Halkaroo," the editor of the *Chabook* lashed the Sethia class with the cutting taunt that "the proverbially long turban of the lords of creation has been in this instance tied up in the short lined head-dress of a mere woman" (the former being fifty times as long as the latter).

It is gratifying to record that ultimately the very Sethias who had so vigorously denounced Meheribai, came to introduce into their own families the reform to which, coming from her, they had thought fit to take exception, but of which they then prided themselves on being the champions. After the enlistment of Bai Meheribai's daughter into the number of Mrs Ward's pupils, people began gradually to open their eyes to the vital importance of women's education. About this time her brother-in-law began to have his eldest daughter Cooverbai taught English by a governess.

Meheribai asked her father-in-law why all sorts of objections had been raised to her daughter's education, when now his own son was allowed to follow her example. His answer was: that "it was not objectionable to have a girl taught by a lady privately, but in her (Meheribai's) case the world-wide publicity of sending her daughter to an English school was the source of objection"; to which Meheribai replied in these pithy words: "Had the question not assumed a prominent aspect in the public newspapers, Mr Manekjee would not even have thought of the same, and, I trust, as you, my noble benefactor, have seen your son in this instance following my footsteps, so you will, God willing, see many other salutary reforms introduced among the Parsees through my instrumentality."

From the original manuscripts now in my possession, it appears that while Meheribai conducted all her arguments in writing, her father-in-law used to send verbal messages through his clerk, manager, or even one of his children.

From all these facts it is evident that the widow lady, Meheribai, was the first to sow the seeds of education and emancipation among Indian women. At that time, however great or enterprising a project may have been, its author never courted popularity through the medium of the public press, as is very often the case nowadays, when every trifling incident is trumpeted forth and rendered unduly weighty. On account of the secluded habits of widowhood, no wonder if Meheribai's name has not appeared at the head of the much-lauded supporters of female education, no wonder if the generations succeeding her have not done her ample justice. However, I will present to my readers a short extract from the *Bombay Courier* of 23rd August 1842, to prove that the matter did excite interest at the time:

> "The announcement in a late number of the *United Service Gazette*, upon which we made some few observations, that a young Parsee lady has been placed for education in the seminary of Mrs Ward, induced us to make some enquiries as to her family and parentage. We have learnt that she is the granddaughter of that old and respected Parsee gentleman, Cursetjee Manekjee, and daughter of Hormusjee Cursetjee, deceased, whose widow is the guardian of the child, and has co-operated with the other members of that enlightened family in procuring every advantage of education for her interesting child. Understanding as we

> do, that Manekjee, well-known to many of our readers as distinguished for literary acquirements, is a near relative of the child, we do not think we strain the point too far in assuming that the distinction attained by Manekjee Cursetjee for literary acquirements on his late visit to Europe, strongly influenced his family to avail themselves still further of the benefits of a liberal education. We shall watch the progress of this girl with deep interest and will rejoice to find the noble example followed by others. We are led to entertain such a hope from the fact that already several Parsee ladies have been to Mrs Ward's to witness the process of education. Would that they could fully appreciate by understanding!"

There are two divisions to the above extract, one of which is faithful and correct, the other erroneous and misinformed. That there was only one Parsee girl in Mrs Ward's school who lived under her mother's care and guidance and that there was no other Parsee pupil previous to her, I emphatically declare to be true. But here is the rub: to assume that Mr Manekjee whose name is well-known among Europeans, by this means diffused female education in his family, is certainly far wide of the mark. For, in the case of Meheribai and her young daughter, he had not the shadow of control or influence over either of them. Sending the little girl to school was the sole and spontaneous act of her mother, and the editor gives credit to Manekjee for a thing he had no share or concern in.

Though the real state of things was as has been above represented, Mr Manekjee was much eulogised by his English friends, and under the conception similar to those actuating the editorial announcement just quoted, the Hon'ble Mountstuart Elphinstone, late Governor of Bombay, wrote in 1843 from England warmly congratulating him on his philanthropic efforts for the spread of female education. Mr Manekjee quietly received these eulogies, while to my uncontrovertible belief [sic] is that he followed the footsteps and adopted the ideas of Meheribai, who being the sole guardian of her daughter, realised in her, to the utmost of her opportunity, her aspirations and ideals in regard to the education of Indian women. Had this not been the case, Manekjee's daughter, who was my superior in age, would have been the first to taste the sweets of English education. Manekjee was not the first of his race to visit England, for Messrs Dinshawjee Furdoonjee Panday, Ardeshir Cursetjee Wadia and several others had preceded him, but returned home without having altered their views in regard to the education of the gentler sex.

When the newspaper further asserts that several native ladies had been to see the system at work in Mrs Ward's school, it is obvious that the statement is equally mistaken; for, as far as we are aware, not a single native or Parsee lady ever crossed its threshold, much less did any other native girl join the school. My view will be readily accepted when one remembers the popular prejudice among the orthodox men, and the still more orthodox women of those times. The school ceased to exist in 1847, and in the following year Mrs Ward left Bombay.

Everyone connected with the old *Bombay Courier*, who may still be living, will no doubt rejoice to see this book, the first penned by her, whose progress they watched with interest over fifty years ago. As my readers follow step by step in its pages the progress of English education and the healthy revolution in the manners and ideas of Indian women, it is to be hoped that they who so enthusiastically hailed the dawn of these good things, will be the more rejoiced to read of its steady and successful growth. Shall we omit to feel behind this record the hand of her who has hastened our social and intellectual evolution by her courageous and far-sighted action?

Of the so-called female reformer of the present day none has, as yet, *originated* any scheme for the advancement or benefit of her fellow-creatures, and, although the younger members of all well-to-do families have had the advantage of a comparatively liberal education, custom still chalks out the path they have to tread.

Ever since my coming of age, I have been accustomed to hear a great deal of controversy on the subject of the rise and progress of female education. I have also read one or two works of Parsee authors, treating of this subject, and the newspapers make mention of many a worthy supporter of the cause; but in no instance has Bai Meheribai had that recognition which is fully due to the prime mover in this reformation. There are several statements made in the books above referred to, which I am compelled to endeavour to refute. In an English work published in 1858 by the late Mr Dosabhoy Framjee Karaka on the manners, customs and ancestral lore of the Parsees, he gives the credit of founding female education amongst us, to a few individuals whom he mentions by name.

It is to say the least strange that an event which caused so much consternation amongst the whole public of Bombay, European as well as native, should be passed over in silence—I refer to the authoress being sent, as a girl, to Mrs Ward's School. But the male sex is ever tardy in acknowledging the merits of a female rival. Mr Dosabhoy has persistently continued in the omission of Meheribai's name, for even in the second edition of his book, which has been revised and considerably enlarged, no notice was taken of the important part played by Meheribai in the emancipation of her sisters, although minute details are given of the leaders in every art, profession, trade or custom, such as the first native schoolmaster, judge, lawyer, ship-builder, manufacturer, and the first traveller to England and China. A parallel example of the same remissness is to be seen in the suppression of the name of the first Parsee lady who ventured to visit England. The omission may be purely accidental, but the episode will be duly mentioned in these pages.

Another Gujarati publication, which appeared in 1874, entitled *Mombai Bahar*, and treating of the pedigrees of distinguished native families, claims for Mr Manekjee Cursetjee (the uncle of the authoress) the merit of introducing English education into the Parsee community, by placing his late brother's daughter in an English school. I have demonstrated to my readers how very differently the case stood, but, notwithstanding that, the fact was too well known at the time to be so soon forgotten. If my Parsee brethren should have been so neglectful of Meheribai's just claim, then it is not surprising that the editor of an English newspaper should have been led into the error of suppressing her name, and giving the honour of her achievements to others. However, all these records agree in one particular—that there was no other Parsee girl attending Mrs Ward's school but myself. In further proof of this fact I give an extract from a letter of my old school comrade, Mrs Mary Crawford, widow of a highly-respected auctioneer of Bombay. The letter is dated 15th January 1885, and runs as follows:

> "I can only send you a few lines, as I have to go out on duty, but I must tell you Mrs Ward had *never* another Parsee girl in her school, either before you came or ever after: this I am sure of."

After Meheribai's example, her brother-in-law, as already stated, had his daughter instructed by a governess at home. Then Sir Jamsetjee

Jejeebhoy gave the same advantage to his daughter, Perojbai. Simultaneously, another well-known Parsee gentleman, Framjee Cowasjee Banajee had his daughter, Perojbai, who was eighteen years of age and married, instructed in English, but so much secrecy was observed that even the members of the family were kept in ignorance of the fact, and the lessons were given to her by her Portuguese master, Mr Amadore Viegas, with closed doors. Thus when the leaders of Parsee society were afraid of letting it be known that their daughters were so privileged, Meheribai publicly espoused the cause of English education and so paved the way for the widespread diffusion of this unspeakable blessing.

We append a portrait of this distinguished pioneer, a faithful reproduction of the first photograph taken of an Indian lady. It was done in 1846, photography being in those days a profound mystery to a Parsee woman's mind. Meheribai is here represented in her widow's weeds, which are always by us retained during widowhood. The likeness is so excellent that those who knew her in her lifetime will doubtless readily recognise her.

IV

Progress Following Meheribai's Innovation—The Passing Away of a Pioneer

The preceding pages bear witness to the important part played by Meheribai in laying the foundation of women's education in India. It would be interesting to my readers to notice the progressive impulse which the cause received immediately after that memorable Parsee lady evinced the foresight and courage so necessary for one bent upon passing one's society through a powerful innovation. We have seen above how Meheribai's example, though its value was minimised for the time being, was emulated in due course by other Parsee parents and publicists. The Jews seem to have been the first to follow the Parsees in this respect, and all honour is due to Sir Albert Sassoon for bringing the means of education to the women of his creed. He lived near Meheribai, and soon an intimate friendship sprang up between the two families.

What Meheribai did for the Parsees, Sir Albert succeeded in doing far more fully and effectually for the Jews. He overcame the prejudices of his old sire, and thus strengthened he spread the light of many a beneficent principle, opening the gate of happiness to the women of his faith.

It is within my memory that Jewesses never appeared in public without closely veiled faces. When the ladies of the Sassoon family came to visit Meheribai, they would never unveil till the male members of the household, servants included, had removed themselves and the coast was clear; but sometimes their fancied security was invaded by a visit of Dr Fogarti, our physician, who would call in as he was wont, unaware of the presence of strangers, and the confusion which then ensued—they attempting to hide themselves in adjoining rooms—caused much merriment.

We cannot but with pleasure compare this with the different customs now prevailing, a new condition of things due in no small measure to the good sense and energy of Sir Albert Sassoon. Jewesses of this country enjoy the privileges of an enlightened education, to which is frequently added the culture of travel. Many having visited England, the Continent of Europe, and the New World, and now live much as English ladies of the period do.

Bai Meheribai's acquaintance outside her own community did not cease here. She was equally intimate with the two wives of the well-known Hindoo citizen Set Khimchund Moteechund, who both were equally desirous of emulating her Parsee dress and elegance. They adopted China or English silk sarees as well as Parsee-fashioned Lahe* sarees, and enjoyed the luxury of slippers, after the manner of the Parsees, as Hindoos they having formerly gone barefoot.

In 1846, a Mr Hinton established a school for Parsee boys, which was mainly supported by the leading gentlemen of the community. Subsequently in 1849, Mrs Hinton opened a similar school exclusively for girls and enrolled several young ladies of the Sassoon family amongst its pupils. By the thorough course of instruction pursued in these schools, the results could be favourably compared with those of European seminaries. The two daughters of Mr Manekjee Cursetjee, who in consequence of their superior acquirements, were held in high estimation, were educated at Mrs Hinton's school.

*This is a minute curious and laborious process of embroidery. The stitches, the size of a pin's head, are made from a pattern on the raw silk fabric, which being then dyed, the minute specks stand out in relief on the uniformly coloured ground. The artisans who worked in this frequently required a whole year to finish a piece of the length of six yards by one. This needlework is almost obsolete on account of its great expense and unostentatious appearance.

The Marathas seem to have adopted English education after the Parsees and Jews, and subsequently the Banias, and lastly the Mahomedans, who, however, do not appear to have made any appreciable progress. Similarly, amongst the Babus, the celebrated Rajah Ram Mohan Roy did much for his countrymen, but even he, as appears from his biography, did not extend his efforts in the direction of education, though now Bengali women are making satisfactory progress. The Bethune Female School at Calcutta did not exist in 1842 and, so far as I know, not before 1848. About 1849-50 the Parsees of Bombay established a female school for vernacular education only, its existence was mainly owing to the handsome donations of Messrs Framjee Nassarwanjee Patell, Cursetjee and Dhunjibhoy Nusserwanji Camaji and others, who thus won for themselves the reputation of being promoters of female education. But I beg to suggest that those whose personal effort, independence and public spirit first made way for the institution of female education among us, are more worthy of having their names perpetuated in history. With regret we note the fact that seven years after the commencement of English female education, this girls' school was founded, and that those who gave it the mere assistance of their purse are held up to the admiration of the world, while the real founders of education by *moral support* are either forgotten or ignored. Such, alas! seems to be the rule of this mercenary world. Amongst Europeans, however, money apparently is of less weight; for amongst them the leader of an enterprise seems to be gratefully acknowledged, and this acts as a stimulus to others to "go and do likewise."

After the events above referred to, we have to record the establishment of several girls' vernacular schools in the principal towns of this and other Presidencies. By degrees the male Parsees, after reaping the unspeakable benefits of education themselves, desired to see their women participating in the same advantages, and with this laudable aim they, who were neither great nor rich, spontaneously came forward with what their limited means could afford and, what was of more value, with their personal exertions, and succeeded in placing vernacular education within easy reach of Parsee and other Indian girls. To them is due the credit of opening these schools in the various sections of the town.

There existed about this time a body, known as the "Students' Literary and Scientific Society," and to the untiring zeal of its members we owe the happy development of the said schools. Amongst its founders we would mention Messrs Dadabhoy Naoroji—the Grand Old Man of India—Nowrojee Furdoonjee, Ardeshir Framjee Moos, Bomonjee Pestonjee Master and Byramjee Cursetjee Ghandhee. Besides these Parsees, Messrs Green, Arnold, Reid and Patton, the time-honoured professors of the Bombay Institute, were members of the above-named society and were, with the distinguished Judge of the Supreme Court—Sir Erskine Perry—the active supporters of female education. Through their encouragement the aforenamed vernacular schools came into life.

Mr Ardeshir Framjee Moos gave up a part of his dwelling-house for one of these schools, and for a period of two years, while the enterprise was in its infancy, several other members of the society most kindly and disinterestedly devoted a portion of their time to teaching the girls. Only subsequently, the plutocrats were roused to a sense of their duty and gave these schools their liberal support, thus again showing that the so-called leading Parsees, the Sethias, were not the organisers of this movement any more than it could be affirmed that the introduction of English education was the work of any Parsee gentleman.

Although the English and Vernacular newspapers, from their ignorance, give forth the names of several Parsee gentlemen, such as Sorabjee Shapurjee Bengali, Dosabhoy Framjee Karaka, etc., as the leaders and advocates of female education, their connection with the movement is but of recent date: those very individuals do not appear to have given a sound education to the women of their own families, while several superstitious customs continued to prevail in their households.

We cannot conclude this brief review of the establishment of female education amongst us, without mentioning a notable instance of the encouragement it has had.

In the year 1860, my uncle, Mr Manekjee Cursetjee Shroff, a well-known judicial functionary, known as "Manekjee Judge," thought of extending the knowledge of English to the females of Parsee and other native castes. For this purpose he opened, at his own expense and at his own residence at Byculla, a school for girls which after some time was by the monetary assistance of a few friends transferred to a suitable building in the Fort and publicly opened under the name of "The Alexandra Native Girls' English Institute." The blessings of this noble institution are open to all castes and grades.

Under the humane influence of Queen Victoria's reign, continued in that of our late Sovereign, the education of Indian women has flourished wonderfully. Some have aspired to excellence in the fine arts and others have even ventured to appear in print. Every facility is now afforded to the pursuit of study. Lady teachers who were formerly much in demand, and used to earn ten times as much as they do now, are no longer *raræ aves*, but are seen frequenting Parsee houses, seeking, in fact, such situations, thus within the reach of those of mediocre fortune. As a natural consequence, Indian girls reap the benefit of their tuition in far greater numbers. Time has to a great extent overcome the old conservatism of the Parsees, whom we now see in the vanguard of progress. These achievements, however, are of comparatively recent date: the school established and conducted by Mrs Ward had but one single pupil from amongst the natives—the humble writer of this book.

But let us revert to the events of the life of her who thus laid the real foundation of women's education in India. During her widowhood, about the year 1848, Meheribai removed to Walkeshwar, Malabar Hill, a step which occasioned as much outcry as sending her daughter to school had done. The Parsee Punchayet, the body conducting the social governance of the Parsee community, gave it out as their grave opinion that it was anomalous for a Parsee lady to live in such an out-of-the-way locality. The newspapers were equally busy in discussing the point, some defending, others opposing Meheribai, all of which had only the effect of encouraging her in the prosecution of what she deemed best and most suitable. The house to which she moved was until recently in the possession of her eldest son and was rented by Messrs Kemp & Co. for a medical dispensary. At the time of which we are writing, that is in 1848, the healthy eminence of Malabar Hill was quite untenanted by any Parsees. Mr Framjee Cowasjee Banajee, it is true, owned a few bungalows there, but they were without exception occupied by Europeans. This beautiful and salubrious locality presents a thickly populated appearance, still it is within recent times that Parsee families have taken to residing there.

In the year 1849, Meheribai had the misfortune to lose her youngest son, Shapoorjee, at the age of eighteen, and a year later her youngest brother, nicknamed Kakajee, who had been the only connecting link for twenty-five years between herself and her estranged family. These two sad events plunged her into grief and solitude for three or four years, but the mutual bereavement had the effect of restoring her to the affections of her long alienated family and, though, at that time her mother was no more, she rejoiced in the favour of her brothers and sisters during the remainder of her life.

It is painful to record that on 9th April 1879, in the eightieth year of her age, Bai Meheribai breathed her last, up to which time she had been in the full enjoyment of health of body and vigour of mind. After her death, the newspapers eulogised her as "the real pioneer of English education amongst native females." In an editorial article published in 1908 the *Indian Magazine and Review* of London paid a fitting tribute to her memory when it observed that she had "distinguished herself by those qualities of which heroines are made. Meheribai realised the advantages of giving an English education to Parsee girls long before other women, and even most men, of her race. But building ideals is one thing, and translating them into action quite another. For this reason her name deserves a prominent place in the history of women's education in India."

V

My Early Life and Engagement

When I came of age I had to discard the childish dress, alike in boys and girls, of short, brightly coloured trousers, jacket and cap, and to adopt the saree—a piece of cloth six yards in length by one or one-and-a-half in width, sufficient to wrap around the whole person and cover the head. As an adult I had also to give up wearing boots and take to slippers instead, a change which I thought no improvement, but custom forbade a grown-up Parsee lady to put her feet into anything else.

I was only thirteen when I left school, but every Saturday I drove over to the Fort and passed the day in the agreeable company of my old school friends. I prosecuted my study of English at home, under the tuition of a governess, who came twice a week for half a day to teach me and converse with me, at a salary of Rs 50 a month. After six months, the lady unfortunately went away and my lessons were suspended for a time.

I next devoted myself to the execution of a large piece of work—a palanquin rug—which took a full year to complete. Then again an opportunity presented itself of resuming my English lessons, but again for only a short period. By keeping up my English friendships, I acquired many English manners and customs which are very different from those of Indians, and my mind became insensibly tinged with English ideas, so that I viewed life differently, in many respects, from those around me. A Parsee lady would not consider it disrespectful or odd to squat on the floor in company, talk in a loud tone while gesticulating freely, stare at others, and so on. My kind mistress inculcated habits of gentleness, respect, order, tidiness and politeness and taught to me to obey and respect my own religion; and I took delight in observing her precepts, which made me honoured and beloved both at school and at home.

When I was present at any Parsee festivity, my manner of sitting appeared to the others affected and I was requested, in terms by no means flattering, to sit at ease as they did. When I spoke, my modulated voice was considered pretended coyness. But those who then condemned my behaviour now view with exulting pride the repetition of it in their own daughters or granddaughters, and I often hear a grandam announce with her wrinkled face lit up with joy, that Soonabai goes to school or that Aimai and Sherinbai are learning English. Parsee parents are now the most eager to give their daughters every means of improvement. To me nothing could be more gratifying than this complete reversion of feeling in the question of female education.

When a marriage was about to take place in a Parsee family, invitations were issued to between two and five hundred friends and the festivities extend over a period of five to seven days. This used to entail a great deal of unnecessary labour on the ladies of the household. Letters of invitation are sent to the gentlemen, after which a priest goes to each, requesting the honour of his presence on the morning of the wedding-day. But in those days, the fashion of inviting the lady guests was most tiresome and nonsensical; the principal ladies of the house were obliged to go round amongst relatives and friends two days before and again on the morning of the wedding-day to proffer and reiterate their invitation, and not until they were nearly prostrate with fatigue, would the guests consent to come—such was the perverted notion of politeness.

To make an end of this most stupid and trying custom, my mother, on the occasion of the marriage of one of my brothers, sent cards of invitation to ladies as well as gentlemen. The greater number responded to her invitation, but others held aloof at the innovation. In this case my mother, as a widow, could not have paid the visits and she wished to spare me the fatigue as I was quite a young girl. Our house not being large enough to accommodate so many guests, my mother was allowed the use of the adjoining Engineer's office, an arrangement which was quite unaccountable to the Parsees, who began to think there was no end to the wonderful things my mother could do. Since that time, a few families have adopted the plan of written invitations, but it is by no means general yet.

After the wedding festivities were over, my mother and I retired for a time to Walkeshwar, Malabar Hill, where we lived in a tent. This being the first time for a Parsee family to sojourn under canvas, many visitors drove out to see us and satisfy their curiosity. We continued to live in our tent, till a small bungalow, my mother had in course of erection, was completed. We were the first Parsees to settle in Malabar Hill. In time, we made the acquaintance of our European neighbours, who were as astonished at our advent as if we had come from another land.

While living at Malabar Hill my youngest brother and I were attacked by cholera and, as no medical assistance was to be had in those days in that remote locality, we were removed to our house in the Fort, where, by the timely assistance of our physician, we recovered. Had it been otherwise, people would not have been slow in laying the blame on our distant abode. In the treatment of this terrible disease, our doctor had strictly enjoined us not to drink water, but being unable to endure our intense thirst, we contrived to elude the vigilance of our attendants and drank copiously of some water which had been left standing in the empty room for two months. With the deepest gratitude to Almighty God we remember our miraculous escape from this premium paid to death.

How often in my life have I experienced that the heaviest storm succeeds the most unruffled calm. In 1849, my youngest brother, who had escaped the malignant seizure of cholera, died of a slight attack of fever. This was an irreparable loss to our now limited domestic circle, and my mother's health completely gave way under the burden of grief. It was at this time and under these unavoidable circumstances that I took a sorrowful farewell of my studies, at the age of seventeen.

The care of my invalid mother and the domestic duties of the house now devolved upon me.

After a death in the family, the Zoroastrian religion requires that for a year the survivors must observe numerous ceremonies for the benefit of the departed spirit. Different viands must be prepared every day for the deceased and every monthly return of the day of death a special ceremony is held, for which many sorts of sweetmeats are requisite, over which the priests recite appropriate prayers. This is called "Baj." It is necessary on these occasions to treat fifteen or twenty priests to dinner. In these observances, for the express behoof of the departed, rich and poor give willingly and with no niggard hand, glad to have the opportunity of showing their regard for their dead. All the viands must be prepared under the direct supervision, often too by the hands of the ladies of the family and in strict accordance with the rules laid down by our religion. It fell to me to superintend the preparation of these offerings to the memory of a beloved brother, and with a full heart I entered into the melancholy duty and soon imbibed a taste for culinary operations.

I became an adept in the making of sweetmeats and of soups for my mother, who could not at first be brought to believe that what she so much relished was the work of my hands. Even in the quiet retirement of mourning and sick-nursing, my liberal education stood me in good stead, for with keen zest and enjoyment, I performed the household duties which others felt to be drudgery.

After my brother's death, we left Walkeshwar and occupied an airy and commodious house which my mother purchased at this time. Over against this house the gloomy structure of the ramparts projected, at this point at an acute angle, and very much impaired the comfort and value of the house. The ramparts were of solid masonry and surmounted by heavy artillery. My mother, accordingly, at the advice of Colonel Jarvis, petitioned the Government for the removal of this obnoxious corner, offering to defray the expense herself. This request was at once acceded to, much to the surprise of other Indians, who could not believe that a widow, who forgot her position so far as to memorialise the Government, would have a ready ear lent her and succeed in her efforts. Thus Bai Meheribai, by her boldness and independence, once again incurred the envy and raillery of her native townsmen, though by God's grace all her endeavours in the cause of female reform were invariably crowned with success. Considerably after this date, in 1860, the ramparts were totally demolished and the moat filled up.

The year 1850 was an auspicious and momentous one for me, as I was then pledged to a partner for life. Up to the date of which I am writing, early marriages, or rather infant marriages, were the universal rule; it was no uncommon sight for me to see a babe at its mother's breast pronounced by the priest a married person. Twelve years was the maximum age for a girl to marry. If, through untoward circumstances, a daughter remained unmarried up to fifteen it was a grave sorrow to the parents, and the girl herself became the butt of cruel taunts, while scandal was busy with her name. Setting all the force of her character against this pernicious custom, my mother would not hear of marriage for me till I had reached my sixteenth year. Marriages were then entirely arranged by the parents, the young people having neither voice in the matter nor cognizance of it till all was settled.

By my association with English ladies, I had come to the conviction that I had a right to either assent to or decline any proposed union that I too had something to say in a matter of such grave importance to myself. My father had destined me for his brother's son, and such a connection would not have been distasteful to me, but, on account of my mother's separation from the family, I was not sure how the case stood.

I was much in favour with my uncle, the father of the boy, and from my childhood I had been invited every week, as well as on my birthday, and all festivals, to his house where I spent the day in much enjoyment with my cousins. This could not fail to please me and so impressed was I with my uncle's kindness that I used constantly to exclaim to my friend: "What a good uncle I have! He gives such grand entertainments on my birthday." I afterwards discovered that my natal day was also the anniversary of my grandmother's death, and that the festivities were in honour of her, though my uncle killed two birds with one stone by making me believe I was the heroine of the day.

On these occasions I would converse and associate freely with my cousin, but our long-contemplated union was, according to Parsee custom, never broached between us. One day, acting under my mother's advice, I asked my uncle to make me his daughter-in-law, according to the express wish of my father, but he answered that though he loved me as his own child, he could not, on account of his objection to my mother, consent to my union with his son. From this I understood plainly that only if my revered and beloved mother were no more could I aspire to be the wife of my cousin. Under such painful circumstances I tried to dismiss the subject from my mind, while my mother sought elsewhere for a partner for me. I may here mention another custom which thwarts the happiness of many a couple.

As soon as a child is born, the parents have its horoscope prepared by a Hindoo astrologer; and when, therefore, a marriage is in contemplation, the first step is to produce the two children's horoscopes, submit them to the opinion of competent astrologers, and either proceed with the proposed match, or give it up, according to the verdict of these authorities. This idle superstition has made many an ill assorted marriage, and marred many an auspicious one.

After my brother's death, at which time I was seventeen years of age, we received numerous visits of condolence from our relatives and friends. Amongst the number was a cousin of my mother—a rich, elderly widower. He avowed to my mother his affection towards me, offering to make over to me all his property and wealth, if I would become his wife.

This was a tempting bait to my mother, who believed my happiness would be secured by this generous proposal. I, however, thought otherwise, but dared not say so, as it would have been held in the highest degree undutiful and unprecedented to decline an offer already accepted by a parent. In my distress, I turned to Bai Baiai, wife of the late Jehangir Framjee Jessawalla, my mother's most intimate friend, and with tears streaming down my cheeks, I confessed to her my repugnance to the contemplated union. She entered into my feeling and lovingly consoled me by promising to use her best efforts, to dissuade my mother from carrying out her intention and fortunately her endeavours were successful, for I never heard another word of this unequal match.

Only a month after this happy release an incident occurred, which serves to prove the secret workings of Providence in the events of human life. The aforementioned lady, my mother's friend, had the misfortune to lose her young and beloved daughter-in-law, who was cut off in the prime of life and happiness, leaving six children and a young husband to mourn her untimely loss. This sad event plunged the whole circle into profound grief. They were a large and united family, all living together in love and harmony, in the parental homestead. In consequence of the mourning in both families, there was a cessation of the daily visits Bai Baiai paid us, and I, as an unmarried girl, could not go out alone, the custom of our race being that after the occurrence of a death a full year must elapse before the relatives may pay even the nearest friends a visit.

We were then living at Khetwady and our friend in the Fort. An idea all of a sudden struck my mother, that her friend might make me her daughter-in-law and, simultaneously, a rumour arose, that my mother had betrothed me to the widowed son of her friend.

One day Bai Goolbai, sister of Bai Baiai, visited us and broached the delicate topic to my mother, subsequently our friend herself came at dusk and all preliminaries were discussed and arranged between her and my mother. The only objection which presented itself to my mother was the charge of six motherless children, which she considered too great a burden for me, but on being assured that the paternal and maternal grandmothers would divide the care of these little ones, and that they would be provided for, she was relieved, and all anxiety was set at rest, by my declaring that of my own free will I chose this friend's household as my future home and selected her son as my future partner for life.

I may mention in passing, that Parsee ladies, who have attained the dignity of grandmothers, always cherish and take entire care of their grandchildren, during the remainder of their life, thus helping and relieving the parents to a very great extent. Amongst Parsees or, properly speaking amongst all native women, till recently there used to be no acquaintance with the opposite sex, outside the immediate family circle. Thus, my mother, though on terms of affectionate intimacy with Bai Baiai, had never seen any of the male portion of her family, and I naturally had not seen, much less talked to him who was now my affianced husband.

In the weak state of my mother's health, she thought it advisable to hasten the betrothal on, and she did so by sending, according to Parsee custom, the following items to the bridegroom—a diamond ring, a nosegay, a packet of sugarcandy, "Kunkoo" (red powder applied in a circular form on the forehead), a cup of curds, some salmon, artificial fishes of Chinese workmanship wrought in silver, betel nuts and leaves, both real and of silver. All these things were sent in a copper box, instead of on the usual tray, so as not to wound the feelings of the late wife's parents, who lived in the house with the bridegroom's family, as it was considered quite unusual to think of a second marriage, for one year after the death of one so young as the first wife had been when she died. A few days after this, my future mother-in-law sent me in return costly suits of silk, and so the betrothal was ratified and soon became noised abroad. With a grateful heart I bow to the decrees of the Divine will, and trust my future, as my past, to the great God who has kept me hitherto.

In those days, the Parsees did not allow an engaged couple to meet or correspond with each other, from the betrothal till the marriage tie proclaimed them one. So in this interval my intended husband went on a tour to inspect his father's branch establishments in Upper India and the Punjab. These were situated in Kurrachee, Sukkur, Mooltan, Rawalpindi, Kabul (He was present at the battle of Kabul in 1843), Ferozepore, Delhi and several other places, and in those days, before railways and posts were known, travelling was arduous and tedious. My husband, who had been in the habit of making journeys from his seventeenth year to his thirty-second, used to go from Bombay to Kurrachee in a small sailing ship and from thence up-country on horse or camelback, returning to Bombay for two or three months in the summer.

It was then unknown and unthought-of for a son to follow a different business or calling from that of his father, and each son vied with the other in maintaining the prestige of the paternal house as handed down from one generation to another. During the long engagement between my husband and myself, of nearly two years, no correspondence passed between us though I ardently longed to see him or, at least hear how life was faring with him. From his mother I received assurances of his unchanged love for me, and with that I had to be satisfied, but my English friends found it incomprehensible that I could endure such a long and silent engagement. My husband's friend, Mr Arthur Lynch, rallied me upon having chosen a husband without having seen him and who, for aught I knew, was neither comely nor handsome, to which I answered: "It is not so much the body as the mind we love, and, seeing that my betrothed is highly spoken of by everybody, my mother thinks she gives me into good hands and I myself expect to be happy." Mr Lynch was pleased with my reply and then, in right earnest, praised his friend and congratulated me on my choice.

But, in the midst of all this happiness, a heavy calamity fell upon my mother, spreading distress through our family and causing me much anxiety and pain before entering on my new career. After a prosperous service of seven years in the old Oriental Bank, my eldest brother assumed an independent position; he then began to treat his mother lightly and bad companionship drew him on to evil. In his blind folly and ambition for wealth, he brought indelible disgrace on a hitherto untainted name by appropriating a very large amount of money belonging to the Bank—a lac of rupees, equivalent to £6,666. He was tried and sentenced to a long term of imprisonment. This was a heavy blow to our aged mother and she was much harassed by the loss of 60,000 rupees, which she had to give over as a guarantee to the Bank, besides being stung to the quick by the stigma on her family and by the cruel remarks which reached her ear. Before dropping a curtain on this painful episode, I may state that the heavy sentence of twenty-one years was, through the unceasing efforts of my aggrieved mother, the recommendation of influential friends, the untarnished name of our family and my brother's evidently reformed character, commuted to seven years, at the expiration of which period he was released and restored to his family.

The house which my mother had bought and for the benefit of which a part of the rampart had been removed, had to be sold while under reconstruction. It was purchased for Rs 65,000 by Sir Jamsetjee Jeejeebhoy who subsequently presented it to his son. It was for many years the seat of the Presidency Magistrate's Court. Before the existence of the Parsee Matrimonial Court, Set Cursetjee Manekjee Shroff, my grandfather, used to sit in judgment on family feuds in this self-same house. This reminds one the Gujarati proverb: "The camphor-box is but filled with camphor again."

VI

Insight into Married Life

It was in the year 1850 that my fiancé started on a tour in the Punjab, whence returning in 1852, the marriage day was fixed for the auspicious seventh day of the ninth month (30th May), considered in the family a lucky day, as it was the birthday of my uncle, Sir Cowasjee Jehangir Readymoney. The marriage was celebrated at Girgaon, where my mother and I were then living. This long looked-for day would have seen my mother supremely happy, but for the ever-present thought of her guilty son. The fact, too, of this being a second marriage on the bridegroom's part, called for a moderated expression of rejoicing.

Although the festival was kept as unostentatiously as possible, my mother lavished upon me, her only daughter, all that the fondest love could suggest. All our friends were duly invited, but on my husband's side only his two sisters, his sister-in-law and my mother-in-law's cousin and Bai Kooverbai, the sister-in-law of the late Lady Jamsetjee were present. It was the last named lady who, after putting the red mark of "Kunkoo" on my forehead, with her own lucky hands garlanded my head with flowers and invested me with the bridal dress, and thus adorned, the marriage rite was performed according to Parsee form, at 7 p.m.

Soon after the ceremony, my husband's relatives departed. After midnight benedictory rites were performed, following upon which my husband and I were escorted to his father's bungalow at Tardeo, where his family had taken up their abode two days before, so as to make ready for our reception.

It is not customary for the young couple to walk together, but the bridegroom heads the male portion of the procession and the bride follows with the ladies. Thus I reached the bungalow, where I was heartily welcomed by my new relations. My husband continued his way to the family residence in the Fort, where I followed next evening. Before crossing the threshold of my future home, flowers, cocoanuts and rice were scattered over my head, a ceremony known by the name of "Anchoo-Meechoo." From that day, I became a member of the large family, consisting of between fifty to sixty persons, all living under one roof.

Some of the presents which my mother gave to my husband, on the occasion of my marriage, may be enumerated as an example of what is customary in Parsee marriages. Thus, she presented each member of his family, male and female, with handsome suits, and sent shawls and turbans to the managers and clerks of his firm. On each intervening holiday, during the first year, she gave my husband a suit, a costly shawl and a diamond ring, at the same time bestowing suits on each of his children by the first wife. To me she gave all sorts of culinary utensils, such as pots, chatties, trays and large copper vessels, ornaments of silver such as cocoanuts, dates, betel-nuts and leaves—a suite of carved black-wood furniture comprising tables, chairs, couches, etc., and a valuable bedstead, with silken hangings and coverlets—a milch-cow and a she-goat—sewing materials in rich abundance, a work-table, a writing desk and a large sum of money. Thus my loving mother gave expression to the joy she felt at seeing me united to such a good and exemplary man.

From the year 1852 down to the time my partner departed this life, the course of my existence was a happy and easy one, blessed with the unceasing love of my husband and the pleasant intimacy of a large family circle. All the female members of the family were old-fashioned in their ideas and way of living, but nothing was wanting on my fond husband's part to insure my comfort—indeed love prompted him to anticipate my every wish. Thus, on the first day of my new life, he handed me the key of a cupboard, which when I opened, I found stored with all manner of things just suited to my taste, for instance, silken fabrics, stockings, kid gloves, pieces of lace and tulle, velvets, bottles of otto of roses, handkerchiefs and every requisite of sewing and writing. It was a delightful surprise as I certainly never expected to see such luxuries in a house where old customs prevailed, but my husband's liking for English fashions agreed with mine.

On questioning my husband whether his former wife had also been of the same mind, he smilingly replied that "she had been simplicity itself."

He further went on to say: "My family is a large one and quite of the old school; you, however, blessed with an English education as well as trained up in Parsee usages, will wisely discern how to maintain the family concord, without depriving yourself of anything to which you have from infancy been accustomed."

These kind words of confidence in me soothed my anxieties, and I offered fervent praise and thanksgiving to Almighty God for the happy lot he had ordained me. It would be out of my power to describe the thrill of ecstasy which the love of my husband excited in my hitherto virgin breast—what could I do, but strive to live in harmony with all the members of his family and act a mother's part to my step-children? And these endeavours brought their own reward, in the good feeling manifested to me by my numerous relatives, though no doubt, the new customs I introduced sometimes annoyed them.

My fond mother had accustomed me from childhood to dress carefully and in good taste, both at home and abroad, and now that I was under the authority of my parents-in-law I continued the same habit, dressing as a young and happy wife, in bright silken stuffs at home and bedecked with diamond and pearl jewellery when at feasts or entertainments. The only ornament in general use amongst the ladies of my husband's family were the ear and nose rings while their house dress was simple in the extreme. To wear costly suits when at home was then comparatively unknown.

My mother-in-law, whom I affectionately called "Aunt," supervised my meals herself and looked after my comfort in every detail. In the family, the old-fashioned mode of eating together, squatted on a low cane couch, out of the same dish, prevailed—the luxury of table, chair, drinking glass and separate plate being unknown. My indulgent mother-in-law, foreseeing that it would be difficult for me to take part in such meals, provided for my exclusive use plates, cups and tumblers, besides allotting me my meals in a separate room and often providing an extra dish or two for my benefit, secretly, however, to avoid kindling envy. When at home, my husband would join in the repast, which, though now a common custom, was then unprecedented, as males and females in those days ate apart. To me it was a source of keen pleasure to see how his views ran in unison with mine, and owing to my condition at this time, the affectionate solicitude of my two mothers and husband was redoubled.

In her joy at my blissful hopes, my mother presented me with a set of splendid diamond and pearl ornaments and my husband's parents gave me some in gold, in addition to which every holiday my husband laid a sum of money before me, telling me to lay it out in ornaments after my own taste and design, but as I had jewels enough, these sums remained in my hands and accumulated.

After my marriage, I enjoyed the favour of two neighbouring families, one the long estranged family of my maternal grandfather, now happily reconciled with my mother, and I was a frequent guest here every holiday at the kind invitation of my maternal aunt, wife of the late Sir Cowasjee Jehangir Readymoney and who was then staying at her parental residence. The other was the family of Framjee Nusserwanjee Patell.

At a suitable time I removed to my mother's house, where by God's grace I was in due course safely delivered of a daughter, on the fourteenth day of the fourth month. The babe received the name of "Goolbai," the choice of a name always resting with the child's grandmothers. Forty days after confinement I wished to return to my husband's house, but to this my mother was most averse, desiring me to stay with her till the child had completed her fifth month. To this I would not consent and my mother was angry with me, saying if I persisted in going away she not only would give none of the looked-for presents to the child, but she would detain the ornaments she had given me at my marriage. My fond husband on his daily visits soon discerned that something was amiss and on my acquainting him with the matter, he eased my mind by telling me to provide everything for myself and the child at his own expense, and that we should then go home at the appointed time.

Within a week I got all completed, *viz.*, a rich complete costume for my mother-in-law, garments for my infant, large tapestry coverlets for taking the child from one place to another, toys, cups and saucers, plates and milk jug all of silver, a brazen bath for the baby, a trayful of sugarcandy, a basket of wheat, a cradle with netted curtains and a cot.

"All this," I said to my mother, "I have to thank you for," with which polite fiction she was somewhat mollified. However, when I set out for my husband's house, accompanied by a nurse carrying the baby and my husband's sisters, who had come to call me home, my mother did not relent, so that grief lay heavy at my heart and I was reluctantly compelled to appear with the few simple ornaments I had received from my husband.

The first day of the new moon is considered auspicious by Indians, and generally chosen for any special event, and on such a day I returned to my home, but it failed to cheer me, for there was a cloud between me and my beloved mother. The unfortunate disagreement I managed to keep a secret and continued to pay her a visit every fourth day, as I had always done since my marriage. My happiness would have been complete but for this coolness on my mother's part and for anxiety on account of my two brothers, Heerjeebhoy and Furdoonjee, who lived with her and were without employment. I tried to help them and whenever my mother was ill I went every day to take care of her.

As already mentioned, I brought some new fashions with me into my husband's family, amongst others the use of stockings—Parsees of the old school never wore them. As I had been accustomed to wear them all my life, it would have been impossible to give them up entirely. I had there always kept them on in my own room, but taken them off when mingling with the family, but now my husband's express wish was that I should wear them always and go in them everywhere. My sisters-in-law saw with displeasure my husband's growing inclination for new ways, but as the time wore on and his love increased his ideas ran more and more in the same channel as mine, inspiring me with confidence and making me independent of his sisters.

In 1854 on the occasion of a second pregnancy I, agreeably to my husband's wishes, remained at home, under the tender care of his mother, but being prematurely confined my babe did not survive its birth. My mother was much annoyed that I had not gone to her and the suspicions of my husband's family were aroused. It being at the same time discovered that my husband was in the habit of lavishing money on me they began to regard me with dislike, so much so that whatever I did or my husband gave me seemed to augment their jealousy. But the love of my husband and his worthy mother towards me was not lessened one iota.

Of the four children, two sons and two daughters, of my parents-in-law, my husband was the eldest. He was also the chief worker of the firm, and was invariably consulted on all matters, commercial and domestic. He was so busy during the day as never to be able to join any pleasure party, only occasionally making an exception when requested by his father to accompany him, otherwise he devoted all his leisure to his aged parents, whose love for him was truly touching. Through his unwearied exertions the prosperity of the firm considerably increased and his father's confidence in him was so great, that the direction was left almost entirely in his hands. But woe succeeds weal as uniformly as night the day, and an all-wise Providence decreed it so in my case, lest a life of uniform bliss should make me proud and selfish. Cut off as I was now from communication with my mother, I was obliged to conduct all transactions with jewellers, embroiderers, clothiers, tailors, goldsmiths and so on for myself, in my own private room.

Shopping being in those days unknown, all purchases were made by the men of the family from pedlars and artisans plying the streets, the women and children wearing without word or comment what they were given. Hindoos and Parsees dressed pretty much alike in flaring red, green or yellow stuffs, the tailor's taste being unquestioned and his ugly, badly-sewn garments the universal mode.

After my advent amongst my husband's relations, my sister-in-law, wife of the other son, felt it awkward to accompany me in walks and visits, she being so differently attired from myself, so by the kind permission of her father and mother-in-law she had some dresses and ornaments made, similar to mine, but even in this trifling business she herself had no voice, one of her husband's sisters, Bhikhaijee, undertaking the order and supervision of the work, while I, by my husband's favour, was at full liberty to have any sort of ornament fashioned according to my taste; and having had an insight into the workmanship of jewellery from my early years, I had no recourse to Bhikhaijee for assistance, who on this account was far from kind.

In a Parsee family the husband's sister used to hold even a more arbitrary sway than the mother, in consequence of which unfortunate dissensions often arose; in my case my independent dealing with the tradesmen was the innocent cause of scandal and enmity. My mother-in-law was most good-natured and simple. Long before there was any thought of my becoming so nearly connected with her, she gave rise to much merriment amongst us by reason of her sheer artlessness. On one occasion, when she came to visit our mother, we stuck upon our clothes little bits of black wool of the size and shape of caterpillars, on seeing which she screamed and warned us of the danger of their poignant stings, but when we put the supposed caterpillars into our mouths her apprehension knew no bounds and she predicted certain death. When we revealed the secret, however, she only laughed and enjoyed the joke as much as any of us. She was perfectly without guile and therefore an easy prey to the evil-minded.

Three years after my marriage the only brother of my husband fell dangerously ill. It is customary in cases of illness, before resorting to medical aid, to consult the invalid's horoscope and a handful of wheat is passed over his head, from which a Brahmin astrologer pretends to prognosticate whether he will recover or not. To serve their malicious purposes, my sisters-in-law made their mother believe that the grains of wheat had plainly manifested that her son's illness was caused by me—the new daughter-in-law. My kind mother-in-law would not at first credit this assertion, but the invidious workings of dislike and ill-will impressed even her guileless mind and alienated her affection from me. A deep melancholy settled upon my dear mother-in-law, which I ignorantly imputed to anxiety for her son.

My third confinement was just impending, and ignorant of the gathering storm I resolved to remain for the approaching event in the family house, but my mother-in-law, hitherto kind and considerate, did not condescend to ask my wishes or intentions and this most unaccountable silence seemed to me like hail in harvest. I adjured my husband to have all the mystery cleared up by going direct to his mother and asking her the cause of her dissatisfaction with me, but he, who is kind to a fault, would rather bear injustice than take anyone to task. So he advised me to let things take their course and said that if his mother did not restore me to her favour we would remove to our bungalow at Tardeo.

At last my husband resolved to ask his father's permission to go temporarily with me to the Tardeo bungalow; he feared however that the expense and luxury of a separate establishment would be considered unseemly for a lengthened time and that his father would be opposed to such a plan. But as I knew enough of the management of a house from my maiden days, I did not fear to be my own mistress and liked the idea of having a home to myself and husband and our children, for although I had tried from the very day of my marriage to conform to the antiquated habits and notions of my relatives, the result had been failure and disappointment. But in one instance I had, by dint of persevering courtesy, won a friend to my side.

The aunt of my husband who was at the same time his first mother-in-law, lived in the same house, and had at my coming assumed a hostile attitude towards me, turning away her face when we chanced to meet and showing plainly that she resented my presence, which was perhaps natural, on seeing me in the place of her dear departed daughter. I was very desirous of pacifying her angry feelings, so with the idea of doing so, I one day encountered her and embracing her affectionately, begged her to "think of me as her daughter and love me as such." She speedily relented, and in proof of her favour gave me the next day a handsome costume, and during her protracted illness suffered me to nurse and serve her like a daughter. Before she breathed her last, she told the entire family that I was possessed of sterling merits and had been like her own child to her. Our close intimacy lasted for a period of two years.

VII

My Embroidery Work

On the first day of the second month of 1855, I bade adieu to the family residence. My mother-in-law seeing my preparations for departure was about to dissuade me from this step, when the intriguing members of her family prevented her doing so and managed to get her out of the house at the time appointed for me to leave, so that I was compelled to go without her farewell and benediction. I accordingly set out for Tardeo with my daughter and two step-sons and the wife of the second son, who, in conformity with the prevailing custom, was married during his minority.

Our bungalow had only one storey and was furnished very simply, but as regards air and sanitation was greatly superior to the family mansion. Here had I passed the first day of my married life and here was to be my future home and the birthplace of my succeeding children. My husband joined me at 7 p.m. and from henceforth we made it a rule to dine together with our children at one table every evening. Not only was it the custom in those days to eat apart but driving together, except in a close carriage with the panels and venetian-blinds closely shut, was undreamt of. No Indian lady had ever been known to drive in a phaeton or any other open carriage.

The luxury and benefit of living in a bungalow was then

comparatively unknown. The Zenana of Borahs and Mahomedans of the present time affords an illustration of the life of Parsee ladies of that period. Our change of residence gave rise to ill-natured remarks, but on the other hand it added to our enjoyments, chief among which was the pleasure the garden afforded us. We would not go the length of taking a drive together, as the parents of my husband would not have approved of such a step, and although he was regardless of public opinion he was always obedient to the will of his father and mother. In spite of great coolness on the part of my mother-in-law I paid her a visit every few days. Of the six children by my husband's former wife four remained at the family house and two accompanied me to the new home. Nusserwanjee, the eldest, cherished me as his own mother and used to visit me daily. My husband was called to Baroda on business, relative to his sister's husband, and during his absence I was delivered of a daughter. At this juncture neither mother nor mother-in-law attended to me. I had to depend entirely upon the servants, while the frequent visits of friends and relatives mitigated the loneliness of the forty days' retirement. My husband returned from Baroda and the short-lived child breathed her last on the termination of the said period. The sting of this sad loss was in some measure blunted by the restored affection of my dear mother-in-law whilst my father-in-law was a daily visitor at the bungalow. Surrounded with domestic comfort and with good and efficient servants, my life now became a very happy one. At this time I began a piece of needlework which has had some little renown. It was a saree of white English satin, entirely covered with embroidery, representing variegated flowers and birds. It occupied me for more than six months and no fewer than forty-two different coloured silks were used. The saree was six yards in length by one and a quarter in breadth.

Shortly after our settlement in the bungalow, my father-in-law sent us an invitation to pass the Muktad Holidays at the family house, adding that at the expiration of the festival, we might, if we chose, revert to our new style of living. To this my husband like a dutiful son replied, that "the bungalow was his father's but that if he had any objection to our remaining in it we would move, only wherever we were it would be our constant aim to deserve his esteem."

"If such is your will," replied his kind father, "make the bungalow your home, but it would be wise to establish your right to a moiety in the firm as also to take a sum monthly for the maintenance of your family."

But my husband, with characteristic humility declined to raise any claim during the life-time of his worthy father. After this we were permanently domiciled at my father-in-law's bungalow and time went smoothly. The simultaneous marriages of my husband's sister's sons, who were born when their father was on the shady side of sixty, were celebrated with great pomp at our bungalow. On this festive occasion I appeared in my new hand-wrought saree, to the general surprise of the large assemblage of guests, to whom it seemed surpassingly novel and beautiful. My sisters-in-law, who had ordered for the occasion costly Chinese sarees were totally eclipsed. They had expected that as the new saree could not be finished by the time, I would as a matter of course appear in a saree of similar type to theirs and which I had worn on the day previous to the wedding. I here formed the friendship of Bai Maneckbai, wife of Set Byramjee Jeejeebhoy. My needlework was much talked of and many mere casual acquaintances thought it worth their while to call and see it.

This reminds me of two other pieces of embroidery which I worked when at the age of fifteen—one a rug, suited for a palanquin, which my mother made a present of to our worthy friend Colonel Jarvis, who, on accepting the same, said that a spacious hall would be the appropriate place for such a magnificent carpet, and that he would keep it in his family house in England. Another piece of embroidery formed an acceptable present to Set Cursetjee Banajee at whose splendid ball-parties—for at that time this was the only Parsee who could give such parties—I was a frequent guest. Another piece I made for my uncle Dhunjeebhoy, intending it for a foot-rug for his private buggy, but he like Colonel Jarvis considered it more suitable for a spacious hall or sumptuous drawing-room. Thus my needlework was everywhere prized and admired, which, besides the keen pleasure I found in it myself, spurred me on to greater proficiency in this graceful and useful feminine art.

English ladies were equally astonished at the work on my saree and would ask me how I had the patience to go through such an amount of labour, as one yard of such fine stitching would have been enough to weary them out. Besides this, I had embroidered various suits for children, saree-borders, numerous caps, boots, slippers and so forth, partly for use in my own family and partly as presents for my friends. Such things though not of much value, were most acceptable and prized far above their intrinsic worth. In return, they sent me presents of their portraits, writing or sewing materials or other serviceable and yet ornamental trifles. The interchange of such inexpensive presents was quite an innovation, as up to this time the cost of a present had been its only criterion of worth with a Parsee, anything which did not represent a high figure was unacceptable.

Another irksome and senseless mode of gratifying one's friends and relations was that of sending trayfuls of sweetmeats on the monthly or annual ceremony for the dead. These sweetmeats were very troublesome to prepare and therefore the first recipient would discharge her obligation to another friend by sending them on to her, she in her turn would despatch them to another and so on, the original trayful of sweets sent off early in the morning would be seen knocking about from door to door till even considerably past midday. My friends, contrary to my urgent request, insisted on sending questionable benefits to my far-distant bungalow at Tardeo. As the tray-load consisted of a variety of viands, over which the priest had performed prayers, only Parsees could partake of them, but they reached us at a late hour and were considerably wanting in freshness; they, therefore, went usually to fill the belly of a cow or other domestic animal. To avoid all this, I ultimately made it a rule to decline with thanks such presents, although at the risk of offending the donor. It is gratifying, however, to note the steady decline of such stupid customs, as also of other ceremonies for the dead, entailing heavy expenditure and much waste of time.

Another custom, which I would like to see virtually abolished, is that of sending Europeans at Christmas large quantities of cakes and fruits. These were for a long time sent only in the name of the husband, who threw away large sums upon them. These costly presents coming all at one time serve no other purpose than to be made over to the servants, for the Europeans themselves though receiving them on the one hand, on the other only laugh at the absurdity. It might be reasonably asked why Europeans do not return the compliment paid them by sending to Parsees at Peteti (New Year) or to Hindoos at Diwalee something of the same kind, instead of ignoring these occasions, which are of as much importance to us as Christmas is to them. My husband and father-in-law formed no exception to this rule, and I could not dissuade them from it. Since, however, I am blessed with independence, I have to a considerable extent done away with these expensive follies, and substituted self-made keep-sakes, which I like both to present and to receive. Surely such a gift, trifling though it be in value, should be more acceptable than costly and useless articles, only given to preserve a silly custom.

I was now happily restored to my mother's favour. My brother Heerjeebhoy was about to be married to her sister's daughter, a union at which he at first demurred, but at my persuasion ultimately agreed to. My ever-magnanimous husband on this occasion said to me: "as you are united to a family in opulent circumstances, it will be expected that we give a handsome present." Accordingly he gave my brother Rs 2,000 on his wedding-day, which increased the affection of my mother towards us and won my brother's regard.

After the birth at this time of a still-born child my health was much impaired, and my husband, therefore, gave me for my personal comfort and convenience a carriage, in which I could enjoy the luxury of an evening drive. Before this, I had seldom stirred out for an evening walk or drive, but generally spent these pleasant hours with my children and daughter-in-law at home or in rectifying the irregularities of servants in the domestic economy. After the acquisition of the carriage I used to frequent the Bandstand, where I was the only Parsee lady to be seen. In those days this salubrious resort had no attraction for them, their one idea of enjoyment being comprehended in visiting and gossip—when the inexhaustible topic of discussion was the ceaseless feuds of mother and daughter-in-law, or the sorcery used by some wife to make her husband a slave to her will and inflict on her mother-in-law an incurable malady, or how Meherbai though past sixteen is still unmarried, and Bachoobai waits for her betrothal in feverish anxiety, that Roopabai would not condescend to call her daughter-in-law and that Dinbai's daughter would not go to her new home. Happily, the love of gossip as well as the opportunity for indulging in it exists now to only a limited extent, funeral obsequies most inappropriately affording the best field for scandalmongers. In some families for the ten days after a death has occurred, from two or four hundred females congregate daily, ostensibly to condole with the bereaved. It can be readily imagined that tales are then carried from one ear to another and that they lose nothing in the telling, this and the practice of questioning servants, who casually call at the house with messages, as to the habits and doings of their mistresses, are the two prime sources of mischief-making and tale-bearing now extant. The steady growth of education, bringing with it wider interests and occupations for the mind, has given a fatal blow to the voice of scandal. Much praise is due to the Cama family for having introduced some reasonable changes in our funeral ceremonial, for instance, abridging the ten days of wailing to one or two. Although the benefit of these reforms is widely felt, a few orthodox families tenaciously cling to the old customs.

The life at Tardeo awakened in me and my children a taste for gardening, in which the mornings and evenings were delightfully spent, and the year seemed as if it had been but a month.

In 1859, when anticipating my fifth confinement, I was urged by the Doctor to curtail my household avocations and to rest as much as possible. I, therefore, availed myself of this time of enforced idleness to renew my study of English. In the month of July I was delivered of a son, who received from his grandfather the name of Dadabhoy, after a very jovial and bulky friend. Eleven days after the child's birth, my mother-in-law appeared in company with this gentleman—Dadabhoy Framjee Deevecha—who carried a tray filled up with suits, caps, toys and sweetmeats for his name-child. Before bringing this chapter to a close, I would mention the restriction which used to be observed by young Parsee mothers. For the first three days, the child dared not be suckled nor taken from the mother's arm, for five days the mother desisted from all wheaten food and for ten days from animal food, eggs included. Then a ceremony, called the "ten days Gote," was gone though, after which she could eat what she liked. I threw off this tyrant yoke of superstition and subsequently the whole family did the same. This "Gote" ceremony is evidently borrowed from the Hindoos, like many other customs still practised in Parsee households.

VIII

Contact with English Society

In the year 1859 my husband retired from his father's firm and secured the post of guarantee broker to Messrs Volkart Brothers, a flourishing German firm established in Bombay. His honest and straightforward dealings commanded the esteem of his employers and contributed to the popularity of the firm. Shortly after this appointment, Mr Broadback, the genial and shrewd partner, died; it was, however, a consolation to my husband that Mr George Volkart, who succeeded to the management, was equally well disposed towards him. In 1860 my husband fell ill of malignant fever and by medical advice was moved to a friend's bungalow at Malabar Hill. Here Mr George Volkart was our next neighbour and he called regularly twice a day to enquire for the patient. Sometimes he would drop in about 8 p.m. and chat with us, sitting beside me on the sofa, much to the disapproval of my mother-in-law and other aged relatives who, after he had gone, would expostulate with me on the monstrous impropriety of which I had been guilty. But these friendly visits were very agreeable to me. In those days not only would a Parsee lady not sit in the same room with a European gentleman or converse with him, but if she met him coming along the road she would escape up some bye-lane or into the nearest house. The sight of an English soldier or civilian on the steps of a house would throw its female inmates into hysterics or send them flying like frightened rabbits, whilst the servants hurried to shut up the doors to the great discomfiture of the stranger who could not guess that he himself was the cause of all this confusion. The Parsee ladies could not speak or understand a word of English nor often of Hindustanee and their servants could not command courage enough to ask or answer a question and excused themselves by saying they feared the females would all swoon away in affright. But instead of blaming the domestics, I would attribute this nonsensical timidity to the opponents of women's education, who restricted the acquaintance of their wives and daughters to the limited circle of their nearest relatives.

My husband, under the judicious treatment of Drs. Sylvester and Miller, was soon restored to health. We celebrated his recovery and the first birthday of our son Dadabhoy simultaneously, friends and relatives flocking to us with their congratulations. My mother-in-law though in mourning for her youthful daughter Rattanbai, since whose untimely death a year had not yet elapsed, kindly deviated from ordinary rule and joined our merry-making, rejoicing in her son's restoration.

My husband now resumed his official duties, taking his second son Cooverjee as his assistant, an arrangement made at my instance.

We returned to our own bungalow at Tardeo in August where I was confined of my sixth child, sad to say, stillborn, and the forty days' seclusion was spent in continual illness, my life was despaired of and I only regained my health after two months of suffering.

In 1860 I resolved to visit Poona in company with my step-children and other relatives to the number of about thirty; none of the party had ever made such a journey before. Although I had enjoyed more freedom than any of my Parsee sisters, I had never been further than a couple of hours' drive from Bombay. The Parsee population of Poona then consisted only of traders, and but in rare cases was the luxury of this cool retreat enjoyed by any of the outside community. We set out on our journey in October and, taking a short halt for dinner at Khapolee, at the foot of the Bhore Ghaut, we continued our way up and over the Ghauts in hackney coaches. These, to us novel vehicles, jolted pitilessly, now sinking into a deep rut, then perching on a high mound, but we were a merry party and these ups and downs only added to our hilarity. At 6 p.m. we reached my father-in-law's bungalow at Khandalla. Spending two days very comfortably at this place, we left for Poona.

We reached Poona, once the renowned capital of the Peshwas and the city of unparalleled historical importance in the Deccan, at 6 p.m., and it presented a most unique and interesting appearance to us in the evening twilight. Set Edulji Colabawalla had kindly placed his bungalow at Bhowanipeth at our disposal and we arrived there at 7 p.m. Here we enjoyed ourselves to the best of our wishes. My hosts praised and made much of me and seemed thoroughly to enjoy themselves. It was always an unfailing source of pleasure to me to receive praises from my elders, as I had been accustomed to do so from my earliest years. It is good to rise superior to the fleeting joys money gives by attracting to ourselves the love and esteem of our elder relatives, as well as of those nearer and dearer to us.

We took long drives and rambles on foot in the city and freely resorted to every kind of amusements to hunt away the tedious hours which we were required to spend indoors after dinner, but in this round of pleasure a sigh would often escape me, for my husband, the author of all these gaieties, was not sharing them with me. Among the most interesting sights of Poona may be mentioned the temple of Parbutti, the waterfall at the Bund constructed by Sir Jamsetjee Jejeebhoy and the beautiful public garden known as Hirabagh, with its shady avenues and smooth green lawns, in which stands a palace called Ainabagh, built by one of the Peshwa's prime ministers, but the only noteworthy thing about this building is that its walls are hung with large mirrors. Poona was not then as now embosomed in gardens, but as during our visit which took place at the end of the monsoon, a nice drizzling rain often fell, the city and its neighbourhood looked fresh and inviting. We paid our respects to the Parsee High Priest of the Deccan and Set Pudumjee, visited with the customary offering of sandalwood the Fire-temples of Sir Jamsetjee and Dastoorjee, finding both edifices well built and excellently managed, and in due time returned to Bombay the same way as we came.

In the following March my daughter Goolbai was to be invested with the sacred shirt and thread—Sudra and Kushti—and this being the first great family festival since I became independent, I wished to celebrate it with something like pomp; my desire was, however, frustrated. My husband's youngest sister had died about a year before and my father-in-law resolved that the daughter of the deceased should be invested on the first anniversary of her mother's death and my daughter one day before, so that the spirit of the departed might reap a two-fold advantage. Thus the investiture of my daughter at the age of nine took place with formal ceremony but entire absence of festivity.

Parsee females in accordance with custom continue their mourning for the dead for a much longer period than the men. If a woman loses her husband she passes the remainder of her existence in grief and seclusion, whereas a widower after one month resumes his wonted life, entering again into all the gaieties and amusements of his bachelor days and if he chooses, soon finding another partner. When a near relation—parent, brother, or mother-in-law—dies the woman is thrown into a year's mourning during which long period she abjures all new and coloured dresses, jewels and visiting, never even going out for a walk. After the death of a beloved child, grown up son, or husband, the mourning is still more severe and prolonged; for the first month she tastes no food during the day, only partaking of a sorry meal at night and tea in the morning. A widow always retains her garb of woe, that is an entirely black saree unrelieved by any jewels or colours, and she would on no account be present at a marriage or other auspicious festival, as is presented in the portrait of Bai Meheribai given in this work. The young people of her household participating in her mourning to some extent are shut out from legitimate pleasures, and these undue restraints are partly the reason why so many youthful couples now remove from the parental roof to small homes of their own, thus asserting their independence and shaking off many old usages.

My cup of matrimonial bliss was often alloyed by bitter dregs from my mother's house. On account of my eldest brother's misconduct, the other two, Heerjeebhoy and Furdoonjee, failed to procure employment and my most ardent desire was to assist them to some honourable occupation and thus keep them in the paths of virtue. My husband was at this time a Director of *The Times of India* and he most kindly exerted his influence in getting Heerjeebhoy employed in the office of that paper, his wife still continuing to live with my mother. Their domestic peace was unhappily often disturbed and at length matters assumed a serious aspect. One day Heerjeebhoy came to my house much agitated and after upbraiding me for having persuaded him to marry, threatened to put an end to his misery by taking his own life. As the disagreements seemed to originate between our mother and his wife, I invited him to come with his wife and live with me, which they gladly did, but my mother was so enraged at this that she cursed me. My brother Furdoonjee had in the meantime, being idle, incurred a good deal of debt and made off to Penang, leaving my husband to settle as best he could with his Marwaree creditors (Jews of the East). Dorabjee who was undergoing his term of punishment at Penang, had with him a good deal of his ill-gotten gains unknown to his mother who used to send him assistance to the full extent of her means. He led a comfortable life during his penal servitude as may be seen from his numerous and now moth-eaten letters in my possession. After spending a couple of months with me, Heerjeebhoy and his wife removed to the house of my father-in-law's sister to whom, unknown to my brother, I agreed to pay a monthly sum of Rs 30 in addition to a like amount paid by himself towards domestic expenses. Subsequently the illness of my mother called me every day to her side and she then requested me to summon Heerjeebhoy back to live with her. Peace was accordingly once more restored between the mother and son and Heerjeebhoy continued living with his mother as before. It is perhaps superfluous to mention that my brothers were all perfectly obedient to me, though they were older than I, and my sole wish was to benefit them without wounding the feelings of my mother.

Through the kind intervention of our uncle Dhunjeebhoy, who had been for years in the Army Clothing office, Government most leniently cancelled the remaining fourteen years of the sentence and set my brother at liberty to the extreme joy of the whole family, who all hoped the liberated convict would earnestly strive for the remainder of his days to atone for his sin by leading a devoted, charitable and penitent life. Since his conviction I had been a voluntary exile from English Society, but now that he was pardoned, I returned with keen zest to this pleasure, of which I had been deprived for seven years. To complete our joy my husband with his own unfailing kindness engaged my brother's services in the firm to which he was attached. So once more my eldest brother was at home and a great sorrow was raised from my mother's heart. He with his wife and children lived with our mother, as did also Heerjeebhoy, but with reluctance I must admit that the bungalow at Malabar Hill instead of being the abode of peace and love soon became the scene of serious discord. It would be far more agreeable to me to suppress these sad and humiliating episodes, but on account of the bearing they have on the concluding part of my story, they must be brought to light. One night the quarrel assumed so serious an aspect that my mother had to call in the protection of the police against her enraged sons. They were taken to the Commissioner of Police, Mr Forjett, and kept in custody for the night and next morning on being released they came to me and with tearful eyes related all their grievances. I consoled them as best I could and kept them at my house, my husband exerting himself on their behalf, as we thought if their time were more occupied there would be less quarrelling at home. But my mother was much displeased with me for this no more than sisterly conduct. At my husband's recommendation and through the influence he had with Mr Rich, the Manager of the North Western Bank, Heerjeebhoy was employed there and my eldest brother was transferred to Messrs Volkart's branch establishment at Kurrachee. Both brothers professed the most unfeigned love and gratitude and when anyone asked their relationship to me, they made answer that I was their *mother*. All my monetary transactions such as buying and selling Government securities, shares, etc., were conducted by Heerjeebhoy in his own name, unknown to my husband. With the other two brothers my dealings extended no further than assisting them with loans of money, which Dorabjee honourably refunded, but Furdoonjee, far from giving anything back, only saddled us more than once with his debts.

In January 1862, I gave birth to a son, and two months later I had to mourn the death, after protracted illness, of my beloved mother-in-law. In consequence of this sad loss the care of all my step-children now devolved upon me, they accordingly moved to our bungalow and we were very happy in each other's company.

One night in November of this same year during new-moon, an incident occurred which mystified us exceedingly. On this evening I had gone with my friend Manekbai, wife of Byramjee Jeejeebhoy, to see the Diwalee illuminations from which I only returned at about eleven o'clock. Two hours or so after I had retired to rest I awoke, thinking someone was in the room, but seeing no one I concluded the child's ayah had slipped in to look after her charge and soon I was lost again in sleep. Early in the morning one of our gardeners woke us with the tidings that many trunks and boxes were lying exposed in the compound. I then saw my sewing case lying on the floor of my bedroom, furniture misplaced, and trunks missing from their places. At that time ornaments to the value of from two to three lacs of Rupees (£20,000) were in my possession, and in the pocket of my husband's coat there was a bundle of notes amounting to Rs 30,000 (£2,000). Every one of the Chinese boxes and cabinets had been opened and ransacked, one of these full of English silks had been eased of its contents which were scattered all over the rooms, showing that each fold of every piece had been searched. On the table lay, amongst other things, caps embroidered in pearls, diamond rings, lockets containing watches and so on, none of which were abstracted or even disturbed. In the compound we found similarly that the boxes had been wrenched open, their contents thrown aside after minute examination; a curious heterogeneous display of gold embroidered clothes, silver knives and forks broken and twisted, pieces of China silk all unfolded mingling with the dust, leaves and dew of the garden. But of all this nothing, not so much as a needle, was missing.

My jewels had evidently been the object of the thief's search and nothing less would satisfy him, but by a lucky coincidence they were safe in an unlikely receptacle, quite beneath the notice of their would-be possessor, and the notes were still in the pocket of the coat hanging upon a peg. And as it is usual to put on every available item of jewellery during the Diwalee holidays, I had put all mine ready for use into an old cupboard, not even locking them up, and so their insecurity was the means of saving them. As nothing had been stolen the police could not trace the audacious culprit. That it must have been someone well acquainted with the interior of the house, was plain, for he had evaded the Ramosee (night watchman attached to every big private house), had entered through the verandah and open doors—being midsummer all were unclosed—and prosecuted his search in exactly those places where I was accustomed to deposit my jewels. My suspicions fastened upon a cook we had recently dismissed, and I believed he was in collusion with the Portuguese ayah of my infant. The former, although an excellent cook and a hardworking servant, had frequently incurred my displeasure for his audacious and unceremonious conduct in entering my private apartments, in spite of repeated instructions to ring the bell before doing so, his defence always being that in none of the other Parsee families where he had served had he ever seen a bell which made him forget to act up to instruction.

Soon after his dismissal the daring burglary took place, although the bungalow was at the time fully occupied by ourselves, step-sons and grand-children. From that night sleep fled from my eyelids until a storey was added to our bungalow and its security greatly increased. Subsequently my son Cursetjee died at the age of two years and in the same year we lost a sincere friend and beloved patron in the sudden death of Mr George Volkart. Just a few days before his intended departure for England he breathed his last after a slight indisposition and with heartfelt sorrow his name lives in our memory. When I went to condole with his widow, she told me that a week before her husband's death, when he was in the full enjoyment of health, she dreamt that she was travelling to Europe with her brother-in-law and her husband was not with them; full soon alas! she had this dream realised, for within a week she left for England with Mr Pearson. After Mr Volkart's death my husband left the firm on account of some disagreements with the succeeding Manager, but on the arrival of Mr Ahlers to assume the management he was reinstated in his former position. Like Mr Volkart, Mr Ahlers was very kind and polite to my husband. Every morning he came to our bungalow to take my husband to the Cotton Green where, being young and inexperienced, he was initiated into the rules of cotton selection by my husband, and thus he was soon on a friendly footing with us. It greatly pleased and interested him to see me so unlike other Indian ladies, mixing freely in English society and so on. Mr Ahlers being Consul for Holland, entertained a party of Dutch travellers shortly after his arrival, who were making a tour of India to observe the manners and customs of the inhabitants and the capabilities of the country.

As Mr Ahlers wished to show his friends a Parsee family at home, we invited them to luncheon one day and had a large party of English and Indian officials, as well as several Parsee ladies and gentlemen to meet them. In those days no Parsee would eat in the presence of aliens nor appear at a table where prohibited food (beef and pork) was served as it was on this occasion; our Dutch guests were therefore surprised that their host and hostess did not share the repast with them, and were much interested in the explanation which I gave them of our religious prejudices against certain articles of food. Sir Jamsetjee and Set Cursetjee Cowasjee Banajee were amongst the first to invite Europeans to their houses, and on several occasions the then Governors of Bombay with their staff, graced with their presence the supper tables, but the host was a mere spectator at the feast or at most served his guests with wine, and perhaps once or twice pledged their health but did nothing further. In my young days, I was always a welcome guest at the parties of Set Cursetjee, but along with the ladies of the house merely enjoyed the sight through the venetian blinds of the adjoining rooms, though I would have had no compunction in eating with strangers, provided that no beef or pork were on the table. In my school days I used to invite my companions and be in return invited to their homes, and many a merry feast we enjoyed in each other's company, but the two objectionable viands never appeared in the bill of fare, out of consideration for me.

The luncheon over, I led this "little gallant troupe" as Mr Ahlers called his Dutch guests to the houses of several of my relatives and friends and to the residence of a Bania. All these houses were found by the travellers tasteful and sumptuous beyond their expectations. They were especially surprised to find that a Bania (Hindoo) lived in such comfort and luxury as they saw in the house of Set Kalliandas Manmohundas. He and his wife, Kesarbai, were the first of their caste to adopt the style of living of the English; like ours their bungalow was tastefully furnished, a gatekeeper patrolled in front of the house, the hall was magnificently decorated, and our European friends also found to their amazement comfort and refinement in this Hindoo abode equal to any English home. The Dutchmen on seeing the superb bedroom asked me if the bedstead was kept for use or only for show—a silly question which made me laugh at their conceit. When Europeans see with their own eyes how incorrect are their surmises about Indians, their supercilious superiority is taken down a peg. The travellers were quite amazed to learn that the faultlessly appointed carriage and pair which took them from place to place belonged to none other than my Bania friends. After these gentlemen had taken their leave of us, I received a letter from Mrs Ahlers expressing thanks for dishes, plates and other things I had lent her and also for the hospitality I had shown her and her Dutch friends, not omitting to convey to me in the same letter the expression of very favourable opinion entertained by her friends about me.

IX

Kesarbai—A Progressive Hindoo Lady

With unfeigned pleasure, coupled with melancholy regret, I would here offer a tribute to the memory of my beloved and lamented friend Kesarbai, in whose character were blended the most admirable traits of her sex and the noblest influences of Hindooism. Between her and myself a truly sisterly affection subsisted; it was a unique sight when she and I went out together, a Hindoo lady and a Parsee lady in one carriage, attired exactly alike in saree, "cholee," slippers, etc.; and she, Kesarbai, even acquired the habit of putting on stockings, and had all her ornaments fashioned after my pattern; it would have been impossible to distinguish our caste, but for the white kerchief worn on the head by Parsee females. Her own caste ridiculed her for having become a "fashionable Parsee lady." Our intimacy drew forth much comment, and we were respectively designated "Dosebai's Kesarbai" and "Kesarbai's Dosebai," but nothing cooled our attachment, and a separation of a week was enough to create uneasiness in either mind.

Her disposition was sweet and child-like. Our short friendship of eight years was brought to a close by the untimely death of my dearly loved friend in 1869; she survived her husband only eight months, leaving one son to inherit and perpetuate her good name. The late Kalliandas *alias* Killibhoy's uncles Narotumdas and Vurjeevandas

Madhowdas, the leading well known Hindoo citizens of Bombay, stood guardians to the surviving son. Thus the happy pair left their joint concern with this world in one and the same year. I give a portrait of Bai Kesarbai, and while saving my reader the task of perusing the English version of her notes to me, I should only mention here that they fully testify to the unique intimacy that subsisted between us.

In 1863 Mr Ahlers and my husband wished to go to Surat and proposed that I should accompany them for the benefit of a little change of air and although at the time in mourning of my child, I consented to go. When Parsee families are going on an excursion, they need a week for their preparations and then carry along with them a host of children with ayahs and servants. I was told in the evening, and the following morning saw me fairly equipped for the journey—the children were left behind under the care of my step-sons and their wives. At that time there was no railway from Bombay to Surat, but the *S.S. Taptee*, of which my husband was the owner, plied between these ports; we accordingly embarked on it. Our party consisted of Mr Ahlers, Mr Johnson, my husband and myself. The weather was calm and the conversation with the two Europeans was animated and interesting, Mr Johnson being elderly, Mr Ahlers witty and of a jovial disposition. There were other Parsee women on board whose remarks reached my ears. "See, see," they whispered, "the female yonder sits and walks in the company of Europeans." Arrived at Surat, my husband and I took up our quarters at the house of our friend Mr Pestonjee Burjorjee Antee, while the two gentlemen went to the travellers' bungalow. We found the town dull with no interesting feature to engage a traveller's attention and smothered by dust which found its way into our eyes and even into our mouths when talking. Indians frequented Surat and Nowsaree in ignorance of more salubrious resorts; since then those who can afford a sojourn at Poona, Matheran, Mahableshwar, the Nilgiris or Simla, have learnt the benefit of these our natural sanatoriums. We left Surat after a stay of four days, but on our way were doomed to serious trouble. Going to the steamer in a small boat, the wind suddenly began to blow a hurricane and the waters threatened to engulf us, our crew were thrown into a state of fright and consternation and could not discern the *Taptee*. Thus we drifted about from 6 p.m. till 4 a.m., our lives were despaired of, and we ourselves encountering no boat or other means of rescue, gave ourselves up for lost. As to myself, I could scarcely give utterance to a word, so bewildered was I, but I tried to fix my thoughts upon Him, the Protector of all mankind.

Ultimately at four o'clock the storm abated and we could perceive the lights of the steamboats and in half an hour we were, by the infinite mercy of God, safe on board. Alarmed at our prolonged absence in such a tempest, boats had been put off in search of us, but none had crossed our track. We reached Bombay the next day full of gratitude to Almighty God for our miraculous escape from a watery grave. This year the safety of both our life and property had been in jeopardy, but the Creator of the universe had preserved us from the hands of robbers as well as from the raging elements. Thus it is that he who fearing and remembering God frequently, walks in the paths of virtue and overcomes all obstacles.

From this time forward I began to order out from England silks, stuffs and ornaments, in the sale of which I commenced privately to deal. In addition to this, I turned my attention to the care and management of horses. Every morning I made it a rule to go into the stable and supervise the grooming and feeding of our horses, treating them to slices of bread from my own hands. This would fully occupy me for a couple of hours, much to the annoyance of the grooms. After my round in the stables, I devoted an hour to culinary matters, teaching the servants how to cook various dishes to our taste, and instructing them in habits of cleanliness and order. Then I would go to my room and repeat the necessary daily prayers, after which I set to my needlework, patterns for which I transcribed with such alterations and additions as my taste suggested, from English and Parisian fashion-plates. I never made extravagant use of my money at the milliner's shops like many English ladies, but purchased raw materials, from which I made curious and artistic garments for myself and others. Even this elicited unpleasant remarks—confident however that soon hundreds would imitate and adopt my fashions, I did not care an iota for what the ignorant said against me.

In 1862 my husband's partner wanted to send a competent man to examine the accounts of his business with a firm in England. This fact reaching my ears, I earnestly requested my husband to recommend my brother Dorabjee, who was so clever at accounts, and this was, I am glad to say, acceded to. To me his employment for nine months in a princely city of the Western World was highly satisfactory, as if by these means his future prospects should be improved, it would redound to my credit. I therefore left no stone unturned to further his felicity and prosperity. My brother Heerjeebhoy saw himself—through my husband's intimacy with Mr Stevens, the senior partner of Sir Charles Forbes and Company—installed in that office. My joy at my brothers' good prospects after the shadow that had so long rested on our family, can be more easily conceived than described. Subsequently my brothers persuaded me to get my husband to sell them at a nominal price a piece of vacant ground about a stone's throw from our bungalow, "so that" they said, "by living near we may prove more serviceable to you and worthy of the thousand favours you have heaped on us."

An offer of Rs 25,000 had already been made by a rich Indian gentleman for the ground. When I brought my brother's request to my husband he said that nothing commensurate with the high value of the ground could be offered by them, but if I chose I could give it to them as a present—to this they would not accede. They next day brought a legal conveyance, made out in due form, which they presented to him for signature, taking off their turbans and laying them at my husband's feet in token of great humiliation.

On perusing this document, my husband found that the purchase money was therein stated to be only Rs 1,500, whereupon he tossed away the deed saying: "Rather than selling the ground for such a trifle, your sister can give it to you as a free gift." They, however, reasoned that a sum, though merely a nominal amount, should be set forth in a legal conveyance, so that none of my husband's heirs could ever lay claim to the ground. So, after more discussion, my husband signed the deed, which elicited such expressions of gratitude from my brothers as are not to be described. "Could we with our very lives serve such a good and benevolent man willingly would we offer them," they said, reiterating again and again how they would make up the full sum of the purchase-money if ever the "good time coming" brought them the means. "Yes," said I, "when you are worth a lac of rupees (one hundred thousand) or more, you can make up the full price Rs 25,000 and then it will be accepted." "Oh, dear and kind sister," they replied, "how can beggars roll in luxury? We are no more than your servants; but if ever we can command a lac we will with alacrity pay down our debt, even over and above that sum."

On the ground so acquired they put up a temporary abode and removed there from their residence in the Fort. Through me they regained the good graces of their uncle Dhunjeebhoy, and when the latter used to say in joke that my brother would order out from England a diamond necklace for me, my brother used to say that I was already loaded with jewels, and nothing of the sort would be acceptable to me, but an equally valuable present to my only son would gratify me. This assured me that in his easy circumstances he would not fail to repay his obligations. He then requested my uncle to advance him money, which he willingly did, and with this and a loan from me of Rs 10,000, he built a very handsome bungalow on the newly acquired ground. Heerjeebhoy purchased the title and interest of his brother in this property, and became the sole proprietor. From that time forward, fortune seemed to favour him, but prosperity did not change his evil disposition nor soften his heart.

The new bungalow, which was open on all sides, was very cool and airy, and was consequently much liked by Set Dadabhoy Byramjee Banajee, the tenant. Heerjeebhoy made up his mind to persuade Set Dadabhoy to purchase the bungalow at a big price. He informed Set Dadabhoy that the bungalow was about to be sold, and that he would be unhappily compelled to part with his good tenant. He had produced one letter purporting to be from a Bania, making an offer of Rs 1,10,000. Dadabhoy expressed to my husband, his desire to purchase the bungalow rather than be turned out of it; but my husband told him, that he would not desire one of his caste to be a purchaser of it at such an exorbitant price. Set Dadabhoy expressed himself willing to offer Rs 10,000 more, making in all Rs 1,20,000; and calling for pen and ink, proceeded to draw up an agreement. The signatures being affixed, he drew out a cheque for Rs 20,000 and gave it to my brother as earnest money. My brother's joy at the near prospect of so much wealth knew no bounds.

Soon after this, Dadabhoy ordered out from England splendid furniture to fit up his drawing room. Dadabhoy, however, could not act up to his agreement. He suffered serious losses, and four months after the agreement, he, in a private note to Heerjeebhoy, expressed his inability to complete the purchase, giving up the Rs 20,000 and forfeiting the agreement.

Heerjeebhoy desired to go to law. We strongly advised him to be content, and have pity on the sorely perplexed Set Dadabhoy; but his covetous nature urged him to the extreme, and he filed a suit against his unfortunate tenant. Through the intervention of my husband and uncle, a compromise was effected by making over to Heerjeebhoy all the furniture of Set Dadabhoy. Heerjeebhoy was now worth a lac and a quarter but when I reminded him of his promises to pay for the ground he always evaded my remarks. One who builds his fortune on the ruins of another can easily forget old debts.

At the time when my eldest brother was engaged in the Bank, my mother had to stand security for a large amount, representing the liability of his position in the Bank; and on his fraud coming to light, she had to make good the loss sustained by his employers. Her bungalow at Malabar Hill was put to auction and bought by one Vithul, a Hindoo broker, but subsequently transferred in the joint names of her two sons, Heerjeebhoy and Furdoonjee, with a counter-agreement binding them to make over the same to their mother whenever she should demand it. All this was then unknown to me and would have remained so, but for disputes which arose when they refused to give peaceable possession of the bungalow to our mother.

In 1863, she was constrained to file a suit against her rebellious sons, and while the case was proceeding the eldest brother, Dorabjee, joined the defendants. The suit lingered on; at times they agreed to abide by arbitration, and anon they would disagree again. No less a personage than the patriotic Professor Dadabhoy Navrojee accepted the post of arbitrator and his opinion on the case, with all the other documents relative to it, lie with me. After going carefully and at length into the details of the case, he gave his decision in favour of their mother, but this did not please them, and in disgust at their disputes he threw up all further concern in the matter. The case once more appeared in Court. But the mysterious machinations of certain individuals led to the missing of a precious document, the only one of vital importance to my mother's claim. This was an agreement in Gujarati, signed by the two brothers. When the suit came on for hearing before Justice Sir Matthew Sauce, the document was wanting, and the case was accordingly dismissed with full costs, amounting in all to Rs 12,000 (on the plaintiff) for the defendants.

Indignant at the unfilial and unnatural behaviour of my cruel brothers, I ardently requested an interview with my dear unfortunate mother, but she refused this request until I positively and forever severed all connection with my brothers.

I feel it uncouth to introduce such dark, uninteresting episodes in my smooth and happy career, and nothing but a desire to paint me as I am, induces me to do so.

X

The Memorable Share Mania in Bombay

Happiness is as transitory as the rays of the evening sun. Time in its ceaseless course often spreads woe where hitherto prosperity has reigned supreme. Such, indeed, is the lot of mankind. The year 1866 was at once the most propitious and the most disastrous known in Bombay—the mania for speculation, raising many a one to the pinnacle of opulence only to whirl him down to a poverty before undreamt of, as we see warfare sometimes reducing royalty itself to pitiful and abject imprisonment. The bright sun of prosperity, whose blissful influence had irradiated all Bombay, became suddenly obscured by a black cloud of adversity. As the whirlwind throws down the most stately ancient edifices, leaving the mean shanties untouched by the storm, so the respectable, high-standing classes met the calls upon them to the utmost stretch of their ability, ruining themselves thereby, whereas the mushroom public took advantage of the Insolvent Act, and whitewashed themselves clear of all liabilities, pocketing whatever they could lay hands on. The general credit being thus shaken, those who would have been able in time to pull through their difficulties were compelled to take advantage of an Act, known as the 28th, specially framed to meet the emergency of this panic.

My husband, unknown to all, had, in partnership with unprincipled persons, become seriously involved, and his entire personal wealth was swallowed up in the general ruin. The friendly support of the office officials was our only comfort at this terrible crisis. Several banks stopped payment, the credit of native merchants was gone and hardly one in a thousand escaped the universal ruin and stigma of insolvency. The Europeans concerned in these failures made their way home as best they could, and thus the once smiling Bombay fell into the grasp of the fell fiend—despair.

Those, however, who remained steadfast and honourable throughout this time of trial must surely eventually receive the blessing of Divine favour. I did not give way to despondency, but gathering courage and patience from reverse of fortune, willingly parted with all the joys and jewels showered on me by my fond husband in happier days. These proving unequal to our heavy liabilities, a mortgage on the family estate became inevitable. Kind Mr Ahlers came at this juncture to our aid; he furnished us with a loan to a very large extent and continued my husband's interest in the firm intact. From this time, I took the domestic economy entirely into my own hands, parted with some of our carriages and horses, and as occasion required made use of a sum of money which I had, unknown to my husband, in my brother's hands.

The circumstances under which I gave up my joys and jewels were as follows: On the strength of my father-in-law's signature, the bank had honoured several drafts payable on sight; at the time when they fell due, payment was demanded; this threw my father-in-law and husband into a dilemma from which they could not extricate themselves; so in the nick of time, I came forward and parted with all my jewels, realising a large sum, to the intense relief of father and son, who overwhelmed me with expressions of eulogy and gratitude. This fact never transpired in public before. It was during these troublous times that my husband's younger and only brother died; his aged father took this sad bereavement much to heart and we all participated in his sorrow.

At this time, an affliction of the chest from which I had long been suffering, assumed an acute and dangerous character; all other remedial measures having proved abortive, the physicians recommended as a last recourse my being taken to sea, and it was decided that I should make a sojourn on board my husband's steam-boat, the *Taptee*, but my debility was such as to preclude all possibility of transit. It seemed that I was in the last stages of consumption and I was weary of my life, when at last succour came. My mother's family physician, Dr Yule, was brought to see me; he gave me a number of minute white pills (which now I know to have been homeopathic medicines) ordering me to take a certain number three times a day; to live entirely upon milk and confine myself to my room. By these means a marvellous improvement was brought in the short space of one week. The doctor gradually allowed me to revert to my ordinary diet and mode of living and within a month I had regained my health. From this it will be seen that a change from one pharmacopoeia to another sometimes does good, though it is God who controls the application of remedies and sometimes ordains astounding results by the most trivial agency.

Previous to Dr Yule's visit, when my case was pronounced hopeless, my daughter's father-in-law had telegraphed to his son to send his wife home to Bombay, to take a last leave of her mother. At this time, almost in a convalescent and weak condition I had to assist at the delivery of my step-daughter-in-law, and it was there that I was apprised of this when she had arrived at Aden, and a week after she was by my side. Seeing me so far restored, she concluded that my danger had been exaggerated, and the presence of my dearly loved first born soon dispelled any lingering disease.

My daughter had given birth to a son in London, the child was only nine months old and had been left in the care of his father and a nurse. My daughter's jewels were in sad case; the major portion of those I had given her on her marriage were missing, she had but one bracelet and one earring and her necklace and rings she had lost in London. Out of maternal love I got what jewels she still possessed reset and replaced with new, those that were gone. She was in the habit of wearing a little skull cap instead of the white kerchief of Parsee matrons, so I made her one to her taste embroidered in pearls.

At this time my brother Heerjeebhoy met with a severe accident by falling from a wooden stand; when the news was brought to me, leaving all domestic concerns, I ran to my brother's side and found him lying in a state of insensibility and seriously injured, but by the skilful and instantaneous help of Dr Mackenzie, he recovered in the course of a month. The first ten days I never left his bedside, and thus my brother's illness considerably curtailed the short time I could enjoy my daughter's company.

After about two months' stay, my daughter took her departure, we all escorted her on board the steamer and took farewell of her. Her journey to and from England alone and unattended, and while still in her teens, furnished a topic of interesting gossip. In those days a Parsee lady would not go in a carriage from Mazagon to the Fort unaccompanied by her mother, elder sister, or at least an ayah, and it was seldom that Parsee females stirred out without several clubbing together to countenance and protect each other. My daughter's courage, therefore, gave rise to scurvy remarks, but only she who moves in good society can venture on such untrodden paths. My Hindoo friend, Bai Kesarbai, wittily versified this incident; her rhyme may be rendered thus: "Amongst Parsees, one Meheribai Supla gave birth to a daughter named Dosebai, in whom reforms doubled. She in her turn gave birth to a daughter named Goolbai, who thinks it not much to go and come alone from England, and this trebles the reforms. When Goolbai brings forth a daughter, all social reforms will have gained their extreme ends, and then all Parsees—orthodox and reformed—will agree."

After my daughter's departure, my venerable father-in-law was once more plunged in grief by the death of his eldest daughter who had been his constant companion in his old age. The work of adding a storey to our bungalow, which had been kept in abeyance on account of our pecuniary losses, was now resumed and completed, all expenses being defrayed from my private funds. In the course of this work, I actively superintended the same and, in a measure, acted as head builder, in which novel capacity I spent most of my time.

The grief which I naturally felt at my mother's unfriendly attitude towards me was changed into joy in 1869, when, at her kind suggestion, I gave her a call and a complete reconciliation took place between us. To ensure her comfort in the autumn of her life, I sought to install her in the house of her sons, but when I made them the proposal they turned the tables on me by saying: "As we have each by the grace of God a considerable family, we could hardly accommodate our mother, whereas you, with your spacious bungalow, could do so easily." I, however, remonstrated with them on the impropriety of a mother-in-law making her son-in-law's house her home, when the custom is for her to live with her own sons, so on this occasion they were obedient to my will.

The High Court had decided, when my mother's case was non-suited, that she had a right to half the rent and proprietorship of the bungalow at Walkeshwar, but reduced to a state bordering on distraction by poverty, and the unnatural conduct of her sons, this fact had escaped her memory and it formed no part of the duty of her sons to remind her of it. I now compelled Dorabjee, the eldest, to pay her Rs 60 a month, the rent being Rs 120 per mensem. From this pittance she paid outstanding charges to Heerjeebhoy, leaving only twenty rupees for her personal needs. I, therefore, took upon myself all her expenses for dress and medical attendance, in addition to refunding a sum of money advanced by Set Ardeshir Hormusjee Wadia to enable my mother to prosecute her case. These matters all being settled, I felt convinced that further differences would be avoided, but alas! the mother's curse that her sons should prove as ungrateful to me as they had been to her and that she should live to see it, was yet to be consummated.

At the close of December 1868, we left Bombay for Nassick to pass the Christmas vacation there. We reached the Nassick Station at midnight, and as we could not command a conveyance at that late hour, we all slept in the waiting-room. After a few hours while the Queen of Night still held full sway, we started in a tonga and pair of mules and reached the city at break of day. It was then the depth of winter, and the cold was more intense than we had ever experienced before, more like what one heard of the English climate. The presence of my beloved husband gave much additional pleasure to the excursion. The city of Nassick is very ancient, it is considered sacred by the Hindoos, and is situated upon the river Godavery. The climate is highly salubrious, as was evinced by the keen appetite we all developed there; its soil produces fine fruit and vegetables. Its principal features of interest are the magnificent pagodas with idols they contain, and the large water tanks made in the Moslem fashion.

Being then in a delicate state of health, I had to return sooner than had been intended. Subsequently, in March, I gave birth to a daughter, she was named Baiai after my mother-in-law. During the forty days' seclusion, I could not see any of my European friends, except those ladies with whom I was on intimate terms, and whose curiosity prompted them to come and see the strict observance of the rules our religion enjoins. Mrs Ahlers and Mrs Baker (wife of Col. Baker, Under Secretary to Government in the Public Works Department) were my particular friends then, and they frequently visited me and conversed with me. During previous occasions of this nature, Mrs George Volkart paid similar friendly visits. To them it seemed incredible how anyone could voluntarily pass such a long time in a low, comfortless prison-like place and they would ask me how I, who loved English freedom, could have patience to comply with such a tiresome and senseless custom, and why I did not set it aside as I had done other old Parsee usages. To this I replied that, though I liked to deck myself out in English array and though I advocated many salutary reforms, it by no means followed that I would deviate from any rule laid down by our religion; no matter though the observance entailed trouble and discomfort. It is, therefore, my humble advice to all Indians to abide in the religion in which they were born; let them dress and enjoy themselves as they like, but never for a moment trample on or ignore their own old-established beliefs. As it has been willed by an All-wise Providence to create us each in our respective ancestral religion, so it is but right to continue steadfast in the same; by so doing, we will assuredly endear ourselves the more to Him.

The year 1870 was a memorable one for India, for it marked the visit of an illustrious guest, H. R. H. the Duke of Edinburgh. The news of his advent was hailed with delight by Her Majesty's loyal subjects and fitting arrangements for the reception for the first time of one of her children were at once set on foot. Government resolutions were issued requesting the people to whitewash their houses, observe cleanliness throughout the city and make a suitable display, all of which they cheerfully did as they were eager to behold the benign features of the sailor-prince. Accordingly, after visiting other cities, His Royal Highness came to Bombay, where an august assemblage of Feudatory Chiefs and Princes had gathered to pay their respects to the Queen's son. On this occasion, Parsee women, casting off their awkward reserve, were seen threading the streets and entering into the spirit of the day, and I who had for a while taken leave of gaiety returned to it now with fresh zest. I first saw His Royal Highness from the balcony of a Hindoo temple near Byculla Bridge as the royal procession was passing along Parel Road and the next time when he was going to visit an Indian Prince, the Thakore of Bhownuggur, who had taken up his temporary abode in a bungalow adjoining ours. On this occasion several other Indian ladies and myself stationed ourselves at the gates of our compounds, presently the carriage of His Royal Highness and the Governor of Bombay came slowly along. On seeing us, Sir Seymour Fitzgerald saluted, His Royal Highness with his wonted courtesy raised his hat and returned our salaams, while I fervently invoked benedictions on him and his gracious Mother.

After this joyous event, I received the welcome tidings that my daughter and her husband would shortly come and settle in Bombay, such being the will of her father-in-law. My daughter and her little son arrived first, and according to her father-in-law's instructions took up her quarters with me, where after two months she gave birth to a daughter. She was here made to conform to Parsee usage and spend forty days in retirement, which at her previous confinement in London she had failed to do. The child was given by her grandfather the name of Ruttonbai, after his mother. Soon after this my son-in-law Dadabhoy reached Bombay, but his mother, Bai Soonabai, whose whole wishes centred in seeing her son domiciled in Bombay, died ere this could be accomplished while I was spared to enjoy this happiness.

My pleasures were now entirely of a domestic character, for having within a comparatively short period undergone eleven childbirths, my health precluded me from taking long journeys, and for the same reason, coupled with my husband's exceedingly retiring disposition, I gradually left off going to the large entertainments of Government House and elsewhere; in fact, I had ceased to hanker after such gaieties. When it became known that a ball was to be given at Government House, everyone desirous of being invited went there and registered his name, and invitations were then sent to those whom the Government thought fit. Up to the fourteenth year of my life, I was a constant guest at these parties to which I went in the company of my good grandfather; afterwards I never ventured alone into such an assemblage, and it was but seldom that I went with my husband. Now, in the companionship of my daughter and son-in-law, my chief relaxation was an evening drive.

After having lived six years in England, they found it irksome to be cooped up from morning till night in the parental home, so they spent every third or fourth day at my house, when I was careful to have everything prepared for them as they liked best. Every week or two I gave a small party to my son-in-law and a few of his friends who had been to England to finish their education (Messrs Pherozshaw Mehta, Hormusjee Wadia, the two sons of my uncle Manekjee Judge were amongst the number); for, like a dutiful son, he was ever obedient to his father's will in living under his roof and dining every day with him, so being thus dependent he could not invite any of his friends; therefore, I sought to please him by entertaining them at my house. With a mother's pride I delighted to bedeck my daughter with jewels and dresses, exactly the same as I wore myself; thus, being of identical height, we were generally taken for sisters. Our worthy friend, Sir Frank Souter, always made the absurd mistake of addressing me as Mrs Cama, and my daughter as Mrs Jessawalla, declaring it was impossible to make out who was the daughter and who the mother.

A very pleasant picnic to the caves of Elephanta lives in my recollection; the party consisted of our relatives, including my uncles Dhunjeebhoy and Manekjee's family, and the young friends who met periodically at my house; we set sail before the first peep of dawn—a merry party—and our servants had preceded us, so that everything conduced to make our enjoyment complete. However, ere the day was over, every one of us was chilled to the heart by the dread that the finale to our picnic might have to be played in the law courts of Thana, twenty miles distant from Bombay, for in the exuberance of youthful spirits, my cousin Jehangir said something in fun to a stranger; this personage resented the liberty and would have dragged us all before the Thana Judge if the more sedate members of our company had not known how to pacify him. With somewhat subdued feelings we reached home safely at 7 p.m.

Amidst such days of gladness the gloom of bereavement again broke in. In June 1871, I lost my beloved daughter Baiai, after one day's illness from diphtheria; she was two years and a half old, but so healthy and precocious as to have been always taken for double her age. This equally sad and sudden blow plunged me into inexpressible grief and I could only derive consolation from the thought of the immutable will of an all-ruling Providence and the instability of earthly joys. As an antidote to my grief, my husband took me for a change of air to Sewree, my daughter Goolbai and her children bearing me company. The love of my dear little granddaughter did much to alleviate my grief. My son-in-law and cousins used to frequently visit us; two of the latter (Manekjee's sons) were ready-witted and jovial, and in this agreeable company, I in a measure "steeped my sorrows in forgetfulness." On account of its airy and pleasant situation, Sewree is now and then resorted to by pleasure-seekers, but it has no permanent residents. Every variety of fish and in the freshest state, such as is very seldom to be had in Bombay, is here obtainable. There are two or three bungalows for the occupation of Customs House officials, also a large cemetery for the Christian population of Bombay, where I used frequently to go in the evening stillness. The general aspect of this small suburb is refreshing and calming. After a stay of a month and a half, I returned to Tardeo.

In October of the same year, 1871, our small coterie of friends, including my daughter, her husband and children, both my sons and myself, made a short sojourn at Matheran. We took the morning train, and after partaking of lunch at the Neral station, completed the remainder of the journey by road, my daughter and other children riding on ponies, the other females and myself being accommodated with palanquins.

On my daughter's return from England, she frequently appeared at the Bandstand and other places of public resort in Bombay on horseback, habited in an English riding dress. This unprecedented behaviour kindled the ire of the other Parsees, some of whom were so silly as to send verbal messages to her father-in-law complaining of the liberties he allowed her to take in the face of day. These wiseacres would probably have raised no objection, if she had preferred to take her ride at midnight! To a Parsee the idea of a female riding and in an English habit is dissonant; albeit history tells us that women in Persia affected this mode of locomotion, their descendants discard it with fury and contempt. But with me it was otherwise—it gladdened my eyes to see her enjoying this graceful exercise and her father-in-law, far from prohibiting gave her full scope to indulge her taste for this and other healthy recreations.

But to resume—we reached our destination at 6 p.m. and took up our residence in the bungalow known as "Arnold Lodge" which was placed at our disposal by the Hon'ble Framjee Nusserwanjee Patell. We first partook of the cup that cheers without inebriating and soon forgot the fatigues of the journey. At supper, I pledged the health of all my comrades and offered hearty thanksgiving to God for having restored my daughter to my side; through His grace, man nowadays can roam like an aerial creature from place to place, the good Providence of God guarding and protecting him and bringing the wanderer at length to his loved ones at home. My uncle Manekjee's family and other friends were at Matheran at this time and there was great interchange of hospitalities amongst us. Dinner was invariably served up on some moonlit eminence, where, amid the bright effulgence of the Queen of Night, under the serene canopy of heaven, with the salubrious air of the surrounding valleys and mountains playing around us, we all met together and spent the last hours of the day in harmony and joy.

A trip to Matheran is now common enough, but in 1865 only about a couple of Parsee families had ever been there. To my great regret, my kind husband could not, from press of occupation, participate in our enjoyment on this occasion; after a stay of six or seven weeks we all returned to Bombay, young and old, all much invigorated by the mountain air.

Shortly after this, I heard the glad tidings of an approaching marriage in the family of the Hon'ble Set Byramjee Jejeebhoy and according to my wont I immediately set myself to invent some new sort of fancy work for the occasion. Devoting much time and thought to the task, I at length commenced an entirely original design for a cap to be worn by my son at the approaching festivities. The ground of the cap was black velvet, upon which eighteen coloured miniatures of the family were to be arranged; each tiny picture was set in a golden rim with a thin glass over it (as the face of a watch is covered with a glass fixed in a ring) each profusely surrounded with small pearls set in gold embroidery. In the centre of the crown came my husband's likeness with his seven sons ranged round him; my father-in-law's portrait was placed in front, on the rim of the cap, beside this I placed my own, and the pictures of my daughter, her husband and children filled up the remaining spaces. It took me two months to complete this unique picture gallery, and soon after the marriage festivities commenced at my friend's house.

Being still in mourning for my little daughter, I could not take part in the entertainments with which marriages are heralded in, though there was no objection to my daughter and other children doing so. My kind friend Bai Manekbai was no more, but her daughter-in-law Bai Heerabai, Mrs Nanabhoy Byramjee, was equally intimate with me; she came in person to entreat me to put off my mourning for the time and come to their festival; accordingly on the marriage day itself I went in my usual evening dress. August was the assemblage that day at Set Byramjee's house; the Governor of Bombay, Sir Seymour Fitzgerald, with his full staff was there and a large gathering of the leading Europeans of Bombay. My friend Lady Sassoon with her daughter Mrs Gubbay was present and saw my daughter for the first time since her return from England and a warm friendship sprang up between the two daughters on that day. The cap was by this time the focus of attraction; my son who was wearing it was positively fatigued by the innumerable calls upon him to satisfy the curiosity it excited amongst the large and brilliant concourse, who had assembled to celebrate the nuptials. Three days after I received the following note written on behalf of my father-in-law:

> Respected Bai Dosebai, Hearing from Set Dadabhoy Hormusji Cama of the elaborate workmanship of a cap embellished with our family photographs which was worn by your son Jamsetjee on the occasion of the wedding at Set Byramjee's, grand-father desires to have a look at the same. We shall be glad if you will kindly bring it with you when you come in the evening.
>
> Faithfully yours, Rustomjee Jamsetjee Pesikaka.

The writer of this was my husband's sister's son who was living with my father-in-law.

Frequent visits from all and sundry testified to the widespread interest produced by this unique fancy work; it was assiduously copied, though at first the services of men versed in delicate handiwork had to be hired to get the work done through them.

XI

Some More Innovations in Parsee Society

On 4th April of this year, Mr and Mrs Albert Sassoon gave a splendid ball to Sir Seymour Fitzgerald, the then Governor of Bombay, to which my daughter and I were invited. The only other Parsee ladies present were the two daughters of Judge Manekjee, who from their early years had accompanied their father wherever he went. Before this none of the Parsee ladies are known to have taken part in a ball, but on this occasion my daughter, better known as Mrs D. D. Cama, danced just like a European lady. She was therefore the first Parsee lady who publicly took part in dancing and this constituted a novelty in the eyes of both Indian and European. The fact was widely commented upon in the European and native journals, the former of which were all in favour of the movement and gave us their hearty congratulations. Some of the native newspapers vehemently condemned the innovation and sarcastically criticised my daughter's conduct, while private individuals lodged complaints with my father-in-law characterising our conduct as scandalous and indecent. My aged relative at first regretted these proceedings, but on my explaining to him the merits of English society, he showed himself content and said, "Nothing but rank envy could put such a dubious interpretation upon such an innocent pleasure."

At this ball I was restored to an old friend, namely, Mrs Moses, sister of Sir Albert Sassoon. She was one of my mother's old Jewish friends whom I again met after a lapse of years. On seeing my daughter grown up to womanhood she asked with a smiling face, "Is she your daughter? In my eyes you appear still a mere girl." In conversation with me she remarked, "Your mother was the first Parsee female to give her daughter the benefit of English education, now it has spread far and wide, but in those days your mother was subjected to unjust calumny and to a downpour of sarcastic remarks." I was much pleased with this tribute to my mother, though bitterly pained at being alienated on account of my brothers from a fond mother who had patiently borne so much for my sake.

My interview with Mrs Moses took place in an ante-room of the ball-room, where I had the further satisfaction of learning from other members of the Sassoon family the esteem in which my dear mother was held by them all, and from this time forward they renewed their affectionate regard for me. After the unfortunate and ruinous lawsuit, my mother withdrew from the world and ceased to see her friends, but this unexpected interview revived their old interest in her and they expressed their desire to see her. On 12th April, when we were on our way to a ball at Government House, we heard from the mounted policemen who were stationed at short intervals along the road, the dreadful news of the assassination of Lord Mayo. The eager guests turned round and wended their way back home, with hearts oppressed with sorrow; indeed the entire populace evinced genuine horror and sympathy as soon as the tragic event became known.

It may be worth my readers' perusal to insert here a strange prediction of this appalling event. Invitations to the ball having been issued four days previous to the date of the entertainment, I was busily engaged in preparing a dress suitable for the occasion when our friends assembled as usual at our house.

One of them said in jest: "It is still four days till the ball, wherefore should you work so hard? If someone were to die in the meantime, all your trouble would be for nought!"

To which another gave this melancholy response: "The death of any of us could not prevent the ball, but that of the Governor or Viceroy would."

The fulfilment, alas! of this warning voice we saw ere the four days were over, and we were not a little bewildered that the sad prophecy of a sudden fatality should be so exactly verified.

I may here add that in those days just a few invitation cards were sent out amongst Indians on such occasions, and these bore their own individual names, without the necessary formality of "Mr and Mrs"

In the following June my daughter gave birth to a son; she had come to my house for her confinement and we duly observed all our customary religious restrictions during the ensuing forty days, notwithstanding her severe indisposition. She was then removed to her father-in-law's bungalow at Cumballa Hill, but the change did her no good, thence she was taken by Dr Mackenzie's advice to Poona; she was too weak to walk a step and had to be carried to and from the railway. I, of course accompanied her to Poona, where we put up at the bungalow of her husband's uncle, Pestonjee H. Cama, in the Civil Lines, my son-in-law, his sisters and our kind host being with us. As night advanced we began to feel the cold, which is here intense, my daughter then lost herself in profound slumber, and by the bracing air and salubrious climate, so marvellous a change in her failing health was effected, that at the end of a week she was able to dispense with the medicines and by a fortnight was so far restored as to accompany me in a drive. My own experience is that a change of air is ten times more efficacious than medicine.

During our two months' stay, our host's courtesy and regard were unwearied, he thought of everything which would possibly contribute to our comfort and my daughter's recovery, and we gratefully felt that the good results were mainly owing to him. The carriage and horses which we brought from Bombay added much to our enjoyment and convenience, though previous to this time, no native lady had ever driven in an open carriage in Poona and the antiquated people did not much relish our doing so. Mr Manekjee, Judge of Bombay, used to drive in an open carriage with his daughters, but as they were minors they escaped the taunts of the public, whereas I was in the prime of life and used to drive in an open barouche with my daughter and her husband.

In Poona as in Bombay females only drove in shigrams or broughams, of which they would occasionally let down the panels, but the carriage still remained a closed one. Without being lengthy on this subject, I would point out one glaring inconsistency of the busy bodies who jeered at us for taking the air in an open carriage. Everybody conceded to the Parsee female the liberty of walking on the streets, but if she were seen sitting in an open carriage silly remarks and ill-natured innuendoes assailed her; though it must be admitted that her face being seen by all would have constituted the objection, whereas in walking she was scrupulously veiled. What a droll figure this veiled female walking on the streets cuts, and if she were thus attired to sit in an open carriage, in the ordinary ill-mannered way, taking off her slippers and bundling up her legs, I grant there would be reason in the outcry! It costs native ladies a deal of trouble to leave off their awkward habit of sitting, but as I had, from my earliest years, mixed in English society, I had always conformed to their refined manners. But the rapid spread of education has dispelled many obnoxious customs and some Parsee girls of the present generation appear lovely both walking and/or driving, with their sweet youthful faces exposed to God's air and few grudging them their freedom.

In November, the new Viceroy of India was expected in Bombay and a grand Durbar was to be held, at which the native Princes and Chiefs were requested to be present. Magnificent tents were erected on the Esplanade for the occasion and Bombay wore a gay appearance. Besides the Rajahs, some influential natives were honoured by invitations from Government. My husband, daughter, son-in-law and I were present in this august assemblage, and it was gratifying to note the admission of Parsees for the first time into such a grand state ceremony, though their number did not exceed ten. Neither Mrs Ardeshir Wadia, who was ever prone to criticise my movements, nor any of her family was present on this occasion. All the Princes and Chiefs, heartily responding to the invitation, were there, bearing costly presents. The Begum of Bhopal was also amongst them, but veiled, and she was then and there invested with the order of G.C.S.I. by the Viceroy, by command of the Queen.

On 19th November, Sir Albert and Lady Sassoon gave a splendid ball in honour of Lord Northbrook, the Governor-General. Amongst guests were to be seen representatives of several sections of the native community, such as Parsees, Banias, Memons and Purbhoos.

Nevertheless there were no other native females present, but my daughter and myself. We were kindly encouraged by the English, who assured us that if we would lead the way hundreds would soon follow. We were always treated with the utmost kindness and consideration, both by ladies and gentlemen; indeed our presence in their midst seemed to give them pleasure.

The year drew to its close with lightning speed. I was kept constantly occupied in preparing with my own hands dresses for myself and my daughter, for although she had lived for a considerable period in such an enlightened city as London, she had no refined taste like mine. This additional trouble on her behalf gave me only pleasure. She would be satisfied to wear anything—awry or ill-fashioned—so that acquaintances made the remark that she had been in England without avail; many supposed that I had imbibed or rather copied English manners and customs from her, but that was an ignorant mistake, for my inclination towards English fashion dated from a time long before her birth, when my good mother sent me to an English school.

Unlike the Europeans, native females do not annually change the fashions of their dress; I, however, do so every three or four years, consulting nobody's taste but my own, both in my clothes and jewels. I both design and make my own things, without any foreign agency whatever, and without being egotistic, I may say that there are very few Parsee females capable of doing the same. Even European ladies think it worth their while to come and see my handwork. Since 1870 other Parsees have begun to introduce changes in their ornaments, wearing English-made jewellery in place of that of native manufacture. Indian jewellery is odd, and of cumbrous shape and size, and very costly. Through Messrs Volkart I ordered out new fashioned ornaments for several of my friends and others, by which I reaped a golden harvest.

Now English jewels as well as dress fabrics are much affected by Parsees, Banias, Hindoos and Mohamedans; thus India's money finds its way to England, millinery establishments are daily increasing in India, and native pedlars frequent the streets offering English goods for sale. Previous to 1865, a Parsee lady was seldom seen in a millinery shop, her husband used to bring her, according to his own discretion, whatever he thought she needed. To see me frequenting such shops filled the people with astonishment, although up to the present time I have never bought anything but the raw material, out of which I have made more curious and durable apparel, than anything I could buy at an exorbitant price. Fashionable girls of this generation squander large sums at their milliners', having their dresses made there, although anyone with a little ingenuity could make them for oneself.

About this time the Alexandra Native Girls' Institute was founded, for the purpose of giving sound education to the middle classes. The rich, who at first had a disinclination to the spread of education amongst their daughters, veered round and ardently desired what they had formerly rejected. Amongst such were Set Ardesir Hormusjee Wadia and pre-eminently his wife, whose daughter in time entered the school. With their knowledge of English, the Wadia family tried to gain a footing in English Society. They had looked at my position amongst the English, and they saw the advisability of sending their daughters to an English school. This was in 1870, and even then Set Ardesir was against the step.

Nowadays English schools are springing up in all directions and governesses are within easy reach of all, but the adage "All learning and no knowledge" illustrates the present state of things amongst our girls. They do not evince the least interest in domestic affairs, and think their duties are summed up in attending schools and learning their tasks. This gives rise to serious complaints from those parents who are not in easy circumstances; their daughters learn English but ignore the necessity of helping their mothers at home while their superior acquirements create in them an intolerable pride. They ape the extravagant dress of their rich companions, though the parents have the utmost difficulty in making both ends meet. It is sadder still to find the fond foolish parents running into debt that their daughters may flaunt about in silks and satins, or when the young girl's demands cannot be satisfied, she resents their poverty by taking away her life. The case is not improved when these senseless girls marry, and many a young man is driven to dishonesty by the extravagance of his wife. It is madness to pull down our humble cottage on seeing the palace of the rich. These girls make a misuse of their education. The daughters of the rich again, though they learn the language, do not, it seems to me, acquire the polite manners of the English. They walk with a peculiar thud of their boots, dangling their cambric handkerchiefs, a bodice fitting tight after the English style and adorned with lace and thus they think themselves reformed away into European ladies, but like the loud note of an empty vessel, their very appearance is enough to convince one of their limited knowledge. It is easy to dress like an Englishwoman, but to imitate her virtues should be the aim of my countrywomen.

When English education was first introduced and only three or four Parsee ladies had taken advantage of it, they never exhibited a shadow of pride, though their learning had a wider range than that of many of the present school misses. The total ignorance of the present generation of housewives in the most important of their duties, *viz.*, cooking, gives rise to bitter complaints, and the appearance which these young matrons present in public is a great contrast to the dismal state of their households. Several of our religious ceremonies, in particular those pertaining to the dead, require the condiments to be prepared only by Parsees; in former days every lady considered it her prerogative to direct and often with her own hands perform this service. Not so now, everything is left to servants, who in their turn exact their share of work from others under them. As it is the duty of the husband to provide for his family, so it is equally incumbent on the wife to look well after her household affairs; and I think, if parents had brought up their daughters in the fear of God, they would not have forsaken the good old ways. And another growing vice amongst the Parsees is a supercilious disregard of their religion, the most trivial points causing them to forsake it altogether, though they invariably incur ridicule and contempt by so doing. Many are the castes and creeds created by God, and he who piously continues in the religion of his forefathers will assuredly reap Divine favour. Such is my opinion. Everything in this world is subjected to change and I admit that some changes in religious observances seem inevitable, but this should never induce us to lend an ear to the sly whisperings of deceitful tongues which traduce Zoroastrianism as imposture and uphold Christianity only as the embodiment of truth. Society would honour us if we were faithful to our religion, God himself would honour us, I believe. As in every clime the self-same sun illuminates the earth, so it may be said of the various religions of the earth, the one living and true God inspires them. Those who are wise are contented with this plain truth, it is only the weak-minded who are swayed by designing persons. He therefore who forsakes his religion not only suffers condign punishment in this world but will do so, too, in the life to come.

In former times parents spent very little on the training of their children and laid by as much as they could for the autumn of their life, but now the education of a family swallows up the greater part of a handsome income. The sons readily find employment and the fond parents believe that their first desire will be to reward the self-denial of years by ministering to their wants, but in most cases the son no sooner begins to earn money than he separates himself from the paternal home and ceases to have a care for his aged father and mother. Thus it will be seen that advancement and enlightenment have not brought us unmixed good; I attribute this state of matters rather to imperfect education. "A little knowledge is a dangerous thing," and these foolish children with their "little" think themselves greatly superior to their parents and their conduct therefore is often most undutiful, while the parents, fearing the disgrace of exposure, pass over in silence much which ought to be checked. Formerly Parsee children were most subservient to their parents; for my own part though not married very early, I honoured my father and mother-in-law and always strove to please them, willingly undertook the cooking for religious feasts and ceremonies and looked carefully after my household; after that I had my share of legitimate pleasures, but duty came first.

From the year 1872 my little weekly parties increased so that we mustered about twenty intimate friends. We visited each other frequently and met every evening at the Bandstand to converse on the topics of the day, though it was an innovation for native gentlemen to stand at the carriage door and openly chat with ladies, but as on so many previous occasions, I was first ridiculed and then imitated.

In May of that year Captain Merello of the Rubattino Steam Co. invited my husband with his whole family and friends to an entertainment on board the steamboat "Persia"; we to the number of twenty accepted this generous hospitality and spent a day of much enjoyment. My father-in-law's sister who had never seen, much less partaken of an English dinner before, provoked the liveliest merriment by her comical remarks. Mistaking the Italian waiters for important personages, whose great courtesy led them to forget their position and serve their guests, she constantly addressed them in titles of respect and performed the most profound bowings and salaams to them. At 6 p.m. when we took our leave of our kind host, the fun and merriment had quite fatigued us. In the same company we now and then enjoyed a trip to Mahim or Bandora. The young members of this small jovial party evinced quite a filial regard for me and their merry spirits made our meetings very animated and joyous. My husband was quite averse to going on any pleasure excursion without them, so it became a matter of course to go all together. In February 1873 Bai Bhicaijee, wife of Dossabhoy Framjee, invited us to join them in a pleasure trip to Bhandoop, a kind invitation we most thankfully accepted. Accordingly we made a trip to Bhandoop, which is seventeen miles distant from Bombay, with the usual merriments and hilarity and during our sojourn at that place we visited the Vehar Water Works.

After this I made preparations for the Navjot of my youngest son, Jamsetjee. Our bungalow was painted afresh and I was busily engaged in making new suits, as it would apparently be long before another such joyful ceremony could take place in our family. As I have always been of the opinion that my sons should only marry when they are in a position to maintain a wife, I resolved to celebrate the investiture of my youngest son with as much rejoicing as if it had been a wedding. The birthday of my aged father-in-law was fixed on for the ceremony and all our friends and relations were invited. My son was then nine years of age. Several European ladies and gentlemen were invited and attentively observed this interesting ceremony; my aged father-in-law although still mourning the untimely death of his children, came at our earnest request and the day was passed in the greatest rejoicing. In April, our "Society of friends" went to Matheran. We rented "Wadia Lodge" belonging to the well-known millionaire lady Bai Motlibai, and, as usual in this delightful place we enjoyed many picnics on moonlight nights to the different adjacent hills. On one of these occasions my son-in-law stumbled and fell, had he gone one pace further he would have been plunged into a bottomless abyss.

At that time Mrs Nolke, wife of Mr Nolke, Manager of Messrs Volkart's Bombay firm, stood on terms of great intimacy with me and besides visiting each other we used to drive together in one carriage of an evening. But we never used to trouble our heads about office affairs. After a time my husband's legitimate rights and privileges were curtailed and this was felt by both himself and me as extremely discouraging, as generally one grown old in a service sees his condition bettered rather than made worse. My second step-son, whom at my urgent desire my husband had taken as his assistant, was now engaged by the firm at a salary of Rs 300 and my husband was reduced. Being well experienced by this time in all his father's duties he undertook to discharge them at a considerably smaller salary. We felt keenly the ingratitude of both sides. Disagreements springing up between Mr Nolke (the Bombay Manager) and Mr Volkart, the former suggested to my husband to combine with him in starting a cotton mill. This, it was supposed, would turn out a highly profitable undertaking and my husband, therefore, unknown to me, severed his eighteen years' connection with Messrs Volkart. When I heard of this I was deeply grieved and thought the smaller income at Messrs Volkart's preferable to the uncertain riches of his new business. However, it was too late to retrieve the past, as Messrs Volkart were pleased to find that the son on a low salary could fill his father's place. Thus led into a doubtful and chimerical enterprise, my husband resolved to set up the mill at Oomrawuttee and Mr Nolke returned to England to be the home agent. But, in the month of December, my husband was laid aside by a severe and protracted attack of fever which necessitated his instant removal to some airy locality. By God's grace and by constant changes of air he recovered at length.

In 1875 I resolved to visit Mahableshwar, but before leaving home, I wished to place my business matters on a more satisfactory footing, as it will be remembered all my immovable property (bungalow, etc.) stood in my brother's name. No one knew this fact except my daughter, her husband and Mr Pherozshah, barrister, to whom all my dealings with my brother were pretty well known. When my uncle broke off all connection with my brother he said to me in warning voice, "You hold too much intercourse with your brother, beware!" Accordingly I suggested to my brother one day that the property should now be reconveyed to me, instead of nominally standing in his name, as I intended to effect a deed of trust on it. My brother then with great suavity began to expostulate with me, thus—"In so doing it would be necessary to pay the amount of value into the bank and thus your resources would be exposed to your step-sons who might some day or other render the trust deed null and void. To do away with this objection and as you are disinclined to keep the property longer in my name, a better plan would be for me to make you a *free grant* of the bungalow. I owe my prosperity to you and your good husband, and as I am now reputed opulent it would not seem unreasonable for me to bestow the bungalow upon you and in this way your trust deed would be more valid. It only remains for you to pay the bank in my name and then, with the property locked up in trust, no harm can come to it."

But all his subtle reasoning could not persuade me to accede to his proposition, for his behaviour towards my uncle filled my mind with misgivings. The bungalow, bought by me, stood in his name, while I had not a single scrap of his hand-writing to show my right and title to it.

I therefore consulted Mr Pherozshah, and by his advice next day I summoned my brother and said to him: "I have taken the opinion of Messrs Pherozshah and Dadabhoy, which assures me that no one can lay claim to property bought by private personal money and that a female can effect a deed of trust as well as anyone else. I therefore wish to do so without delay."

He replied, "Very well, all in good time. When you are once involved in legal difficulties none of your many advisers will help you much then. The best course is what I have already suggested."

At this moment Pherozshah and Dadabhoy suddenly came up and seeing that he must have been overheard he acknowledged that the bungalow only nominally stood in his name, and thus compelled, he released the property out of the Land Mortgage Bank by means of my own monies which he had in his hands still. In the course of a month a trust deed was drawn by Ardesir Framjee, Solicitor, and my brother Heerjeebhoy, Pherozshah and my son-in-law Dadabhoy were nominated trustees of it. The document was duly signed and attested by the Government Solicitor, Mr Cleveland. This being settled I felt uneasy about my shares, promissory notes and money still in Heerjeebhoy's possession. I had to keep a vigilant eye on them and, as a safeguard, from this time forward all transactions were conducted in writing, but from the time that this scrutiny and precaution on my part began, my brother was seized with uncharitable intentions towards me, although in his exterior bearing he continued sweet and urbane.

XII

On the Heights of Mahableshwar

After the execution of the trust deed, my mind was comparatively at rest; our small company of friends accordingly started for Mahableshwar on 1st April. Amongst us we saw Mr Pherozshah's family and the brothers and sisters of my son-in-law. We reached Poona at 5 p.m. and halted for the night at Set Byramjee Jeejeebhoy's. Before the break of day, we started on our further way. Hearty thanks were given to Mr Dorabjee Dadabhoy Bootee for the satisfactory way in which he managed the transport of our luggage and procured us good conveyances. It was at the outset a pleasant drive through hilly country and with the moon still shining, but as day advanced we experienced great heat, and I felt apprehensive on account of the seven young children of our party. At noon we halted at Wai and refreshed ourselves with the provisions we had with us, and after a couple of hours' rest we started again on our way.

On reaching the Ghauts the horses were taken out and men were yoked to our carriages, which to our eyes seemed uncouth, but these stalwart fellows found it apparently no difficult task to pull us up the steep actively. It took over an hour to reach the summit where our horses were put to again, and we proceeded along a high mountainous road full of novelty and interest to us. We soon came to fields where raspberries and strawberries were growing in profusion; the farmers who are emigrant Chinese, on seeing a carriage approaching, ran to us with baskets of these delicious fruits; as they are only obtainable in a cold or temperate zone, we had never seen them before and their cultivation here is an index to the prevailing temperature.

Evening came on laden with cool zephyrs. Our road became more and more mountainous and wild; it presented an awful picture as seen at dusk with jagged rocks overhanging us and terrible precipices, first on one side, then on another; we were thankful when we reached our journey's end at 7 p.m. We there established ourselves at the bungalow named "Glen Ogle," hired for the season from Mr Elias Sassoon; our servants who had gone on in advance had a good dinner ready for us, and after doing it ample justice, we drowned the fatigues of this long journey in refreshing sleep.

The cold of Mahableshwar is like what we had heard people tell of the English spring or autumn. Next morning we all set out for a walk, the paths overhung with dense foliage, and the moss-covered hills clad in an eternal green, made up a picture so lovely and interesting, as to throw into oblivion the dangerous impression of the preceding evening. God has in His infinite mercy created such heavenly retreats for man during the sultry months, and it is to be regretted that the well-to-do natives do not avail themselves as they ought to of these healthful resorts—some ill-founded dread prejudices the majority from undertaking the journey. Only three or four native families then visited this delightful place, though it has the advantage over Matheran, both in point of scenery and situation, being 5,000 feet above the sea. The invigorating air soon improved our walking powers, for, whereas in Bombay half a mile's walk was enough to tire us, here we could perform our three or four miles' ramble with ease.

Like ourselves, the families of Sir Jamsetjee and Set Dinshawjee Petit were here for the first time, the ladies of all three houses used to meet and form quite a procession on the early morning promenade. Lady Jamsetjee who was well-known amongst the Parsees for her sweet endearing disposition, gained the respect and affection of all. She is of such a pure and gentle nature, that in this respect I have seen none to compare with her. We made many new acquaintances among the Europeans, who were much surprised to see my daughter riding in full English equipment, and our boys and girls playing Badminton together. Our evenings were spent in wandering amid the Elysian scenes, resting on some inviting eminence, where fruit and sweetmeats were partaken of and finishing up with a long drive and outdoor dinner.

But a sad incident rudely interrupted this pleasant routine. At such crisis, relying on Divine assistance, I always exert myself to make the best of circumstances, for to try and alleviate human sufferings is the paramount duty of man. It is easy to get a name for philanthropy by giving of one's superfluity, but he only earns it, who by self-denial and personal exertion helps his fellowmen. Along with our Portuguese servants, we had sent a Parsee cook to Mahableshwar; this man had been with my son-in-law in London, was an adept in the culinary art, and was the only child of an old and faithful nurse of the family. He was in perfect health when we left Bombay and continued so for a fortnight, after which time he was seized with fever. I called in Dr Mackenzie, Superintendent of Mahableshwar, to see the poor man and he advised his instant removal to Bombay; however, on account of some internal malady, it was found impossible for him to endure the transport.

I did all that I could to give him ease, but his malady grew worse, and in spite of all our efforts to save him, the poor fellow breathed his last. Sorely perplexed as I felt at this melancholy event, I at once set on foot the religious ceremonies which have to be performed directly after death takes place. The kind assistance rendered by the family of Set Dinshawjee M. Petit and other Parsee residents made the absence of a Parsee servant less felt. In going to up-country I had made it a rule to take such things as our religious ceremonies for the dead render necessary and they were now of the greatest service to me.

On producing them, my caste fellows exclaimed: "Were you forewarned of poor Ruttonjee's fate?"

I proposed to take the remains to Bombay, so that the unfortunate mother of the dead should have the consolation of a last look at the face of her only son, but the general voice opposing this plan, Poona was fixed upon and I telegraphed my son-in-law to meet me there with the bereaved mother. I also requested by telegram the High Priest at Poona to commence the necessary ceremonies there.

After reaching Poona with the remains, which we could do after much trouble, the High Priest assuming that the corpse had been defiled by contact with an alien caste, directed us to take it, without entering the city, to the open space adjoining the Tower of Silence. We satisfied him that all prescribed ritual had been strictly observed and the corpse was free from any defilement. In the meanwhile, the mother of the deceased had arrived with my son-in-law, but if I had not accompanied the remains they would not have received a decent disposal. The mother's grief was heart-rending, and though half killed by the sudden blow, her grief was much lessened when she knew that all ceremonies attendant on the burial were rigidly performed. She showered blessings on me for having ensured to her son the last honours of an upright Parsee. Exactly twenty-four hours after death the body was conveyed and deposited in the Tower of Silence. The High Priest, though in the third day's ceremony of his own brother's funeral, rendered us all assistance in his power. The death of a Parsee in an up-country station entails endless difficulties, and had I not bestirred myself, no one else would have taken the trouble on behalf of a poor servant; it was therefore said of me in Poona that even a man could not have done what I did in the matter. We started for Mahableshwar at four o'clock, and after some difficulty reached our destination at seven the next morning.

By degrees the games of Badminton, our picnics and rambles were resumed. My husband's birthday fell on one of these days, and as the Portuguese cook did not suit our taste exactly, I myself took his place and prepared a most *recherché* repast. In honour of the day, Messrs Nowrojee Furdoonjee and Dossabhoy Framjee were our guests, and at dinner the former began to extol our Portuguese cook's skill as far beyond that of Parsee cooks; but Mr Dossabhoy remarked that the toothsome dishes must have been made by some queen, so then it came out that I was an adroit hand at cookery, and the gentlemen were much astonished to learn that one so given up to refined pursuits could also in an emergency fill the place of any one of her servants. I am very fond of making such choice sweetmeats as are novel to my friends, to whom I send them as trifling presents once or twice a year. Thus on this happy day, I sent specimens of my confectionery to my friends in Mahableshwar, and Sir Jamsetjee complimented me by saying that it pleased him to find one so excelled in the refinements of society, possessed of the sterling qualities of a capable housewife. These sober qualifications were soon to be put to the test for our five or six Portuguese servants all abruptly left us, because of Mr Pherozshah having had to rebuke one of them. Though there were numerous applicants for the cook's place, it was quite impossible to find one sufficiently experienced, so I had to turn my knowledge to account. Hotels were in those days little frequented by Parsees. On 10th June, amid cooling showers of rain, we returned to Bombay, pushing on rapidly on hearing of the serious illness there of my father-in-law; otherwise we had intended to spend some days at Poona.

I found domestic anarchy reigning in my own house, and I was much engaged immediately on my return in setting things to rights there, besides which I had to pay a daily visit to my father-in-law, whose prolonged illness demanded my husband's constant attendance. On the 30th day, tenth month, 1244 A.Y. (17th July 1875), he bid adieu to this life, leaving only one son to lament him. Up to the last, he was in the full possession of his faculties, and previous to his illness he used to come twice a week to dine at our house with a select party of friends. His love for my husband continued unabated till the last, and he consulted him on every point, domestic and commercial.

After his death discord arose between my husband and his sons, the children of his first wife, who had been kept in their grandfather's service. My father-in-law had made his will in 1872, and shown it to my husband; according to this, the testator delegated all his possessions and powers to his only surviving son, my husband, directing that the grandchildren should remain under their father's control, do his bidding and be content with as much of the estate as he chose to give them. This was consonant with reason, seeing that, through my husband's efforts the firm had been greatly enriched, and what was his would eventually become his sons' inheritance. The testator further bequeathed Rs 200 monthly to each of his late sons' children, Rs 50 monthly to his only surviving sister, and Rs 10,000 for funeral expenses and charities. This will my husband found just and equitable, and there being nothing to say against it, the subject was never broached again.

During his father's last illness, my husband went to see him at least twice daily, and whenever he appeared, the venerable patient evinced his gratification by affectionately stroking his son's back. Nothing seemed to have ever interrupted their beautiful love for one another, and to the last it was never supposed that the original will had been rendered null and void.

After my return from Mahableshwar, my sister-in-law (widow of my husband's brother) informed me that a new will had been executed and duly signed, and attested by an attorney. I acquainted my husband with this and on his making further inquiries of his sons, they answered their father, telling him the new will was in the possession of Mr Pestonjee Hormusjee Cama, and that it would be read ten days after their grandfather's funeral in the presence of the interested parties. On hearing this, my husband grew extremely uneasy and consulted the physicians as to whether the invalid was in such a state of mind as to allow of his legally attesting a fresh will, but their answer was in the negative. My husband, who never spoke a harsh word even to his servants, now became greatly exasperated, and losing all patience, harshly upbraided his sons. One of them, more forward than the rest, accused me of having incited his father to this outburst; for they had so firm a faith in their father's good nature, that they thought nothing would disturb it—in this, however, they were mistaken.

Ten days after the death of my revered father-in-law, the attorney came with the second will to be read out in the presence of my husband, his sons and nephews but before it was half through, my husband left the room in disgust at the manner in which his rights were quite ignored, and everything monopolised by his sons. This subsequent document was attested by intimate friends of the eldest son, and it bore the signature of a native attorney, whereas the will of 1872 was witnessed by two gentlemen of standing, the particular friends of both my father-in-law and husband; the second made no mention of the testator's sister or grandchildren—the children of his second son. I said to my husband that it was better to pass the unpleasant affair over in silence. My reasoning had the desired effect, and my husband's anger subsided. Money was never an object of his ambition, but he did desire to have the control of his children and to see them obedient to his will as long as he lived. If further proof had been needed of the objectionable nature of this will, it was contained in a paragraph referring to our bungalow. This, as has been related, was purchased by me, my father-in-law himself and four Europeans attesting to the validity of the transaction—this property was mentioned as being still under mortgage, but could become my husband's if released by him.

From this time forward, there remained no love between the father and his ungrateful sons. From the very day I was allied to this family, I treated my step-children with uniform kindness, and participated in their weal or woe; in fact, God inspired me with a maternal sympathy for them. The eldest, Nusserwanjee, was a great favourite of mine, and I often, unknown to the others, made him presents, but neither my father-in-law nor my husband confided in them. During the former's illness, Nusserwanjee frequently tried to get information from me, but I on these occasions always referred him to his father. In spite of all the troubles my step-sons have caused us my wish has always been that they might enjoy long life.

XIII

Visit of His Royal Highness the Prince of Wales

It was at this time that the welcome news of the Prince of Wales' intended visit reached India. That the heir to the Crown of England was coming with royal pomp and pageantry was news indeed. Everyone was overjoyed at the prospect, all ages and classes were filled with joyous expectation, and all equally eager to receive the august guest with befitting honour—indeed, it would be impossible to depict the enthusiasm of the populace. When the Duke of Edinburgh came to India, I had felt the desire that all Her Majesty's sons might follow their brother's example, and now my wish was to be partly realised.

The Native Chiefs crowded to Bombay to do honour to the fortunate English Prince; they, with their retinues of gaily clad followers were to be seen going about our streets, bungalows were let at fabulous rents, houses were all newly painted and whitewashed, streets and public gardens repaired and put in order, in every way trade became brisk and flourishing. Our city hung with innumerable flags and bright Chinese lanterns in the trees, presented a very gay appearance as the day of His Royal Highness' arrival approached. Laying aside my mourning for the occasion, I put on my handsomest dress and ornaments, and took my seat on one of the stands erected on the Esplanade, whence I had a good view of the Prince as he passed along amid the deafening cheers of his exultant subjects, followed by an imposing cavalcade of Rajahs, nobles, leading citizens and high Government officials. This English Prince, coming amongst us, was considered an auspicious omen by the natives, and his advent afforded the Parsee ladies an amount of happiness and freedom unknown before; several salutary reforms arose then amongst the native females and have been preserved ever since.

For instance, widows, who had hitherto been excluded from all public sights, came out and participated in the general rejoicing; others who till this time had only driven in closed carriages with the venetian blinds tightly shut, now appeared in open carriages; others who had never set foot in the streets were now hurrying along eager to catch a glimpse of His Royal Highness. On the Prince's birthday, which he spent in Bombay, the illuminations were magnificent, and many a native female, throwing aside ceremony, was to be seen walking about and enjoying the sight up to a late hour. Thus it will be seen that, although greater emancipation for native females has been advancing with slow step since 1860, His Royal Highness' visit gave a great impetus to the movement. On 10th November His Royal Highness was present at a treat given to the native schoolboys and girls, where some hundreds of Parsee ladies were assembled to meet him, and it was a novel feature of the entertainment that some of our most antiquated and orthodox co-religionists were to be seen there, mixing freely with the company. I saw the Prince for the last time at a grand review, when new colours were presented to one of the regiments. This was a very imposing spectacle, all the Rajahs were present, their position being marked off by many coloured flags, and the whole force marched past them and saluted the Price of Wales. Through the kindness of Sir Frank Souter, I had a card of admission to the enclosure, where there were only three carriages of Parsee ladies. The Prince, attired in martial dress and seated on a beautiful steed, attracted all eyes towards him. This grand review was highly relished by all spectators as a representation of Royal pomp, of which until now we had only known by reading. Our bungalow was temporarily occupied by H.H. the Maharana of Odeypore, where, on the occasion of the Prince of Wales paying him a visit, we had again the pleasure of seeing him. The only thing I missed seeing was the S.S. *Serapis*, which was described to me as of extraordinary luxury. To partake of all the rational enjoyments Divine Providence has placed within my reach, has always been the ruling motto of my life; but I consider it equally imperative to take part in the sorrows of others, which is the first duty we owe to God and man. After a sojourn of a few months in various parts of India, this blessed Prince bade adieu to the shores of India, carrying with him the heartfelt blessings of Her Majesty's loyal subjects; again thousands assembled at Bombay to see him and wish him God-speed, and to bless him and his gracious mother. These benedictions might be considered in the style of the National Anthem, and run thus: "May Her Imperial Majesty's reign last long, may victory attend each and all of her endeavours, may God always befriend her and may her innumerable loyal subjects reap multifarious advantages from her blessed rule in India."

As I have already mentioned, my husband, led on by Mr Nolke, ex-manager of Messrs Volkart's firm in Bombay, was engaged in erecting a mill at Oomrawuttee. Nearly half the shares were bought, but the market continuing uniformly dull, the first call could not be met and the work had to be abandoned, thereby causing us trouble and loss. I made up my mind then never to allow my husband to speculate in any way again and he, too, after the collapse of the mill scheme, was anxious to secure a berth in some European firm, and I had to keep a vigilant look to prevent his being duped again; as he had more than once, through sheer artlessness fallen into villains' hands and lost the greater part of his money. About this time a Mr Massotti left the firm of Messrs Volkart for that of Messrs Knoop and Co., and engaged my husband as a broker, in which capacity he was required to furnish a security. I urged him to quit the firm, but as he was extremely averse to doing so, I offered to stand security for him. Messrs Knoop and Co., however, declined to accept a lady's responsibility. At length my brother Heerjeebhoy, who had enough of my fortune in his hands, was accepted as guarantee, and my husband promised never to conceal any business concerns from me, nor to have dealings with anyone unconnected with Messrs Knoop and Co.'s firm. He was not aware of my brother having funds of mine in his hands and attributed Heerjeebhoy's readiness to stand security for him to gratitude, and he heaped encomiums upon him to which he was not in the least entitled.

In August 1876, the year of Lord Lytton's arrival in India

as Governor-General, our company of friends agreed to make an excursion to Goregaum. We reached that place at night and the rain was falling in torrents, as if it was boding something ill. We had put up at a bungalow which Set Byramjee Jeejeebhoy had kindly placed at our disposal. We were in the full swing of enjoyment, when our gaieties were suddenly interrupted by the receipt of two telegrams announcing successively the dangerous illness and death of Cooverbai, my son-in-law's sister. One of her daughters was with us, and this unexpected news plunged us all into the deepest affliction, and tears began to flow. The day being Sunday, the only train for Bombay started at 5 p.m. in the evening. So we telegraphed back to defer the funeral till our arrival. The whole day was passed in anxiety and mourning. As none of us had tasted food since early morning we were constrained to eat a little. At table someone started the idea that the telegrams would prove bogus, which conveyed some comfort to us. Setting aside the religious restriction, the daughter and sister of the supposed dead partook of everything that lay within their reach, thinking that the next day they dared not eat anything they liked. At the station we got another telegram informing us that through the mischief of some evil or envious person we had heard a false news. Whereupon Mr Pherozshah Mehta begged us to prolong our stay for a couple of days. I was however so much disturbed by the news, false as it proved to be afterwards, that I preferred to return to Bombay at once. On reaching my son-in-law's house, I found a younger brother and his wife running laughing into the house and on alighting from the carriage, Cooverbai, who was reported to be dead, came forward to meet us. It appeared certain that she was innocent of any share in this unpleasant affair, the culprit whereof in her opinion deserved to be traced and punished. I apprised her of my suspicion about her younger brother Muncherjee, who, however, began most emphatically to declare his innocence. I was however firm in my suspicions, and from that day rarely sought the society of any of the juveniles. "A wise enemy is better than a foolish friend."

We tried to bring the delinquent to book by instituting inquiries at the telegraph offices, but a whole year passed away before the truth came to light. Mr Muncherjee fell ill, and in his delirium he exposed the whole proceeding, naming his late sister Goolbai's son and his uncle's grandson as the ringleaders of the plot. The Cama family were alone implicated, and Cooverbai's husband, who had sought to bring the culprit to justice, tendered his apology to Mr Cooverjee Nazir, who had been unjustly suspected and harshly treated. I was greatly relieved when this was cleared up, and my impressions proved correct, for no one agreed with me at first. I never hesitate to speak out my mind, even though my friends may not like to hear it.

XIV

The First Empress of India

In April 1876, Lord Lytton was appointed Governor-General, and shortly after it became generally known that our gracious Queen was about to assume the grand title of Empress of India. The entire Indian population received this news with acclamation. An official announcement was issued stating that the public declaration of this event would take place at a grand Durbar to be held at Delhi, the ancient capital of the Mogul Empire. Immediately, the feudatory Princes, Rajahs and nobles began making arrangements to be present and in due time set out on their way to the northern city with their large retinues and numerous followers. Preparations on a grand scale went on throughout the land and the well-to-do of every caste and creed were eager to be present on the occasion, as indeed they were encouraged to show their loyalty by appearing at the Durbar. It was said that something like half the population of India would be drawn towards Delhi and that the demand for edibles of all sorts would be likely to produce a dearth. To attract the attention of the public and to leave nothing undone that could conduce to the splendour of the ceremony, the subject was daily brought prominently forward in the leading native and English journals. As I had long wished to travel through the various districts of my native land, I determined to avail myself of this favourable opportunity for visiting the historical cities of the north. Two months before the time appointed for the Durbar, I introduced the subject to our social coterie and requested my daughter and her husband to bear me company, but they did not enter into the project, being apprehensive of the great difficulties of the journey as well as of the expenses at Delhi and *en route*. Mr Pherozshah also declined to join me, so on hearing this I kept my own counsel and said no more on the subject. In the face of these discouragements, my kind husband readily consented to the plan, saying, we could dispense with other company, and go by ourselves.

Accordingly, I set all necessary preparations in train and kept our intention scrupulously secret to ward off the storm of ridicule and scandal which a rumour of this new departure from old custom would have called down on my devoted head. I fancied I could hear the jeering queries. Is it a Parsee female's business to mix in such demonstrations? How can she be so unwomanly as to venture on such a journey? Parsee men were notoriously selfish and had monopolised to themselves every pleasure and indulgence, fancying that women were only created for household drudgery.

I kept a lookout to see if any of the noteworthy Parsee gentlemen who were honoured by an invitation to the Durbar would take their families with them, but none apparently dreamt of such a thing and thus I was the more bent on going. I have ever taken the lead in matters of female reform and have tried to stimulate the dormant energies of my sisters and to open up to them paths hitherto debarred, leading to innocent pleasures or enlarged interests. It is quite unaccountable to me why native ladies in affluent circumstances should be backward in taking their legitimate place in grand state ceremonials, but they seem devoid of interest and curiosity as regards such things. Every new act of female emancipation at first meets with disapprobation and sarcasm and that frightens many a one from gratifying her inclinations, and on this occasion no other Parsee lady, incited by a keen desire to witness so grand a spectacle, had the courage either to face the ridicule of her people or to undertake the long journey. For my own part the encouragement I have always met with from another quarter, the Europeans, from my youth, has more than compensated me for the sneers of my countrymen. Seeing me busily making arrangements for leaving home, my daughter and friends were given to understand that

I was preparing for a sojourn at Nowsaree, a place about 150 miles distant from Bombay. Thus, everyone being on the wrong scent, I often proposed in jest that ten or twenty of our club should go to the Delhi assemblage, to which they made answer: “It is not for us to encounter such difficulties, even if we could go to Delhi, we females would not be able openly to enjoy any of the sights.” This simplicity made me laugh but responding in the same strain I would say, “Ah yes, a trip to Nowsaree or Gandevi is all that we women can hope for while our husbands roll in luxury and deny themselves nothing, so, in spite of our being reputed of higher culture than many of our sisters, we lead the same dull and tasteless life.”

In due time all was ready and our party of seven, comprising my husband, his old aunt of the comic disposition, our two sons, my brother Heerjeebhoy and an old tried servant of the house, took our departure from Bombay on 22nd December. As my husband’s business affairs did not allow of a very long absence it was necessary to have my brother’s company during our tour after the assemblage was over. He expressed his inability to meet the expenses of such protracted travels, but on my indignantly demanding, “Who asks anything from you?” he made up his mind to escort me. The manager of my husband’s firm had been very unwilling to spare him and was only persuaded to do so on condition that he (my husband) should return, in case urgent business compelled his being telegraphed for. This my good husband kept to himself, lest by his inability to remain with us the whole project should be upset. At the last, feeling sore at the thought of enjoying so much without my daughter sharing it with me, I asked her to come with me, but she again refused on account of the difficulties and troubles into which she thought I rushed willingly. It seemed unnatural to be without her, as she had till now always accompanied me in all my pleasures, I willingly defraying all expenses, but my husband’s company kept up my spirits. He took the management of everything and right well did he discharge the self-imposed duty. He wrote to his cousins in Delhi to secure suitable accommodation and make all suitable arrangements for the reception of a European friend and his family whom he would accompany down to Delhi. He also wrote to his two friends, Shapoorjee and Jamsetjee Eduljee Chinoy, who were in the service of the Nizam’s late uncle, Amir-i-Kabir, co-regent of

Hyderabad, and held in high estimation; these two gentlemen were intimate with my husband and had frequent intercourse with him in Bombay and they were also given to understand that a European and his wife were coming, thus the secret was kept to the last. I wrote to Bai Sakerbai, wife of Set Manekjee Rustomjee, at Calcutta, informing her of my intention to sojourn there for a time after the Durbar at Delhi and requesting her to hire lodgings for me. An intimate friendship had sprung up between us while she stayed for about three years in Bombay. She had honoured us by her company at my daughter's marriage and we frequently visited each other at that time. Through this letter the fact of my intended visit to Delhi became known to friends in Bombay, two or three days before our departure, for the daughter-in-law of my friend in Calcutta, extremely surprised by this unexampled proceeding on my part, at once wrote to her mother and brother in Bombay asking if the news could be true. The brother in his turn interrogated a Hindoo teacher, who came to my house to instruct my two sons; he, however, was quite in the dark as to our intention and could not satisfy the gentleman's curiosity. Meanwhile I received a favourable reply from Bai Sakerbai, kindly inviting me to stay with her while in Calcutta.

Before setting out on this tour, I paid a visit to my kind friend, Lady Sassoon, and on informing her of my projected journey she could not at first give credence to my words, but on being assured that it really was so, she expressed herself pleased, saying she also would have gone if she could have found suitable lodgings there. Here I met Lord Kilman, brother of the late Mrs O.T. Burne, wife of the Private Secretary of H.E. the Viceroy of India, who also expressed himself pleased with my going to Delhi, but he did not know that I was the only Parsee lady who should be there.

On 22nd December we started from the Boree Bunder. Amongst many loungers at the station were Set Dhunjeebhoy Framjee Patell and other members of the Panthakey family whose surprise on seeing our tickets for Delhi knew no bounds and they asked how we could venture to go into such immense crowds as would be assembled there, especially as no other Parsee female would be there. At 5.30 the train started, and on reaching Byculla my daughter, who had escorted us so far, alighted. Next day our departure for Delhi came to be generally known by an announcement of the fact in the local papers. This brought many congratulatory letters from my well-meaning friends, but it cannot be denied that many others were much incensed against me; however, I would not allow their envy and folly to deprive me of one iota of the enjoyment placed within my reach. We reached Jubbulpore the next evening at 9 p.m. and on alighting, my husband as he apprehended received a telegram, calling him back to Bombay on urgent business. This was extremely dejecting, but my husband comforted me somewhat by promising to hasten after us if his affairs allowed; he therefore parted from us, taking his youngest son who desired to go back to Bombay with his father.

We continued our journey and next day at 7 a.m. reached Allahabad; this railway station was then considered the largest and finest in India. We breakfasted there and spent the day in the city. We hired a carriage and drove to the fortress which to me presented a grand imposing appearance. There was a regiment encamped in it and there was much life about the place. At a particular spot near the fortress there is a spacious subterranean cellar which we also visited; sacred rites and ceremonies are performed here by the Hindoos. We saw human skeletons hanging up here and there, it looked dark and gruesome and I would not venture far, though other members of our party went with lighted tapers and saw the whole vast extent of the place. Thence we went to the Bazaar, which is held in an open space without roof or structure of any kind. Of the fruit of this place the pear is a speciality; it has a sweet, delicious taste and is four times the size of those we get in Bombay; it has a small collection of stones like those of the date or greengage in the middle. We next proceeded to the confluence of the Ganges and Jumna where many Hindoo devotees were bathing in the holy waters with their clothes on and performing various religious ceremonies—all this is worth seeing. After this we went through the streets and saw houses and shops of curious architecture and plan. The dust, however, was the prevailing element and sadly annoyed us. At dusk we returned to the station and partook of a meal prepared by our own servant, then rested a little and started again on our way at 9 p.m., reaching Toondla next morning.

At all the stations the station masters and hotel keepers rendered us every possible assistance and attention; they unanimously declared that thousands of passengers had passed through their station on their way to Delhi during the last two months, but that they had seen no Parsee lady till I came. The English passengers freely commented on my appearance till they became aware that I could talk their language, thus many new friendships sprang up in the course of this journey. At this station two new passengers entered our carriage, one of whom was a barrister practising at Cawnpore, the other was the Principal of the Martiniere College at Lucknow. The amusing conversation which they carried on together caused me to smile, whereupon the man of learning whispered to his friend of the long robe that he thought I understood what they were saying, the other retorted that such a grown-up Parsee lady was certainly not so accomplished; this created much merriment and we soon were chatting together and feeling quite at home with one another. The schoolmaster showed me much consideration by rendering me assistance whenever he could. The nearer we approached Delhi the more the number of passengers increased, so that the crowding and bustle of the last hour were such as to throw into oblivion the troubles of the three preceding days' journey; however, by God's grace we arrived safely at our destination.

At the Delhi station the great concourse of people, the shouting and excitement made me think that the timorous folk in Bombay were not so far wrong, that this was really no place for a native female to be in, especially without her husband. But I caught sight of my husband's cousin, Mr Eduljee Cowasjee Jamsetjee, hurrying towards us, and my courage revived. This gentleman carries on the business of my late father-in-law under the name of Jehangir and Co., a name well-known throughout the Punjab and Kabul. This "friend in need" had made all fitting arrangements for the reception of an English lady and gentleman, whom my husband was to accompany, and had come to the station to await them. He was glad that his exertions had been made on my behalf and he skilfully steered me through the great crowd and drove me to the small bungalow in the compound of the United Service Hotel which he had secured for the supposed English couple.

Though the miniature bungalow was cabin-like in its dimensions, it was nicely furnished and answered all our requirements, but the cold was so severe that I was glad to bring into requisition the extra bedding we had brought with us. Early on the morning after our arrival, I was awakened by someone knocking at the door. This turned out to be a Hindoo clerk in the service of H.H. the Amir-i-Kabir, co-regent of Hyderabad; the poor man had been on our track all night and was glad to find us at last. The explanation of the matter is that, on my husband's return from Jubbulpore, he had telegraphed my coming to his kind and good friend Mr Shapoorjee, but the message arriving too late he had failed to meet me at the station, and had employed this clerk to find out my whereabouts. Shortly afterwards, his brother, Mr Jamsetjee, followed in his carriage. He insisted on our leaving the Hotel and making use of the beautiful tents which they had erected for us. I thanked him kindly but had resolved to stay where we were.

On the 26th I had a long drive in Mr Shapoorjee's open mail phaeton drawn by a pair of beautiful studs through the principal thoroughfares of the city, and wherever the eyes were cast dense crowds of people were to be seen, to whom the sight of a Parsee female was a novelty, thus we reached the large open space studded with innumerable tents. Here we saw two of those tents, which Mr Shapoorjee had so kindly provided for our use, they were most comfortable and inviting, supplied with every convenience and our heartfelt thanks were offered to our hospitable friend, but I excused myself from accepting the accommodation on account of the extreme cold which would have been experienced in such an open and unprotected plain.

Returning thence we re-entered the city by the high spacious Cashmere and Lahore gates, once no doubt grand and imposing but now falling into decay. Proceeding through streets teeming with people we came to Chandni-Chowk, flanked on each side by houses and reminding me of the Bhindy Bazaar or Parell Road of Bombay. We saw a great many Hindoos and Mahomedans, a few Baboos and a very few Parsees. They were taken by surprise on seeing me drive through this city of antiquity in an open carriage and the gaping crowd that gathered round the carriage made it a matter of difficulty to proceed. I heard several passing their opinion as to my identity; some said I was a European, some took me for a Chinese, some for an Egyptian, a Turkish lady and so on, but very few knew me as a Parsee, as they did not believe a Parsee lady would venture through such populous thoroughfares in an open carriage.

It was exceedingly droll to listen to the rejoinders made by my old aunt to these openly expressed opinions; she did not hesitate to scold back the curious crowd saying, "If you want to see persons like us come to Bombay."

The general astonishment with which we were beheld wherever we went in this city was due to the gaily coloured sarees we wore and to the fact that none of the native females had ever been seen in an open carriage before, but according to custom they never appear in public nor go from one place to another without being caged up in a carriage with all venetian blinds and shutters fast closed.

At four in the afternoon of this day Mr Shapoorjee again came to take us sight-seeing, I took my place on his open mail phaeton and my aunt with my son and brother on that of his brother's. We met several Princes and Rajahs with their retinues, as also some of the handsome four-in-hand coaches of Englishmen. Of these, the turn-out of the Lieutenant-Governor attracted most attention from its novelty.

The State carriage was drawn by six camels ridden by grooms in gorgeous livery much bedecked with gold fringe and silver lace; in the carriage, which was a large open brake, a number of beautiful young ladies were seated. This unique show was very striking to us, but apparently more so to my old aunty who in the exuberance of her delight showered down blessing on me for having afforded her such enjoyments at her advanced age.

On our return we saw several old buildings, the most remarkable being the fortress of gigantic magnitude. The strength and stability of this ancient fortification, most part of which has been destroyed by war, prove that the architects of old understood the secret of setting time and decay at defiance. We had a grand view of the Jooma Musjid, the largest mosque in India. Proceeding further we had to make our way through streets literally teeming with people whose smiling faces turned towards our carriage wherever we went. The clouds of dust somewhat marred our enjoyment although the roads had been so plentifully watered as to present a monsoon appearance. A cold breeze and thick fog came on the accompanying darkness rendering it necessary for us to return home by seven o'clock, Mr Shapoorjee and his brother making their way as best they could to their tents, carrying with them our grateful thanks for the delightful and interesting drive.

After taking some tea to keep off the cold we mixed in the

company at the Hotel, where I found some acquaintances, and in animated conversation the time passed pleasantly. Amongst them was Mr Dadabhoy, son of the late worthy Manekjee Nowrojee Setna. Before retiring to rest, I offered prayer and thanksgiving to God for having allotted me a share in such rare enjoyment.

On the morning of the 27th we started for an early walk but had to beat a hasty retreat. The cold was more than we could bear. After dressing ourselves in warm woollen garments, one above the other, and I enveloping myself in a long over-coat such as European ladies wear, we ventured forth again and took a brisk walk which soon made us warm and comfortable. Returning at ten o'clock we took breakfast, afterwards taking a drive in a wagonette. We arranged with the Hotel-keeper to have a carriage and pair retained for our use, besides which Mr Shapoorjee placed a carriage and horses at our disposal. Everything was procurable for money, but I found the prices little in excess of those usual in Bombay and below what report had led us to expect. I met another old acquaintance here, Mr Hormusjee Shapoorjee Bookbinder, for many years clerk in my father-in-law's firm in the Punjab; he left this service and had set up a hotel, known as the Prince of Wales Hotel, a coach factory and livery stable at Lucknow and had in a short time amassed great wealth and become a leading citizen. He was to be seen driving about with great pomp here in Delhi, his fine carriages and horses and English coachman attracting much attention. On seeing me, he began to eulogise my husband under whom he had once served: "It is with heartfelt joy," he would say, "that I see my patron's family here and my pleasure would be enhanced if I could execute any of your commands." And he also desired us to make use of his horses and carriages. To Mr Sorabjee Mody, Manager of my late father-in-law's firm, as also to Mr Eduljee, I was indebted for many kind services and much assistance and consideration.

This evening we again drove in an open carriage to other celebrated quarters of Delhi, but it grew cold and foggy as on the preceding day, so we returned early to our apartments. On Thursday the 28th we bent our steps early in the morning towards the garden of the city where the tombs and monuments of rich nobles who flourished in the past are daily strewn with fresh flowers and fragrant herbs. At 11 a.m. I started in company with my brother to pay a visit to the Hon'ble

Mrs Burne in the Viceroy's camp; we unfortunately forgot to take the guide book of this vast encampment and had therefore much trouble and unnecessary fatigue before we could find her tent. I was most kindly received by Mrs Burne, who invited me to a supper party and also asked me to come and be presented to Lady Lytton in the evening. She further invited me to take a glass of wine or a cup of tea or coffee; for all these civilities I expressed myself, as I felt, deeply obliged. Returning home, I selected suitable garments for the visit to Her Excellency and at half past four drove with my son to the Viceroy's tents in a splendid carriage and pair lent for the occasion by the aforementioned Mr Hormusjee, but in consequence of the circuitous route which had to be taken the appointed hour was long past when we reached our goal and Lady Lytton and Mrs Burne had gone out. So we had to return in disappointment. On the way we saw several Rajahs with their retinues and had an opportunity of learning something of the intricacies of the vast encampment. The streets were more crowded than ever, indeed every day seemed to increase the number of the populace. While sitting reading the newspaper of the day in which was detailed everything going on in Delhi, a trooper rode up with a note from the Viceroy's camp. It was from kind Mrs Burne regretting having missed my visit and hoping I would fix another time for being presented to Lady Lytton.

XV

The Delhi Durbar

Next morning I wished to go out for my usual walk, and those of our party who could not on account of the cold easily shake off sleep, were cajoled into doing so by the diligent use of a pin, for I was anxious not to lose a single hour, when there was so much of interest to be seen. First walking to Mr Shapoorjee's where we partook of tea and coffee, we drove to the vast plain where the native princes and chiefs were encamped and we could not sufficiently admire the orderly distribution of these quarters, even the horses, elephants and camels were comfortably established in separate tents, signboards were set up here and there with the name of the Rajah whose tents adjoined, many of these, particularly those of the Viceroy and his staff, and of H.H. the Nizam, were more like palaces, so spacious, well built, well-furnished and lighted. Others were fitted up as places of diversion, others again as places of business, telegraph office and so on and yet nothing gave the impression of newness or temporariness, for every tent was covered with evergreen creepers and surrounded by tastefully laid out gardens; wells were sunk here and there and all the paths were sprinkled with sand, at every turning rows of artillery met you and flags bearing distinctive designs floated over high officials' quarters. The tents were fitted with fireplaces and chimneys and the fire had to be kept continually burning as the weather was so cold; they were all tastefully decorated and, in the evening, when lighted up they presented a very brilliant appearance. It would need the descriptive powers of a novelist, coupled with the imaginative mind of a poet, to do justice to the scene. I could not but feel intense admiration of the organizing genius of the English, who in the short space of three months, had converted a barren plain into this world of tents, set down in a smiling garden.

Though India boasts of many noble chiefs, I doubt if one could be found who would bring order out of chaos as the English do, at all events a native ruler would take years to do it. Good substantial roads were constructed through this city of tents and away up the hill, from which point one had a good view of the labyrinthine encampment. To assist the public, a directory was published giving the street, number and name of occupant of each tent, but even then it was no easy task to find one's way.

In the afternoon of this day we went to the Exhibition which, considering the former condition of the city, was quite creditable, the entire collection represented local talent, most noticeable being the miniatures on ivory, brassware for domestic use, and jewellery. By five o'clock the crowd was so immense that I was glad to escape from the building. We met on our drive the imposing cavalcade of H.H. the Nizam, headed by his illustrious and accomplished premier Sir Salar Jung; then came the tightly closed carriages of the Begums or royal ladies, followed by a train of elephants with gold and silver howdahs on their backs in which were accommodated a number of young blooming and superbly handsome European ladies. Then came a file of camels. Several Rajahs were to be seen driving preceded and followed by a number of retainers on horses which resembled mules rather than the nobler animal.

In the two-horse State carriage it was difficult to distinguish from amongst the four or six men all sitting with their legs tucked under them, which was the Rajah, but the profusion of jewellery worn by one of the number, generally solved the problem. It would be beyond my subject to dilate upon the greatness of the British empire, but it was impossible to witness all the splendour and display of wealth now reigning at Delhi without feeling how powerful was the sceptre of Queen Victoria, Empress of our land.

Next morning, on our early walk, we met several parties of Europeans, and a few Rajahs or Nawabs were to be seen either on horseback or borne along at a slow pace on the backs of elephants. I had heard of the arrival of some of the Parsee aristocracy but saw none, on account doubtless of the inclement weather. I was in a dilemma, as my brother Heerjeebhoy could not get a card of admission to the Durbar, though through Mrs Burne's kindness I had secured several places for myself in special reserved seats and in consequence had written urging my husband and eldest brother to come and go with me to the assemblage. To my chagrin, my dear husband could not get away, but my brother telegraphed that he was coming. On offering Heerjeebhoy one of my cards, he declined to take it, as my name, not his, was on it and he testily expressed that he could readily obtain one for himself from Major Borass with whom he was on an intimate footing.

Mr Eduljee had kindly obtained permission for us to see the fortress and we accordingly accompanied him thither, and on our way visited the magnificent Jooma Musjid, which with its massive ancient gateway and marble court, stairs, sculptures and baths called forth our liveliest admiration. We were indeed lost in wonder at this grand work of antiquity, its vast hall is capable of accommodating between three and four thousand persons. The minarets of white marble and the whole edifice present an ideal of beauty and sublimity. The extensive compound is encircled by a beautiful marble wall with arches at intervals. No one whom God has blessed with means should fail to visit this monument of antiquity and of world-wide renown. The entrance to the fortress was guarded by English sentries and was gained by crossing a moat, the gloomy walls and massive gateway were very imposing and there was an extensive view over the surrounding country. The armoury proved attractive. There was an unusual flood of visitors, many of whom accosted us and asked where we came from; my aunt could not resist this opportunity for jest and created great merriment by her sallies.

We returned at four o'clock to allow of my brother's visit to Major Borass to ask for a card of admission, which however in spite of his arguments and sophistry he failed to obtain, and so returned very much out of humour, so much so that he proposed that I should not appear at the Durbar. Seeing him so unreasonable I kept silence and presently proceeded to the tent of my worthy friend, Mrs Burne. She was unfortunately not at home but I left a message for her to the effect that as my husband was not with me, I should be glad of my brother's company at the Grand Durbar as it would be impossible for me to go alone, and leaving my brother's name on my card, I returned to the Hotel intending to visit Kootub Minar next morning. At night my son Dadabhoy fell ill of cold and high fever and I was obliged to call in Dr Cowasjee Hormusjee of Bombay who had accompanied Set Byramjee Jeejeebhoy. Although my son was much better next day we thought it advisable to postpone our projected visit to the Kootub Minar, believed to be the highest pillar in the world.

With my aunt I set out to see the amphitheatre where the Durbar was to be held. Although this building was only to be of momentary use, thousands were spent on its erection and decoration; the pillars were of gold and silver, handsome carpets were spread on the floor and a costly canopy of velvet with golden fringe was hung up above. The front seats consisted of rich sofas and chairs, upholstered in blue satin and white silk cord and tassels. On the dais only twenty-five persons could be accommodated; it was elaborately carved and richly ornamented; the whole scene was like a magic panorama conjured up by genii. My old aunt was fairly bewildered by the magnificence and exclaimed, "Methinks it is a specimen of Paradise which I see before me."

On our return we found to my joy that my son had much improved. When driving out in the evening, we saw a great concourse of people in the main thoroughfares, flags hung from every nook and corner and there was a great display of regimental uniforms. Lord Lytton, whose lustrous equipage altogether eclipsed these of the Indian princes, presently appeared in view when every European uncovered his head. Handkerchiefs were waved and the Rajahs salaamed with both hands; to these salutations of respect Lord Lytton responded by a graceful inclination of the head. I found a kind note from Mrs Burne on my return saying she had sent up my name and my brother's to the Military Secretary and she hoped we would soon receive another ticket.

On 1st January 1877 rising betimes, that is to say at five in the morning, we found much life and activity at the Hotel and the day's proceedings were the subject of excitement. My brother Dorabjee was amongst the arrivals and both he and my son who had recovered were to accompany me to the assemblage. After breakfast at nine, we drove off in two carriages, my aunt and some other members of our party stopping at Mr Shapoorjee's tent, whence they could command a view of the whole procession, and we continuing our way to the Durbar tent, but so immense was the crowd of people and vehicles that though the road was broad enough for six carriages to drive abreast, yet wheels and horses were brought into close proximity with each other and we could only proceed at a snail's pace. The road was lined with alternate companies of infantry and cavalry and the police were indefatigable in preserving order and keeping the way clear.

Around the tent a circle of magnificent elephants, gaily caparisoned with uniform howdahs on their backs, was drawn up to look like a castle wall, and seated in the howdahs one saw the handsomely clad followers of the Indian princes. Further on, there was a detachment of English cavalry whose handsome appearance and gorgeous equipment were much admired. Standing *vis-à-vis*, in statue-like rigidity so as to form a safe and convenient passage for the Princes, was a detachment of English infantry and at convenient intervals bands were stationed, their divine harmony enlivening the air. Passing slowly along we reached the steps of the amphitheatre at noon, but it was with difficulty that we made our way through the dense crowd on the stairs.

On entering the tent an officer came up and, taking our cards, conducted us to our seats. I was apportioned a very conspicuous place in the front row amongst leading officials and their ladies; on the one hand sat the Governor-General of Goa and on the other Lady Staveley, wife of the Commander-in-Chief of Bombay; my brother sat immediately behind me. Oh, for the pen to describe the scene spread out before me! On entering this stately arena all eyes were turned towards me and recognising in me a Parsee, the Europeans smiled and seemed pleased, and what the small handful of my own community thought on seeing me, the one and only Parsee woman present, I cannot fathom. But they probably got a surprise, perhaps not quite unmixed with jealousy.

A portion of the interior was reserved for Zenana ladies who were screened from view by heavy curtains and had taken their seats at an early hour of the morning before curious eyes were open. Over against my seat were those of the Indian princes, the first and foremost among whom was H.H. the infant Nizam with his able minister, Sir Salar Jung, and his uncle the co-regent, Amir-i-Kabir; there were also the Maharajahs Gaekwar, Scindia and Holkar, the Rulers of Mysore and Cashmere, the Begum of Bhopal and others, all seated according to their rank and precedence with their banners waving over them. Such a princely gathering had never been known in the annals of India. All these Rajahs wore rare ornaments, diamonds as large as a sovereign hung from their ears and their breasts were ablaze with the precious stones and necklaces which literally covered them; their hands and arms glittered with rings and diamond-studded bracelets; their turbans were mounted in gold and bedecked with pearls and diamonds; their rapiers and sword-hilts beautifully engraved and set with precious stones. When a ray of the midday sun happened to light on any of these gorgeous personages, it dazzled our eyes to look at them. Their dresses were correspondingly splendid and the sum represented upon their persons must have amounted to millions. At half past twelve Lord Lytton made his stately appearance and took his seat on the dais. He met with an enthusiastic reception, the entire assemblage rising to do him homage. At that moment the scene was most brilliant and striking, the band played, the soldiers presented arms and the diamonds shone with oscillating splendour amid the rich hues of the ladies' and Rajahs' raiment. Precisely at one o'clock Colonel Thornton came forward and read in clear sonorous tone the Royal Proclamation, wherein the humane policy of the Government was set forth and Her Majesty's resolution from that day forth to assume the title and dignity of Empress of India or Kaiser-i-Hind. Then the national anthem pealed forth followed by the royal salute of one hundred and one guns and a *feu-de-joie* from the infantry. By the clouds of smoke the atmosphere became murky, the elephants and horses took fright and several accidents occurred; serious mischief was however averted, though it had been apprehended as the crowd was so enormous.

At about 2 p.m. the people began to disperse, but what with the interminable cavalcade of the Rajahs and the dense mass of humanity impeding the way it was five o'clock before we entered our carriage and half past six before we reached home. Volumes of dust were floating about, so my costly dress was spoilt, my jewels literally encrusted with it and my voice rendered husky. I felt much exhausted, the chilling blasts attacked me, and my old chest complaint returned with virulence accompanied by high fever. Thus I saw that my departure from Delhi was advisable, the more so as both my brothers, not caring what befell me now their purpose was served, left for Bombay that night. Relying on God's mercy, I took some medicine which I had brought with me, and found some relief, but rose next day little refreshed. I did not stir out till 4 p.m. when I set out to see the races, but in an hour I had to return in a close carriage feeling very ill indeed. The night passed in uneasiness and pain; my son and aunt were greatly concerned about me. I obtained a portable stove and kept it burning near my bed the whole night from which I got slight relief. Being refreshed by some sleep, I felt anxious to remain a little longer in Delhi and resolved to do so if the same medicine as I had brought with me could be got; however, Dr Cowasjee, whom I had again to call in, had not any with him.

At about noon, Mrs Burne and her brother Lord Kilman called on me. Although I was in bed when they came, I quickly rose and received them. Mrs Burne invited me to tiffin and asked when I would come to see Lady Lytton, and offered me tickets to see the fireworks which were to take place that night; but, in reply to all her kind inquiries, I informed her of my serious indisposition which necessitated my quitting Delhi that very night. After the departure of my kind visitors, I had a serious relapse which confirmed me in my resolution to quit Delhi without delay. Mr Eduljee assured me that I would be able to procure the medicine in Agra or Lucknow. Accordingly I made up my mind to go to the former place, so that in the event of regaining my health, I could see the celebrated Taj Mahal. By the assistance of a couple of men sent by Mr Eduljee and a few others by Mr Shapoorjee in two hours everything was packed and ready for the journey. At seven o'clock we dined together and in a glass of champagne pledged Her Imperial Majesty's health as well as that of the hundreds of Indian Princes who had congregated here. Then wrapping ourselves up warmly, we left our comfortable little cabin and drove to the station.

The streets and houses were splendidly illuminated in honour of the Proclamation, and our last look of the grand old city was a favourable one. The number of travellers at the station was so immense that half had to turn back, but by the assistance of our worthy cousin, Mr Eduljee, we were soon installed in a carriage and ready for the start. I felt the warmth returning to my body and being more composed, I entered into conversation with my kind friends, to whom I was deeply indebted for having made my visit to Delhi so felicitous. Accompanied by their good wishes, we steamed out of the Imperial city, viewing from the train the white marble Jooma Musjid resplendent in the light of innumerable bonfires.

XVI

The Taj Mahal—Eighth Wonder of the World

The train was crowded to excess but seated in our first class carriage, we felt no discomfort and our fellow passengers were very polite. We arrived at Agra at 7.30 a.m. and partook of tea and coffee at the station, the cold being less severe than at Delhi. On learning that there was a dispensary close at hand, I sent thither my prescription with instructions to make it up speedily and send it to me. We hired a vehicle, called a "Yekko," to which one horse, with a crested cap over its head, was yoked and drove to our lodgings, a sumptuous residence reserved for the use of the co-regent of Hyderabad, Amir-i-Kabir; however as he was not expected for some time, Mr Shapoorjee had got permission for my temporary occupation of it. I found my invaluable restorative there awaiting me, so I quaffed a glass of it with as much gusto as if it had been nectar, hoping it would give me strength enough to see the Taj Mahal. By the time our man had dinner ready, the acute pain and uneasiness had so far subsided that I determined to go to the Taj after dinner, and we accordingly started at two o'clock.

At the first glimpse of this world-renowned edifice, I was lost in utter amazement; on entering the gateway, the pure white marble, dazzling in the light of the midday sun, burst upon my gaze in all its lustrous majesty. It certainly is a noble structure and well illustrates the lavish and fantastic taste of the old Mahomedan Empire. The very ground was paved with huge blocks of marble uniform in size and colour, here and there large cisterns of water stood beneath an umbrageous canopy of green, lending an air of calm and coolness to the scene. Proceeding up a noble flight of marble stairs, we entered a spacious court surrounded by a low wall; the Taj Mahal itself stands in the centre of this enclosure or chowk, and at its four corners stately minarets rear themselves aloft, their height exceeding that of the Cathedral tower of Bombay or the old Colaba light-house.

Entering the Mausoleum a series of highly polished marble steps conducted us to a platform just under the dome. Below this, a staircase leads to the vault where lie the ashes of Noor Jehan. The relief carving on white marble of the interior is marvellous and realistically represents flowers, trees, birds, etc.; pillars of coloured marble sustain the roof, and the floor is studded with small pieces of bright marble to represent precious stones. Provided with lighted tapers, we descended to the vault and beheld the last resting place of the once beautiful queen. The sarcophagus is a rare specimen of carving, it is enveloped in a costly coverlet embroidered in gold and silk, the whole was surmounted by a canopy of fresh flowers. Frankincense and other aromatic herbs are kept continually burning and the air was heavy with their fragrance. All who enter the vault make an offering of gold or silver coin according to their means. We much admired the spacious baths, supplied with hot and cold water and my old aunt of seventy-five mounted to the top of one of the lofty minarets so as to see everything there was to see, but I, on account of my ill-health could not perform this feat.

If there be anything on earth which can to a slight extent illustrate the beauty of Paradise, surely it must be this unrivalled building. Hundreds of people must have been employed upon it for numbers of years and the chaste white marble inlaid with gems must have cost a fabulous sum. It seems as if the art and skill of these older days were extinct. Under British rule, large and showy architecture springs up as if by magic, the object being to get it finished in the shortest time possible, but nothing approaching the exquisite detail and costly elegance of the Taj Mahal has been attempted in modern times. It is now in charge of the British Government, and kept so well in order that it has all the appearance of having been but recently built; the Mahomedans still perform their religious ceremonies in it.

There is nothing else worth seeing in Agra except a few old palaces, for the most part in ruins. We visited the Motee Musjid and Jehangir's palace situated within the Fort, and found them magnificent in decay, their domes speared over with minarets in the pure Moslem type. We crossed the bridge of boats to see another mausoleum on the other side of the river and found it also remarkable, but of course all other sights fell far short of the "lion" of Agra, one might even say, of India, the incomparable Taj Mahal. Many an abler pen has described graphically and eloquently this pride of our land; and if I, led away by its unrivalled magnificence, have ventured on a feeble and indistinct sketch, all those who have seen the Taj will find my enthusiasm excusable. Those of my readers who have not been so fortunate, I would strongly recommend to go and see it for themselves. As travelling is nowadays safe and speedy and moderate in expense, my sisters would derive great pleasure and profit from a trip to Agra to see a building of stone carved like network and inlaid with gems like jewellery. I cannot refrain from mentioning that the vegetables of Agra are of unusual size and flavour, the cabbages and cauliflowers being often ten times as large as those in Bombay and correspondingly esculent.

It was evening when we returned from our sight-seeing, and the comforts of our commodious lodging, amply provided with beds, lights and every other necessary article were greatly appreciated. I found myself so much better in health and spirits that I gave orders for conveyances and refreshments to be ready in the morning, so that we might all go to see Futtehpore Sikree. A cousin of my own, who had accompanied us from Delhi, assuring us that he knew Agra well and its places of interest, was to be our guide. Accordingly, next morning at seven, we started, my relative directing the coachman to drive to a particular place which we reached in an hour or so, and found to be a barren plain with nothing to relieve the monotony, but the ruins of an ancient palace and the mouldering tomb of the Great Akbar. In vain we looked for the famous waterfall and the stately structure of Futtehpore Sikree; so finding that my foolish cousin had brought us where nothing was to be seen, I asked the coachman if this were really the place. He replied in the negative saying Futtehpore was very far off and well worth a visit; thereupon my too prudent cousin broke in with "As I knew you could not endure the fatigue of such a long and tedious drive I thought it best and wisest to bring you here."

Our time was thus wasted, so we returned home about eleven o'clock after making a round of the city, and lost the golden opportunity of seeing Futtehpore Sikree, as we were to leave Agra that night. I telegraphed to Mr Hormusjee that we should be at Lucknow on the 7th instant, and received a reply testifying to his great pleasure at the prospect of seeing me again. So we left Agra in the evening and next morning saw us at Cawnpore.

XVII

Lucknow—A Landmark of British Heroism

After a halt of two hours at Cawnpore, the junction of the Oudh & Rohilkhund Railways, we took train for Lucknow at six o'clock and arrived there at nine the same morning. Before the train stopped, Mr Hormusjee came up and expressed his heartfelt joy at beholding the family of his good old master Set Cowasjee in that city. He then led us to the refreshment room, where a sumptuous breakfast was waiting, and after duly appreciating it, we seated ourselves in a carriage of our host and drove to his hotel, passing through the principal streets on our way.

The Prince of Wales Hotel, of which Mr Hormusjee is sole proprietor, suited our taste and convenience exactly, and the suite of handsomely furnished rooms set apart for us, with servants to wait, left nothing to be desired and made one feel thoroughly at home. After refreshing ourselves with a hot bath, we rested from the fatigues of the journey. The climate we found most agreeable, and when dinner was announced at twelve o'clock we approached the table with considerably improved appetites. The cookery, brought off after the English and Mogul taste, was excellent and better than that to which we were habituated even at home, and my old aunt relished her dinner exceedingly, expressing her opinion that the best skilled Parsee cook in Bombay could not turn out such savoury dishes. At one o'clock we retired to rest; at two we partook of tea and biscuits, and at three we drove out with Mr Hormusjee in a carriage and pair to see the city.

The Kaiserbagh is a large enclosure with gates of palatial dimensions at the four sides; these gates are of iron and are wonderfully painted and engraved with figures of lions, tigers and fays with outstretched wings. Entering one of these magnificent gateways we see broad roads bordered with trees, water tanks, good two-storeyed houses and a considerable amount of wheeled traffic everywhere. We drove right across this interesting place, and emerging at the opposite gate we crossed a handsome bridge over the Jumna whence we could command a fine view of the city and its surrounding plains. On the way back to our hotel our kind host entertained us with narratives of the city, interspersed with amusing incidents of my husband's early travels. The hotel was much frequented and the continual coming and going of guests afforded us much diversion as my windows overlooked the entrance. After dinner at seven, I sat down to pen letters to Bombay before retiring to rest; and the following morning I had the happiness of receiving good news from my dear ones there.

It was Moharam time when we were at Lucknow and we heard all through the streets the Tazias (elegies) and saw the mosques highly decorated. The Mahomedans of this place take a pride in making a grand display of their Taboots during this festival; they were very beautifully adorned with gold leaf and of most finished workmanship. Attached to every mosque there were bathing places supplied with hot and cold water; they are not exclusively reserved for the worshippers, as anyone can have a bath there on payment of the tariff and if only one bath is wanted as many as four attendants come and await your orders. I could not but wonder on seeing this why Bombay is altogether without such admirable public baths. Taking into account the wealth and enterprise of the Bombay Mahomedans as compared with the pauperism of a large number of the race in Lucknow, the liberality of the latter was far beyond what one witnessed during the Moharam festival with us.

Feeling very tired on our return at nine o'clock, I would have rested but for the desire to leave nothing of interest unseen, and therefore started again at eleven in a carriage. We drove to the Muchibagh (park) within which the celebrated fortress of Chattar Manzil is situated. This building is not so dilapidated but that one can see the plain and solid structure of the fortifications; the ground floor had been used as a magazine. We ascended to the most lofty point and had a bird's-eye-view of Lucknow and its ancient walls. Near the fortress there is a large artificial pond with stone steps leading down to the water and surrounded by caravansaries for the use of the travellers who come to bathe there. We returned at half past two, much fatigued by the climbing up the fortress, but after having refreshed ourselves we started again. Mr Hormusjee's splendid carriage and his English coachman used to be waiting for us with fresh horses at the exact hour, no matter how inconvenient it seemed. We now drove to the Residency, in the large cellars of which the wives and children of the English officers took refuge at the time of the mutiny in 1857, and the appearance of the outer walls shows that it must have been heavily bombarded at one time. It saddened me to think that in that gloomy subterranean place into which not a ray of light could penetrate even at midday, a multitude of tender ladies and children had lived for four days. We next drove to the Esplanade and that part of the city and returned home at seven o'clock. Every day I received good news from Bombay so I could enjoy all these sights with an easy mind.

On the 9th instant I set out early in the day to see the old part of Lucknow. The gates of Great Imambara supported on high massive pillars of stone impressed us by their true artistic character and the tomb and gate of Hoosenabad are also worthy of note. From there we bent our steps to the Martiniere College and while being shown over its extensive premises whom should we see but our fellow passenger of the journey to Delhi. He expressed his pleasure at meeting us again and showed us the whole of the school and introduced me to his wife and children. Nor was this all, he also made us partake of wine and fruit and for his kindness and courtesy I felt deeply grateful. This school originated in a piece of romance. General Martiniere, the founder of it, rose from the rank of a common soldier to be one of the highest military men in India; much of his life was spent in Lucknow and there he was married to a Mahomedan girl. He was blessed with an only son, but by the decree of an all-wise Providence, his beloved wife and idolised child died before him. He was rich and invested the whole of his fortune in the endowment of this noble institution. Portraits of this distinguished philanthropist, his wife and son are hung up in the school; his memory will ever be held dear in India. The school affords an excellent and advanced education and accommodates a number of boarders, but the students were all away for the Christmas vacation when we were there. We returned to our hotel at one o'clock and as we intended to leave Lucknow the following day we sat down to tiffin for the last time there and I therefore in a short toast gave expression to the great gratification I had derived from my visit to this town, and offered my most sincere and warm thanks for the favours heaped upon us by our worthy host. I gave orders for my luggage to be packed and ready and set out again at two o'clock to see the museum and several other places which had escaped us in our former rambles. Mr Hormusjee had made ready for this excursion, an elephant with a howdah in which four of us were accommodated. My old aunty found it rather difficult to mount to this lofty perch, but succeeded at last and took her place in the howdah with considerable pride. We both found an elephant ride a very amusing experience; the huge creature threaded his way through the narrow crowded streets, nothing disturbing his equanimity or causing him to alter his pace. We could easily see into the dwellings as we passed along and we created no little stir amongst their occupants; some ran to see us, others would have liked to cross-question us from their balconies and others with a salute of the hands would call out to us in their patois, "Begum" (Mahomedan lady) "pray stop awhile and do such poor people as we are the honour of partaking of our 'pan sopari' (betel-nuts and leaves), for we never saw such a thing before as a Begum riding on an elephant in public." My aunt was much gratified by the sensation we created and talked to the people in the garrulous fashion of the aged. Crowds of pedestrians began to gather round the elephant in the middle of the street, but as there is a total disregard of sanitation and cleanliness in this quarter of Lucknow and as there issued from the baker's shop nauseating odours of rank oil and meats in the process of being baked, we were glad to hurry along into purer air, and so after a good round of the city ended our singularly pleasant elephant ride.

At our hotel three very interesting children attracted my attention by their good looks and intelligence, the youngest girl of five was particularly lively, of sweet comely appearance and much attached to me. Who could be the fortunate mother of these lovely children was the oft-recurring question which, with true female curiosity I was determined to solve. I found out from the children themselves that their mother lived in a detached dwelling at the rear of the hotel and I resolved to see her, though our host from very bashfulness had never mentioned her to me. This evening I accordingly went to her house but she flew in as soon as she caught sight of me, however I had time to see that she wore a Parsee dress and was very handsome. I broke my discovery to our host who then cleared up the mystery and introduced her to me. She was by birth a Mahomedan and came from Cashmere, but in dress, look and manners she was every inch a Parsee. This fact coming under my own notice confirms my opinion that even before this century intermarriage between different castes was sometimes practised.

We sat down to dinner for the last time with our host and expressing our hearty thanksgiving to God, we pledged the health of Mr Hormusjee and his family, but a sigh escaped me when I reflected that my dear husband did not share in the felicity and enjoyment of my tour in India. Led on by his unswerving love and kindness I had undertaken this journey and it was a source of intense pleasure to me to hear him praised by many whom we met in different parts. Thanks to the kindness of Mr Hormusjee and to the fact that he was well known in and around the city, we saw in those three days everything of interest in Lucknow, indeed without his valuable assistance we might not have seen so much in as many months. The immense trouble he took on our behalf, the sacrifice of his valuable time, the excellent carriages and horses always ready for our use, have placed us under obligations to him which we can never forget. My sincere wish is that those whom God has blessed with competence would follow the example of this hospitable gentleman in such distant climes. We sat up till eleven o'clock conversing on a variety of topics.

On the 10th we were up betimes, breakfasted at six and bidding farewell to the Prince of Wales Hotel, drove off to the station. Taking our last leave of Mr Hormusjee and thanking him over and over again for all his goodness, we steamed out of Lucknow at nine in the morning, bound for the sacred city of the Hindoos, Benares.

XVIII

Benares—The Sacred City of India

What Jerusalem is to the Christian so is Benares to the Hindoo, its temples are famous and attract thousands of pilgrims every year. Arrived at the station, we enquired for the Travellers' Bungalow which we found to be hard by and where we took up our abode for the short time of our stay. We had brought a good supply of provisions with us, so after our servant had prepared dinner we rested a while and then went out for a drive—the hired horses were lean and miserable and their pace slower than that of a Bombay bullock. We were disappointed with the pagodas which we passed and proceeded further to the Bazaar, where we found several curious indigenous products exposed for sale and we spent an hour examining and purchasing some of these things.

We next drove to the so-called "Golden Pagoda" built of stone and surmounted by a shining dome, not as one would suppose, covered with plates of gold, but with some inferior metal, highly burnished. The Hindoo devotees from all parts of India flock hither to perform their holy rites. We, however, did not find this pagoda or any of the others worthy of praise, on the contrary we regretted having made a halt at Benares. The lane leading to the Golden Pagoda was so muddy that we could not avoid having our entire clothing soiled. We had to make our way through a crowd of mendicants in dirty stinking garments and what with this and the disgusting odours filling the air, it was literally unbearable and we fled away. We saw the full force of the proverb "Empty vessels sound much" as regards the vaunted grandeur of these Benares temples which we had heard of from many lips. We went from this to another Pagoda infested with monkeys. The precincts were no better but it at least interested us to see the frolics of these quaint animals.

The city of Golden Pagodas does not answer to the expectations which its pompous title conjures up, it is full of filth and squalor, excepting in that portion where European regiments are encamped. It is therefore more advisable not to take such a long expensive and futile journey only to be disappointed and disgusted. The brass and other wares of Benares are certainly good but they are all obtainable at Bombay.

We returned to the bungalow to tea and made up our minds to leave this city where the most striking features are heaps of rubbish and pools of mud. There is one good palace here, but of palaces we had seen enough. In the meantime I had been seen and recognised by a Mahomedan acquaintance who came to call on us and proffer the hospitalities of his house but I could not stay here any longer. We took a drive in the company of this friendly Mahomedan to the Cantonment and Gardens.

The evening breeze revived our wearied spirits and to some extent removed the bad impressions of the morning. Traversing a succession of dirty lanes and alleys we returned to the bungalow and sat down to dinner, the good-natured Mahomedan supplementing our frugal repast with sweet dishes brought, already cooked from his own house.

After this we left the Travellers' Bungalow and in order to reach the Railway Station we had to cross a floating bridge; the force of the river is said to be considerable and our carriage had to cross at a walking pace. Bidding adieu to this uninteresting town we took train for Mogul-Serai where we halted for the night and as the first train for Calcutta only started at ten o'clock next morning, we had time to see something of the town before we left, the servant meanwhile cooking fresh dishes for our journey. At 7 p.m. we made a halt at Mokama where we took our dinner at the station hotel and entering the train again travelled all night and reached Calcutta at day-break.

XIX

Calcutta—The City of Palaces

Our train steamed into the Howrah station at Calcutta at 8 a.m., and Set Manekjee Rustomjee with several members of his family was there to receive us. This mark of their regard was extremely gratifying to me. On the way to their residence we crossed a bridge over the Hooghly, the cooling breeze from the river was very refreshing and from this place we had a view of many of the notable buildings of Calcutta. Further on, we passed the handsome Gateway of Government House and soon reached the house of my friends in Chowringhee Road, where Bai Sakerbai gave me a cordial welcome. I saw her again after an interval of twelve years, but the hand of time had dealt gently with her, for I did not see the least change in her appearance. We were mutually pleased to meet again. We were led to our rooms, which were most inviting, looking out on the Esplanade. After bathing and dressing, I offered thanks and praise to God, who in His infinite bounty provided us with such comforts and even luxuries, so that wherever we stayed we found it just like home. Mysterious are the ways in which God fulfils the wishes of those who tread the path of virtue and we insure but our own welfare by never doing harm to others.

After breakfast Sakerbai took us to an open balcony on the first floor, from which a panoramic view of Calcutta was to be had. There was Government House standing on the Esplanade, in front of which the main thoroughfare of Chowringhee runs, and all the way along the stately edifices of the aristocracy were discernible. We sat here long conversing with Mr Manekjee on diverse subjects regarding Bombay. This was my first interview with my amiable and intelligent host, for, though a native of Bombay, he had been domiciled here for the last half century. His father is well known in Calcutta as Rustomjee Baboo and his family ranks high amongst the Parsees. Rustomjee had seven brothers each of whom vied with the other in keeping up the honour of the family—of one of these brothers Cursetjee Cowasjee, we have already described the pomp and the greatness, and of another, Framjee Cowasjee, his dignity and munificence made him known even to her Majesty the Queen. This Parsee family is the only one which figures conspicuously both in Calcutta and Bombay, but our host, though on the shady side of sixty had never revisited the latter place and many of his relatives and friends there, who had never seen him since his young days had been urging him to pay them a visit. Another of the happy results of my visit to the Delhi Assemblage was this opportunity of becoming acquainted with so worthy a man as my friend Bai Sakerbai's husband and I recall with gratitude and pleasure the hospitalities of their home and their cordial friendship.

I felt more thankful than ever for having been able to procure the healing medicine at Agra by means of which I had had strength to continue my journey to the most interesting and magnificent metropolis of India—a city which should be seen by all whose means may permit. God, the disposer of all events, granted me this great felicity and to Him I bow my head in humble gratitude and submission. After tea at 3 p.m. we dressed for an evening drive, the carriage and pair of our host accommodated his two daughters, named Perozbai and Dhunbaiji, my aunt and myself and we drove toward the Oval where the Eden Garden and the Band Stand are located. This promenade can be driven round three or four times in an hour and is pleasantly situated on the banks of the Hooghly. In the distance many a stately ship lay anchored. This being a fashionable evening resort many wealthy Baboos with uncovered heads and in plainest muslin dress were to be seen driving in their splendid carriages. The older people adhere to their primitive national dress consisting of a "dagog" around their waist and a thin muslin covering thrown over their shoulders, but the young generation calling themselves reformers wear coat and trousers and cap after the English style.

We returned at 7 p.m. and at eight sat down to dinner at which the mirth which prevailed was even more relished than the choice dainties set before us by our gentle hostess. Next morning, the 13th, I woke at seven and found everything was ready and our host waiting only for us, so after repeating the morning prayers I left my room and found my hostess preparing tea with her own hands. This was much to my taste, all the ingredients being duly proportioned, and I had not met with so good a drink anywhere throughout my journey. Unlike Indians in those days my friend made tea herself, like a European lady, and prided herself upon the excellence of her infusion; for my part, let it be sufficient praise to say that another cup would not have been unwelcome.

Every day at one o'clock tiffin was served, at which the variety and daintiness of the dishes astonished me. After this meal, I generally retired to my room to write letters to Bombay and rest awhile; at four o'clock we drank tea, after which we went out for a drive. The stately houses, the pleasant villas, gardens and the celebrated statues were, as we successively passed them, identified and a brief outline of their history given us by our companion. Similarly, when any European or native notability passed us on the promenade, he was pointed out to us. Thus I one day saw Sir Ashley Eden, the Lieutenant-Governor, of whom I had frequently heard.

Many wealthy Jews and Armenians passed us in their open carriages, with their ladies—the handsome symmetry of whose figures was much enhanced by their European costume. The carriage in which we were seated being a brougham we could not so well enjoy the scene as if it had been an open vehicle, but as our host's family as well as that of the few other Parsees domiciled in Calcutta never appear in an open carriage, we had no recourse but to conform to their ways. My worthy friend, Bai Sakerbai, had not much liking for a drive, but her elder daughter Perozbai who had a taste for it invariably accompanied me and we became fast friends in the course of two days. Returning home at 7 p.m. the interval between this and dinner was passed in conversing with my old aunty to whom all became much attached. At about eleven o'clock we retired to our rooms, but I sat up to write in my diary the events of the day or to pen an account of my doings to my dear husband.

On the 14th in company with Perozbai I paid a visit to Mr Joseph, the son of my friend Lady Sassoon, and her daughter Mrs Ezra. Their establishment I found equally magnificent as that of their father in Bombay and they had moreover adopted all the English manners and customs. They expressed their satisfaction at this unexpected meeting and Mr Joseph, who saw me again after a long interval, at once recognised me and introduced me to his wife. The same day we visited the Court House Museum and other buildings of importance, all of which we found most interesting and far superior to those of Bombay. Returning by the European quarter we were cheered by the strains of the band and the sight of Lord and Lady Lytton driving in state receiving the salutations of the subjects of Her Majesty the Queen-Empress.

The 15th instant was a rainy day and I was filled with apprehension lest my further view of the town should be hindered, meantime in comes Sakerbai and says in a jocular tone, "You are over-fond of a drive and have thus excited the jealousy of Jupiter Pluvius who has thought fit to put a stop to your rambles by his untimely and uncalled for presence." I accompanied her to the balcony where a gentle misty breeze greeted us and from whence the green verdant landscape was spread out before us. Set Manekjee by way of pastime began to talk merrily in praise of Calcutta where he had spent nearly the whole of his life while I on my side stood up for Bombay. He out of fun would cry down Bombay whereupon I responded, "You have not seen it for forty or fifty years, therefore you cannot conceive of its greatness. Mills of gigantic size rear their heads aloft in every direction giving bread to thousands of the inhabitants, while one of or public buildings—say the Secretariat—would throw into the shade of the architectural glories of your Brick and Mortar Calcutta with the exception of its grand Government House." Then, in pretended vexation, he would decline to hear a word more in praise of Bombay, and the whole of this rainy day was passed in discussing different topics of interest, gravely and anon gaily.

Next morning, while still in my own room, I was told that the sons of the house had gone to escort Set Byramjee of Bombay from the station. After offering up morning prayers, I joined the family and soon after Set Byramjee with a number of his friends arrived. Thus the number of guests increased every day under this hospitable roof, and our conversation at the dinner table was most animated and though this day too, which was rainy, was spent indoors, the time sped on quickly and pleasantly.

On the 17th in Sakerbai's company we paid a visit to the Fire-temple founded by Set Rustomjee Cowasjee Banajee and known after his name to this day. I was glad of the opportunity of offering prayers with a grateful heart in this sacred edifice. Passing through many small lanes and alleys narrower than even those of Bombay we reached the old residence of Rustomjee Cowasjee, now untenanted and partly in ruins, but bearing the marks of having once been a grand and substantial building; it occupies an open airy position and is large enough to have accommodated a family of a hundred persons. In the afternoon the daughter-in-law of Sir Albert Sassoon and Mrs Ezra called upon us. The latter showed me much kindness in many ways besides most considerately placing her carriages and horses at my disposal. In the evening we drove to several beautifully kept public gardens, also to the Zoological gardens where we had the supreme satisfaction of seeing the statues of eminent statesmen and generals of whom we had frequently read in books, who, by a judicious use of their authority, had spread peace and prosperity over the land in times gone by.

On the 18th Mrs Ezra came to take me to the mansion of her husband's parents, which is situated in the commercial parts of the town and where old Mr Ezra lived with his family. This locality reminded me of Bombay thirty years ago. At that time there was a street in the Fort known as Mapla Street inhabited solely by the Jews, whither I used to accompany my mother when she went to the house of Mr Moses, the brother-in-law of Sir Albert Sassoon. The mother-in-law of Mrs Ezra was of good social bearing and wore the ancient dress peculiar to her race, though her daughters and daughters-in-law were in English costume. They offered us a slight repast of dried Persian fruits, fresh ripe fruits of Calcutta, home-made sweetmeats, coffee and syrups which, of course, I thankfully accepted. We entered into lively conversation in the course of which I expressed my satisfaction at seeing so many salutary reforms adopted by the children of the chosen race. I could not help contrasting the prevalence of old customs in this millionaire's house with the thoroughly modern and European taste pervading at the residence of her son. It may to the credit of old Mr Ezra be mentioned that he not only allows but encourages his children to adopt whatever reasonable innovation they may affect, as becoming a most affectionate father. Young Mrs Ezra had had the benefit of a sound English education in her parent's house and being of an urbane disposition she shines wherever she appears and lives in the most complete harmony with the different members of her husband's family. In the afternoon of this day we accompanied Bai Sakerbai on visits to several of the rich and worthy citizens of Calcutta. One residence, known as "the Seven Tanks," is specially worthy of mention, within its spacious grounds there are seven reservoirs filled with flowing water and provided with boats; in the midst of the garden, the green foliage fringing the lakes, stands the bungalow, it is sumptuously furnished and I would fain have lingered long in this most delightful retreat where Nature and Art have combined to fascinate all comers.

On the 19th I went to the Government House to see my friend Mrs Burne, but she was not at home; in the course of the evening I was much grieved to hear from her that she was in deep mourning on account of the death of her beloved sister. This afternoon all Set Manekjee's guests were invited to the highly ornamental residence of one of his wealthy Baboo friends. We found the Baboo at home and great as his riches might be we found his urbanity greater; he was very simple in his attire for he only wore a thin richly worked muslin covering, he was the happy father of seven sons, who, like him, were civil and good natured and well versed in different arts. Unlike the greater number of Parsees of the present day, these seven young Bengalees were not spoilt by their wealth nor turned undutiful to their father. On the contrary, each delighted to do him honour and in the palatial residence which was in course of erection each gave the best he had to offer to their father—one son was a painter, another an architect, a third a sculptor, the fourth a botanist and the rest attended to the affairs of their father.

This noble citizen was none else but Rai Rajendranath Malek. His magnificent home had already been ten years in course of erection and it was said that a similar period would elapse before it could be completed, it is built of pure polished marble of the same description as that of the Taj Mahal, the threshold of each room is made to represent flowers, birds, etc., while the floor of the room illumines in varied coloured marble, a well laid out garden with lawns, avenues, lakes, trees, etc., while in the ceiling parrots and other birds coloured in gold, etc., are represented. The pillars used in this magnificent edifice are of marble, black, tawny and white like alabaster. There are several statues of deities and several oil paintings of His Imperial Majesty's family done by the artist son, and alabaster statues of some of our Indian Princes and Princesses. At the rear of the castle there is a curiously carved pagoda, bearing pious inscriptions in gold and silver and fragrant with flowers. There is a rare collection of birds such as parrots, cockatoos, peacocks and many others of graceful plumage and a number of animals the like of which we do not remember to have seen anywhere else. We spent much time in looking over this magnificent place (or should we not say palace?) and took leave of its master thanking him heartily for his courtesy and trouble.

On coming down to breakfast the next morning I heard the news that Set Dinshawjee Manekjee Petit of Bombay was coming with a host of friends to Calcutta and would also take up his abode in my friend's hospitable mansion. Several Parsee Sethias who had been present at the Delhi Assemblage extended their tour as I had done in order to see Calcutta, but the idea of sharing their enjoyment with their fair partners never for a moment entered their heads. Thus it will easily be understood that the bold step which I had taken created some ill-feeling amongst my people, but I did not forego one iota of pleasure on that account nor swerve a hair's breadth from the course I had chalked out for myself. As long as females are ignorant and uneducated their thoughts cannot soar above the narrow limit of their domestic concerns, but, God be praised, the time has come for my sisters to demand with unmistakeable voice their rights and privileges of which their selfish husbands have so long deprived them. Now that steam has obliterated the difficulty and trouble of travel, will they not shake off the foolish antiquated dread of locomotion and exchange for the dull, inactive, monotonous life which they now lead, one in which culture and foreign travel have incited the mind to study and observation; "better to travel and see much than to live long."

XX

Reception at Government House

On the 21st we enjoyed a walk in the city and on the 23rd my son and I drove to the Government House where I was to be presented to Lady Lytton. On entering the Government House grounds, a gatekeeper showed us where our carriage was to halt, and another opened and requested us to alight. Indoors we found everything in the best appointed style. We were conducted to Mrs Burne's apartments. She after a while led my son and me to a suite of room furnished with rich gilded sofas, the doors and windows hung with splendid rich velvet curtains such as we did not remember to have seen before. We had not waited long before Lady Lytton made her appearance.

She was stately in manners and dress, and I was pleased to see marks of improvement in her health since the first time I had seen her on her landing in Bombay. She greeted us very cordially, and making us sit beside her on a sofa, entered into conversation with us on our travel. She expressed her admiration of the Parsee ladies' dress and ornaments, especially of those which I was wearing on the occasion. I requested permission to show her the likenesses of my husband and daughter inlaid on the cover of my watch and set with brilliants; this was admired very much by the ladies.

Lady Lytton asked me about my impressions of Calcutta and how

Bai Meheribai Hormusjee Shroff, the Authoress' mother.

Mr Cowasjee Jehangir Jessawalla, the Authoress' husband.

The Authoress with her son Dadabhoy and daughter Goolbai.

The Authoress' sons, Dadabhoy Cowasjee Jessawalla (left) and Jamsetjee Cowasjee Jessawalla.

Authoress' daughter, Goolbai, son-in-law, and their children.

Tardeo Estate—Property and Bungalow built by the Authoress.

Sir Cowasjee Jehangir Readymoney, Parsee philanthropist and uncle of the Authoress. *Source Wikimedia Commons*
(below) Illustration of the Authoress' uncle, Manekjee Cursetjee Shroff, known as 'Manekjee Judge', by English painter William Brokendon. (1841) *Source Wikimedia Commons*

Bai Kesarbai, wife of Kalyandas Manmohundass and friend of the Authoress.

Sir Hormusjee Naorojee Mody, well-known Parsee businessman the Authoress met at Hong Kong.
Source Wikimedia Commons

The Delhi Durbar (1877)

King Edward VII and Queen Alexandra.
Source Wikimedia Commons

Casket, Cap and Dress Front, designed by the Authoress and presented to King Edward VII and Queen Alexandra at Windsor. (1908)

Arrival of H.R.H. the Prince of Wales in Bombay. (1875)

Dadabhoy Naoroji, the Grand Old Man of India. *Source Wikimedia Commons*

Parsee philanthropist Sir Jamsetjee Jeejeebhoy, 1st Baronet Jeejeebhoy of Bombay, on a 1959 stamp of India. *Source Wikimedia Commons*

The Authoress driving with her husband. (1876)
(below) Mrs R Ahlers and her children with the Authoress and her son Dadabhoy (on their first visit to Europe in 1878) at Bonn, Germany.

Statue of the Authoress' grandfather, Cursetjee Manekjee Shroff Esq. (Khada Parsi) in Bombay.

Statue of 'Victoria the Good' in Bombay

Robert Bulwer-Lytton,
Viceroy of India. (1876-1880)
Source Wikimedia Commons

Edith Bulwer-Lytton, Vicerine
of India. (1876-1880)
Source Wikimedia Commons

Government House, Calcutta. (1850)
Source Wikimedia Commons

Pope Leo XIII of Rome

long I intended to stay, and on hearing that I proposed leaving the very next day, she kindly suggested it would be well if we could remain a few days longer, as on the following 26th she was to hold a reception, where I could see the guests in their novel toilettes—long trained court dresses. She then suggested that I should make good use of the intervening time by paying a visit to Barrackpore, which was certainly worth a visit. I was very much gratified by the kindness and gratefully said that it would certainly give me much pleasure to attend Her Ladyship's reception, and I would certainly therefore defer my departure, employing the interval in visiting Barrackpore. After this we took our leave, and while going into the hall in company with Mrs Burne, she asked me if I would send my photograph to Lady Lytton, whereupon I at once handed her one my son had with him, which Mrs Burne took and hastened to deliver to Lady Lytton, who was passing out of the hall. She accepted the same and said with a graceful inclination of the head: "This will always remind me of your visit."

Mrs Burne then showed us over the Government House, and at last to the Reception Hall to initiate us into the ceremonies which I was so shortly to take part in. From this place she escorted us up the last flight of stairs, and on the landing we met Lady Strachey, to whom we were introduced and at parting we conveyed our deep sense of all these favours to Mrs Burne. She and her noble husband are well known for their courtesy and kindness and what we had previously heard of them proved to be no exaggeration. Our fervent wish flowed towards the mover of all things that He may give them long life, and may the choice of filling such responsible and conspicuous positions always fall upon such worthy heads. Such prominent officials can do much to promote the peace and interest of the people and strengthen the bonds of the British Empire in India.

After breakfast on the 24th, I visited certain shops, and returning at one to tiffin, I found two invitation cards for the Reception, also a kind note from Mrs Burne expressing regret that, in consequence of her mourning she would be prevented from attending the Reception, but referring me to Mrs Ezra, who would acquaint me with the forms and etiquette to be observed; but as I was no novice in such matters, it seemed unnecessary to trouble my friend. Thinking, however, that there might be some difference between the functions here and at Bombay, I saw Mrs Ezra on the subject, consulted her about the dress I should wear; she took me to her dressing room where a number of rich, costly dresses were hanging up, each one of which must have absorbed the cost of a rich gold ornament; but I fear I am under-rating them for they were adorned with lace of such great value as would appear fabulous to a Parsee lady. Though by birth a Jewess, her elegance and taste in dress and in the house were superior to the majority of Europeans, and I felt supremely happy in having such a distinguished lady for my friend. After paying her a long visit, I set out with friends to see that part of the city which was inhabited solely by Europeans.

After breakfast on the morning of the 26th, I set to work to prepare a dress for the evening's Reception, and this was the first time in my travels that I had had recourse to the friendly needle, but I made up for the neglect by plying it busily the whole day, so that at the supper, my friends twitted me for having been so invisible. At half past nine, my son and I entered Government House and ascending the grand stairs came upon an imposing spectacle: there was an immense crowd. In the absence of dear Mrs Burne as well as of my Bombay friends, I was at a loss what to do in this strange place: but I did not long remain in suspense, I caught sight of Sir Albert Sassoon's family and in their amidst [sic] my fears soon vanished. I, however, found much difference between the two Government Houses: at Calcutta many more ceremonies and formalities are exacted.

First of all, all the guests assembled together in a large hall, after which the gentlemen retired to another room. In the Reception Room, on a dais surmounted by a canopy, stood Lord and Lady Lytton, and as each lady filed past, her name was called out by the Aide-de-camp in waiting, and she made her bow by a graceful inclination of the head to their Excellencies, who responded in a similar manner. Later on, the ladies were joined by their husbands or sons, as the case might be after going through the same procedure, and the rest of the evening was spent in the spacious and brilliantly lighted saloons, where the noble hosts moved among their guests exchanging greetings and a few passing words. Seeing only one Parsee lady among such a large gathering, their smiling faces were generally directed towards us.

All the ladies present wore most beautiful dresses, but Mrs Ezra's was the most costly and Lady Lytton's the most charming—such was the general opinion which I formed for me. There was one noteworthy feature of the dresses on this occasion novel to me and it was of the long trains of the dresses, so that when a lady walked her dress occupied a considerable room behind her. Here I saw Lady Temple, wife of the late Governor of Bombay, she looked extremely handsome and young. I made many new acquaintances and my dress was admired by all. Lady Strachey complimented me by observing: "Everyone assembled here is pleased by your presence as you are the first Parsee lady who has come to the Reception Hall at Calcutta." Several other ladies asked my name and address for the purpose of paying me a visit, but I had to decline the kindness and honour by informing them that after a brief visit to Barrackpore, I would take my departure from Calcutta. Thus I lost the opportunity of making many new friends, but the pleasure of that evening and the kind interest everyone present seemed to feel for me awoke in me a feeling of gratitude which will only cease with my life. We returned home late at night.

On the 27th after an early breakfast we set out with my good friend Bai Sakerbai, her daughters, daughters-in-law and grandchildren for Barrackpore, which we reached by train at about ten o'clock. Having enjoyed the glimpse of this endearing place to our heart's content, we returned to Calcutta at 6 p.m. There remained very little time at our disposal, to pack up our luggage, preparatory to our departure. I had telegraphed to Mr Bomonjee, the young son of our well-known citizen Set Muncherjee Bomanji Panthakey, at Jubbulpore, apprising him of our intention to break journey at that place. We left our noble host's place at nine o'clock with every one of his family except himself to see us off at the station.

XXI

The Marble Rocks of Jubbulpore

After a continuous journey of two nights and one day we reached Jubbulpore where we found the manager of Set Muncherjee Panthakey's firm awaiting us at the station, and with this gentleman's kind assistance we made our way to Mr Muncherjee's bungalow, where we received a hearty welcome from Mr Bomonjee and a substantial breakfast was waiting for us. We thanked God heartily for all the good things He gave us.

At eleven o'clock we started to view the noteworthy sights of the city and first we went to see the gaol where good, strong rugs, towels, baskets, carpets, etc., were being made by the inmates. The prisoners on the whole looked far from discontented, busily working at their respective employments. This gaol is very extensive, being as large as a small village.

From there we went to the Bazaars and saw the camp; in the evening we went to the public gardens where the far-famed roses attracted our admiration. In variety, size and fragrance they were far superior to any I had ever seen.

On our return home we arranged to start next morning to see the marble rocks and accordingly retired to rest in good time. By break of day on the 30th we set out in the cool morning air and by a circuitous route reached a hill at seven o'clock. We halted here for our man to prepare tea and then sat down to a comfortable breakfast which we had brought with us. It was most delightful to sit here and enjoy the beauties of nature. At nine o'clock we set out walking up the hill and soon came to the ruins of a pagoda celebrated for having contained no fewer than sixty-four idols; this can be verified from the broken fragments scattered about. We then proceeded to view the famous waterfall and were stunned by the deafening noise caused by the tremendous rush of water. We were bewildered to find such a huge quantity of water continually flowing in such tremendous masses day and night. The waters are gathered together somewhere in these hills and assume the aspect of a swift, wide river here. We hired a boat and went for a sail on the river the better to view the scenery. The rocks rising on either side are all of marble, for the most part white, but interspersed with blocks of black and brown; the river meanders through and around them in the most fantastic manner; further up it widens into a broad basin, like a large lake surrounded by hills about a thousand feet in height. The scenery all along is most striking; sometimes the marble rocks assume the appearance of palaces rising sheer out of the water. My old aunty, lost in utter amazement, would point to these and exclaim: "Are these the abodes of human or ethereal beings?" These wonderful mountains and the great waterfall are but a manifestation of the power and sublimity of the Almighty. I feel it my duty to recommend my countrymen to visit this picturesque and remarkable locality. We rowed back to the landing stage at four o'clock and reached our quarters two hours later.

Next morning, on 31st January, we left Jubbulpore at nine o'clock and, after twenty-four hours' travelling, we steamed into the Byculla station, where I soon descried my dear husband, daughter and youngest son waiting for us. I offered up my thanks to the Almighty at seeing them all in good health, as well as for the happy termination of my Indian tour.

In conclusion, let me say a word about the Delhi Assemblage which is so indelibly fixed on my memory. Such a sight must have been extremely noble to all present, for, though the pomp and pageantry of Royal State is not unknown in England, the sombre garments of black which prevail there must make such scenes dull and uninteresting; whereas the different nationalities represented at Delhi on this occasion, the thousand varieties of dress they wore and the magnificent jewels of the native princes rendered the Imperial Durbar one of the most brilliant and unique spectacles that the nineteenth century has ever witnessed.

XXII

Lord Lytton at Ganesh Khind

The Durbar at Delhi proved a source of countless blessings to the poor, by opening up new industries, while the circulation of wealth effected by the progress of so many Rajahs through the land, as well as by the magnificent preparations made by the Government, served to lessen to some extent the horrors of famine locally. Moreover, the Princes too confined till now to their respective territories must have gained an insight into the order and enlightenment of the English rule, and thereby laid up a fund of experience and knowledge from their travels to and from Delhi.

After my return home, I soon resumed my domestic duties and particularly the management of a small garden in which the greater portion of my day was spent. Notwithstanding this, I never neglected to take my evening walk or drive, even once, for from my early days I have known the advantages resulting from such exercises. At this time a Hindoo teacher, who used to come to our house to instruct my sons, gathered from them some details of my journey, and having heard the leading incidents of my mother's life, strung these together and published them in the form of a pamphlet. This fact reaching my ears I at once took measures to suppress its publication. Though there was nothing in the pamphlet I could take exception to, its appearance marred the prospects of the autobiography which I already had in contemplation. The Hindoo tutor, therefore, listened to my representations and made over to me all the copies of the pamphlet in his possession, while I on my side indemnified him for all probable pecuniary loss. I asked him why the pamphlet in question did not bear his name, to which he answered that to eke out a living, he wrote on diverse subjects and published them, sometimes under his own name, sometimes that of his brother and at other times, as in this case, published them anonymously. I informed my brother Heerjeebhoy of this incident, he approved of my action and took one of the pamphlets for his own perusal.

On 11th July of that year, corresponding to the 26th day of the 10th month of the Parsees, the venerable head of the entire Parsee community Sir Jamsetjee Jeejeebhoy, the second Baronet, breathed his last at Poona. The grief which this event occasioned was universal and genuine, particularly amongst the Parsees; this grief was a homage paid not to the riches and position of the deceased but entirely to his sterling qualities and endearing disposition. Only four days previous to this sad event, Lady Jamsetjee had come down to Bombay, but on hearing of her husband's alarming illness, she had at once returned to Poona but arrived there too late. Lady Jamsetjee was of a sweet, amiable, childlike disposition and wealth seems not to have changed her in the least. God might have spared her this heavy calamity, but the hand of death mows down all, sparing neither young nor old, rich nor poor. On the 14th instant, I went to Poona and the same evening I repaired to Lady Jamsetjee's bungalow to offer her my condolences, my tears began to flow on seeing her in such a sad plight, and we wept together. Although too full of grief herself to discharge all the duties of a hostess, she offered hospitality to every one of the numerous visitors, requesting me too to remain at her house; this however I declined as I had rented a bungalow of my own. I repeated my visits for the ten ensuing days, as is the custom amongst the Parsees.

I returned to Bombay on the 24th and was engaged in making preparations for the approaching marriage of one of my relatives. After this I went to Poona for the season there, and heard that an Exhibition was to be held the day following my arrival. This, 24th August, was my birthday, and I resolved to see the Exhibition and wrote to my friend,

Mr Dorabjee D. Bootee to buy tickets of admission for me. In complying with the request he asked whether his sister might accompany me to which of course, I joyfully assented. Going to the Exhibition next day at four o'clock, I found a guard of honour drawn up near the door and troops ranged on both the sides, and I then learnt that Lord Lytton being then in Poona was to grace the Exhibition with his presence. Several influential Parsee gentlemen who had come there asked me if I had dropped in at that time for the express purpose of seeing the Viceroy, I affirmed that I had not the remotest idea of the Viceroy's being there till I entered the building. After some time Lord Lytton arrived and everyone stood up to do him honour; I was then seated on a couch in a remote corner, and on the Viceroy's walking round to look at the pictures, he recognised me, and after shaking hands with me asked if I was a resident of Poona. I replied that I had come up from Bombay the day before where I usually resided, and expressed my pleasure at this unexpected meeting. His Excellency also shook hands with my companion, and asked me if she was my daughter to which I answered in the negative, but introduced her as my friend. Our kind friend Col. O. T. Burne was also here, and hoped to see me next day at the Government House party. When I enquired after the health of Lady Lytton and Mrs Burne, I was informed that they were well and always remembered me. It was thought by the bystanders that His Excellency Lord Lytton had out of mere courtesy shaken hands and spoken with me, and His Excellency Sir Richard Temple, the then newly appointed Governor of Bombay, entertained the same notion, but it came to be subsequently known that ere this, I had been a guest at Government House, Calcutta.

Shortly after I met Mr Venayek Wassoodew, the Oriental Translator here and told him that as I had come only there the day before I had had no time to enter my name at Government House as etiquette required, and that therefore I feared there would be some difficulty in getting me an invitation card. He however kindly undertook to make all straight and to send me a card without fail next day.

Accordingly, early on the morning of the 25th an invitation for the party to be held at Government House that day was sent me. As neither my husband nor my son were in Poona, I asked Lady Sassoon's permission to accompany me which she readily accorded, so we drove together to Ganesh Khind in the afternoon. Although I had taken part in such entertainments in Bombay, this was my first visit to the Government House at Poona and its gay appearance struck me forcibly. His Excellency Lord Lytton mixed freely with his guests, shaking hands with the ladies. He entered into conversation with me and mistook the ten-year old daughter of my brother for my child.

The company dispersed themselves about the beautiful gardens and the scene was a pretty picture of social enjoyment. I returned home at seven in the evening, and from this day forth my name was enrolled amongst the guests at Ganesh Khind, the Government House of Poona. Soon after this party, His Excellency Lord Lytton left for Madras to set on foot means for alleviating the sufferings of the famine-stricken population there, and this humane action endeared him to all. I remained longer than usual in Poona on this occasion enjoying the pleasures of the season. I had not omitted to bring my own carriage and horses, and in addition I bought a handsome pair of ponies and a Park phaeton, which I used to drive myself, and thus enjoyed a drive both morning and evening.

On 21st September, Lord Lytton returned from Madras and received an enthusiastic welcome. His Lordship and Sir O. Burne caught sight of me and returned my salaams by raising their hats, this did not fail to draw the attention of their officers, who looked towards me with smiling faces. There was to be a ball at Government House that evening, for which I had duly received an invitation, but having no one else to accompany me, I had written to ask if I might bring my youngest son of twelve years along with me. The answer to this was in the affirmative, so we left at nine o'clock for Ganesh Khind.

It was beautifully illuminated, every nook and alley in the garden was lighted up. Captain Anderson escorted us to the Ball-room which was tolerably crowded, and where dancing had commenced. I was late and felt a little embarrassed, but Mrs Rivett-Carnac, wife of the Military Secretary to His Excellency Sir R. Temple, came up and drew me to a sofa beside her, and I soon felt at my ease. I met many of my English friends and conversed with Their Excellencies Lord Lytton and Sir R. Temple and with Sir O.T. Burne, Ladies Staveley and Sassoon, Mrs Gibbs and others who were all glad to see me here. With some ladies of my acquaintance I began to move about and partake of refreshments, and while returning to the saloon in company with Colonel Wood, I met Set Byramjee Jeejeebhoy, Khan Bahadoor Pudumjee Pestonjee and Dossabhoy Framjee.

It was two hours past midnight, when satisfied with this exquisite and refined entertainment, I rose to depart, on seeing which our good Governor asked Captain Anderson to escort me to my carriage. I thanked him for his civility. It was three o'clock when I retired to rest. At this ball I was several times asked by gentlemen to dance, but I had to excuse myself, never having learnt this graceful accomplishment. In my young days, dancing was considered by the Parsees a vile and degrading thing, but moving in English society as I did, I had begun to see this in a different light, and therefore I had my daughter instructed in the art as soon as I became independent.

XXIII

In Calcutta Once Again

At this time I heard from my brother that a sum of Rs 20,000, due to my husband, had been paid up in full, after the suit to recover it was filed. I was pleased at the recovery of such a substantial sum, but above all felt thankful to be spared the trouble and tedium of a law-suit.

After the Poona season, I returned to Bombay. During my absence everything at home had been neglected, and so I had to labour afresh to restore order and harmony. My dear husband was too much taken up with his business concerns to notice what was going on in the house.

I read in the papers that in the beginning of 1878 an Exhibition would be held at Paris. From my very infancy my imagination, stimulated by Col. Jarvis's vivid descriptions, had pictured in fascinating colours the pomp and charm of England; and I had always entertained the hope of one day being able to visit it. My childish dream had been that soon after marriage my husband and I should go to England, but reality proved this to be impracticable. But now, comparatively late in life, it seemed as if my hopes were to be fulfilled.

Although my husband's business affairs would not admit of his absence from Bombay, he joyfully assented to my going. In the year 1866, when my daughter was in England and in the family way, I had resolved to go to her, but had been compelled to abandon the idea as my husband could not accompany me and my eldest son was not of an age to do so. This son was now grown up, and the opening of the Paris Exhibition furnished a good occasion for the long-wished-for voyage. My daughter was then in Bombay, and I felt no hesitation in leaving my husband and younger son; with his father's consent my elder son was to accompany me. I next informed my brother, Heerjeebhoy, the manager of my pecuniary affairs, of my intention. Thereupon he from the kindest of motives offered to apprise his friends in England of my coming, and request them and in particular, Mr Leith (formerly of Messrs Forbes and Co.) to give me a welcome and render me what assistance they could. Mr Leith had frequently seen me moving in English society in Bombay and remarked to my brother that I was the only Parsee lady who did so. My brother also asked for my photograph for the purpose of enclosing it in his letter.

It was agreed between us that my brother should remit by draft the money necessary for my expenses when abroad. When everything was thus arranged, I told my husband to put up with Heerjeebhoy while I was away, and informed him of the letting of the bungalow and the sale of our furniture and to all these proposals he joyfully consented.

During the following month I was engaged in making preparations for my journey, warm clothing were made [sic] and all requisites gathered together.

Before undertaking this long and perilous journey, I resolved to visit the time-honoured temple of Oodwada, which I had never seen. Accordingly I left Bombay by the B.B. and C.I. Railway one evening and reached my destination at day-break. This is the most ancient and sacred Fire-temple,* and is held in great reverence by the Parsees. Here I observed all the religious formalities and repeated my prayers, which, when done with pure conscience, can alone secure happiness in this vale of tears.

From this place I went to Naosari, where a Tower of Silence built at the expense of Set Nusserwanjee Ruttonjee Tata, was about to be opened. Hundreds of Parsees were assembled here to witness the ceremonies of dedication of this final resting place where the rich and the poor lie side by side. I was desirous of seeing the interior of

*Mrs Jessawalla means 'in India'. –*JP*

this tower, and when I saw all the arrangements made therein for the disposal of the dead body, I became convinced that the method of disposing of the dead amongst the Parsees was the best of all. My next care was to settle some pecuniary transactions between myself and my eldest brother Dorabjee who lived at Calcutta, and I made up my mind to revisit that place.

On the 8th of March I left Bombay with my youngest son and safely reached Calcutta on the morning of the 11th. I took up my residence with my brother at the Garden Reach, the most fashionable part of the town. I saw my worthy friend, Bai Sakerbai, who was much surprised to see me, but regretted that I had not taken up my abode with her family. I also had the pleasure seeing my friend Lady Sassoon at her daughter Mrs Ezra's place, and both the mother and daughter were much interested on hearing of my intended voyage to England which Mrs Ezra said was certainly worth seeing.

My friends enquired if I had waited upon Lady Lytton. But as Her Ladyship stayed at Barrackpore, I could not do so during my limited stay at Calcutta. In the evening I returned to my brother's house. I cannot but mention here that young Mrs Ezra had placed her splendid carriage at my disposal, and I made use of it on every important occasion during my stay at Calcutta. Hearing on the 12th from Bai Sakerbai that Lady Lytton had returned to Calcutta that very day I wrote to ask if Her Ladyship would make it convenient to see me.

On the 13th I opened the subject of my visit to my brother and he at once consented to pay me all my dues. In the evening I drove in a handsome open carriage, sent by Mrs Ezra, to the fashionable resort of the city, where I had driven in a closed carriage the year before. I, being the first Parsee lady to drive in open carriage, formed the object of general attraction. Their Excellencies Lord and Lady Lytton drove past me, and at once recognising cordially bowed to me which showed that my interview with Their Excellencies still lived in their memory. On my return to my brother's house I found that a note had been left for me by a trooper to the effect that Her Excellency Lady Lytton would be glad to see me next day.

On the 14th in the afternoon I went with my son to the Government House and met with a cordial reception at Her Ladyship's hands. She expressed her approval of my intended visit to England. Her

Ladyship noticed the cap worn by my son, which was set round with family portraits and was surprised to hear that the handsome and curious hand-work was my own. Her Ladyship told me that she had preserved my photo received a year ago, and I on my side expressed my acknowledgements for the favour done me. I respectfully enquired if she would condescend to accept from me a cap similarly embroidered to that of my son. "If it is costly," she said, "I regret I cannot." But when I told her that my labour was all its value, in addition to some small pearls used merely to enhance the effect of the needlework, Her Ladyship did me the favour of accepting the same and ordered an officer, who was in waiting, to go and fetch the box containing the cap from the carriage. On seeing the cap which was found to be as represented by me, far from costly, Her Ladyship admired it and thanked me for my humble gift. In the crown a portrait of Lord Lytton, her illustrious husband, was set which pleased Her Ladyship the most.

With Lady Lytton's praise of my needlework and her hearty good wishes for a safe voyage to the shores of her dear land and our sincere thanks for her kindness, I took my leave and returned with my son to my friend. After dinner, in the afternoon I went to my brother's place, got all my packing done, and with my luggage went back again to my friend's. While we were sitting together, a mounted sowar came to deliver a box and a note to me from Government House. The former contained a photograph of Lady Lytton in an ornamental ormolu frame bearing her monogram and crest; it was much admired by all my friends, and I penned my grateful acknowledgements for this fresh mark of her ladyship's kindness to me.

The friendship between my kind host and myself instead of diminishing had only been cemented closer by the lapse of time. At nine o'clock, I bade adieu to their hospitable mansion, and accompanied by all Bai Sakerbai's children, my son and I went to the Howrah station, where my brother awaited us and rendered us every assistance. My friend herself could not accompany me on account of the mourning she was in.

My visit to Calcutta had been more advantageous than I had anticipated. I had met Lady Sassoon and her daughter, enjoyed an unexpected interview with Lady Lytton, and my brother had paid me back the money loan, with the exception of the second amount borrowed at his daughter's marriage, which I did not press for.

Two months elapsed and the worry and trouble began to tell heavily upon my constitution. The physicians advised complete rest and a change, as otherwise my mental faculties would have had to suffer; this strengthened me in my resolution to go to England.

I secured a passage for myself and my elder son in a steamer leaving Bombay on the 31st of May. The day previous to my departure, I informed my daughter and her husband of my intention, the latter told me that he had heard Heerjeebhoy one day declare that, if I left without bringing matters between us to a settlement, he had more than one way of preventing me from getting a steamer to take me. This threw me into a sad fright, for he was bent upon ruining me and would not hesitate at anything. I wrote a letter to him and kept it ready to be despatched, in case he should go to extremes, as he threatened to do. I endeavoured in a variety of ways to place obstacles in the way of his appropriating the money of which he was a trustee and with such fair intentions I went to see his master, Mr C. Douglas, but he was not at home. Mrs Douglas, however, kindly received me, and I informed her that my brother in her husband's employ threw all possible hindrances in the way of my going to England, and I was anxious to speak to Mr Douglas on the subject. She promised to give me all possible assistance, and I was completely satisfied with this kind assurance. I, however, communicated my ideas and wishes by letter to Mr Douglas, so as not to intrude upon his valuable time and begged him to speak to my brother about his unjust and ungrateful conduct towards me. Mrs Douglas, accompanied by another lady, came to see me and gave me letters of introduction to Mr and Mrs Geo. Campbell. Mr Campbell was the senior partner of the firm and lived in England, so I should be able to lay before him all the wrongs I had been subjected to, and as he had been long resident in Bombay he knew the natives well and I hoped through his help to bring the tricks and machinations of my brothers to an end.

The same evening I had the unexpected pleasure of an interview with Col. Baker, who was pleased to hear of my going to England and promised to send me an introductory letter to his mother. Many other friends would have introduced me to their relatives at home, but being sore at heart I could not pay any visits, and it was only those friends who casually met me, favoured me with such letters. I had more than one reason for not giving publicity to my departure, and my friends would certainly excuse my slipping away without bidding them "Goodbye" when they learned the reason.

Seeing in the newspaper of 31st May my name in the list of passengers, Heerjeebhoy was much chagrined and exclaimed that he would try to prevent me getting to the steamer. My mother acquainted me by letter of this threat, and requested me to see her. I went to her at 8 a.m., and when I entered, Heerjeebhoy went out furiously shouting: "Well, let us see how you will embark." Passing over this remark in silence, I stayed some little time with my mother, leaving with her what my means allowed. Thence I proceeded to visit my beloved daughter Goolbai; she had been somewhat indisposed, and I was much pleased to find her restored to health. The same evening I started from the Mazagon Bunder, and on reaching our steamer at Apollo Bunder, I saw Mr Douglas on board. He kindly listened to what I had to say. There were several other Parsees on board, one of whom being on friendly terms with my brother would certainly have informed him of my conversation with Mr Douglas. He would also learn that I intended to visit Mr Campbell, and, who knows, he perhaps would forestall me by writing to him and prejudicing him against me. While going to the steamer, I heard that he had left no stone unturned to try and stop my going; the whole day he had wandered from one attorney to another but all to no purpose. It would take six months to bring the office affairs to a conclusion, by which time I should have returned from England; and once his suretyship was dispensed with, he would perforce have to return my money. I had wished to travel for a year, but all these annoyances compelled me to curtail my term of absence. The lifelong, dearly-cherished hope of seeing England was to be realised, but under such difficulties that the dear memory of that brightest period of my existence is clouded over by a mist.

XXIV

In the S.S. *Nizam*

Having hired a steam launch to convey us to the steamer, my elder son Dadabhoy and I embarked on the afternoon of 31st May 1878 on board the P&O S.S. *Nizam*. My dear husband and youngest son kept us company as far as the Apollo Bunder where we bade each other a temporary farewell. Here many of my friends had assembled to wish us *bon voyage* and were disappointed to learn that we had started from Mazagon. Our steamer weighed anchor at five o'clock; the sea at this time was serene and a delightful breeze fanned the sails. After partaking of tea with our fellow passengers we retired to rest. Next morning I rose betimes and offered a prayer to the Almighty and then went on the deck and joined the passengers lounging there. I found that they were conjecturing amongst themselves who I was and what was my destination. Before evening of that day I made the acquaintance of two or three persons whose kindness and attention lasted throughout the whole of the voyage; amongst them let me gratefully name Mr James, Postmaster-General of Bombay, and Major and Mrs Mathew. All learnt with extreme surprise that so far back as 1842 I had had the benefit of English education.

In the companionship of such enlightened persons, ere three brief days were over, I had steeped in forgetfulness the trials and difficulties to which I had been subjected in Bombay. The time on the steamer passed most pleasantly and the sea, by God's grace, had no evil effects on us. My son-in-law as well as other friends had in jest painted gloomy pictures of the troubles I would have had to encounter, as war was declared between Russia and Turkey; they laughingly said Dadabhoy and I would certainly have to fight on one side or the other, provided we escaped alive from the tempests which prevailed at this season on our way to England; but of all this we experienced nothing.

We reached Aden on 7th June at 7 a.m. at which hour the passengers were all in a hurry to get ashore. Some men in the employ of Set Cowasjee Dinshawjee Adenwalla came on board and kindly requested me and my son to take our seats in the boats sent for us by their master who would be glad to see us. We accordingly seated ourselves in the boat and were pulled quickly to shore and escorted to the residence and store of Mr Cowasjee. The two brothers, Messrs Cowasjee and Dorabjee, keeping business for the time aside, came out and cordially shaking hands with us welcomed us to their house. "We did not know of your coming," they said, "or we should have come ourselves on board to welcome you." Thus it transpired that the men recognising our nationality had invited us in their master's name knowing full well that that would please him. We refreshed ourselves by a hot bath and thanked God for all His bounties. Breakfast was spread and after a lapse of seven days we again partook of and enjoyed dishes cooked in the Parsee fashion. After this we took our seats in a carriage and pair which was waiting for us, and accompanied by the son of our host and his manager, we had a long drive and saw a great deal of the city of Aden and its neighbourhood.

At 1 p.m. we returned to the airy and commodious quarters of our host and sat down to pen letters to our Bombay friends and relatives, telling them of our safe arrival so far, and of the handsome welcome accorded to us by our neighbours (for the Adenwallas occupy the bungalow adjoining ours in Bombay). We had been for long on friendly terms with them; I do not know how to give due praise to their hospitality, but the grateful memory of it is always cherished by me.

At dinner, we heard that Admiral Corbett with his troopship was then at Aden; on the previous day he had paid a visit to Mr Cowasjee and had spoken of my friendship with him. He would have been much pleased to see us here, but there was no time for a call on him. After cordially thanking Messrs Cowasjee and Dorabjee we left their place at three o'clock for the steamer, whither they accompanied us. At four o'clock we sailed again. Among the passengers was a Hindoo gentleman named Shivnath, a brother of some Rajah in Oude; he was bound for England, where, under the guardianship of Mr Fitzgerald he was to receive sound English education. This young gentleman was good natured and amiable and consequently a mutual attachment sprang up between him and my son, so that he was much in our company. There were some amateur musicians, singers and instrumentalists amongst our company who kindly enlivened the tedium with their performances.

Our Captain was very genial and the Red Sea was crossed amidst much merriment and pleasure. One night a short entertaining drama was performed; every day brought with it some new amusement. We felt as if we were living together as members of a family in a small place; so much we felt at home. On 12th June at about noon we anchored off Suez and some of our most gifted musicians left us, to continue their journey *via* Brindisi. At 3 p.m. we entered the Canal which, being very shallow, necessitated a very slow progress. At sunset we came to a standstill, remaining stationary the whole night and again in the morning resuming our slow progress through scenery devoid of interest or variety.

On the 13th we reached Port Said and went on shore to see the place. It is an unpretending little town, consisting mainly of one-storied houses. A newcomer cannot fail to be struck by a novel feature of locomotion. The people here ride on mules of such a pigmy size that the rider's legs touch the ground. We could not help laughing heartily at this ludicrous sight. The inhabitants are for the most part Egyptians. Small dining-rooms are to be met with every now and then with girls singing in them; from one of these places I ordered a cup of coffee but it was so bitter as to be most unpalatable.

The novelty of my costume created much curiosity and quite a mob gathered round us, saying that they had never come across such a dress before. We hastened back to the steamer at 8.30. Next morning we were rejoiced to find the steamer going full speed, it had started at midnight while we were asleep. On the 17th at three in the afternoon we reached Malta and our steamer steering through the rows and alleys, formed by a number of ships and sailing craft of all sorts, came to a halt, just as a carriage does on land. This being the time of the Russo-Turkish war Indian forces were mustered in Malta in large numbers and the harbour was crowded. My son and I with our fellow passenger Mr Shivnath, hired a boat and went on shore. After ascending a flight of stone steps we came upon a gateway such as is generally to be seen in large fortresses; this led us to another flight of steps, on ascending which we emerged upon the public road. Here we hired a light, open conveyance; the fares of these public vehicles are regulated according to the length of the time the conveyance is occupied. His Royal Highness the Duke of Cambridge, Commander-in-Chief of the British army, and cousin of the late Queen-Empress, was this day to hold a grand Review of the Indian troops. It is difficult to attempt a description of this imposing display of the British forces which fortunately for us was to take place on the day we landed at Malta. The ground selected for the manoeuvres was surrounded by high stately edifices on all sides, every window and balcony of these houses was crowded to an excess; all available open space around was occupied fully by spectators on foot or in carriages. To obtain a better view we left our conveyance and shortly after His Royal Highness in full uniform, mounted on a splendid black charger, rode up. Standing here I soon attracted attention; from my dress some guessed that I came from India, and others from China. I was seen and recognised by Mrs Hunter, wife of Dr Hunter of Bombay, who came up to me and introduced me to the lady who was with her; she was Mrs Beattie, wife of Surgeon-General Beattie of Bombay.

As soon as the Review was over we drove through the town to have a view of the different parts of it and the next day the steamer weighed anchor. As we left, the town of Malta looked very picturesque in the afternoon sun and gradually receded from our view as we left the shores far behind. Reading, the writing of my travels, and the agreeable company on board the steamer, made the time pass most pleasantly.

Early on the morning of the 22nd of June we reached Gibraltar; it looked like a marble mountain split up into two. We three again went on shore and here, as at Malta, after ascending a flight of stairs we passed through the gateway into a vaulted passage and after passing through it we came to the public road. We hired a conveyance and set out to view the town. The roads go winding up the hills and the same scene constantly recurs to sight. In the highest quarter of the town there is a recreation park which commands a fine view. Proceeding further we came to the Spanish frontier. The most remarkable feature of Gibraltar is the turning of the natural summit of the mountain into a castellated fortress, mounted in every nook and corner with heavy guns. A large garrison of British troops is permanently stationed here. In the course of four hours we had seen all that there was to be seen and at ten o'clock returned to our steamer, and shortly after left the port. Viewed from the sea Gibraltar looks a dreary sort of a mountain rising in a straight line from the ocean.

On the evening of the 26th, our journey being about to terminate, one of the passengers proposed a vote of thanks to our worthy commander, Captain Barlow.

On 27th June, by the dim glimmer of an early dawn we saw the indistinct outline of Southampton and shortly after our steamer came to anchor. Letters were brought to us from land; amongst these was one from Mr Dadabhoy, formerly in the employ of my husband and now living in London, asking me to telegraph to him as soon as I arrived in Southampton, so that he might meet us on alighting at London. We could now plainly see the celebrated Netley Hospital, a large stately edifice. At six o'clock our steamer started again and within an hour had entered the Dock at Southampton and taken up her position near the wharf. All were soon busily engaged in looking after their luggage and, after bidding "Goodbye" to our good Captain, we left the ship and betook ourselves to the Custom House hard by.

When the officials came to inspect our luggage they all began to look at us; I said to them, "I am no merchant, I have no cigars or tobacco with me; you are, however, at liberty to inspect my packages, but, pray, do not detain us unnecessarily, I have come here to see the Paris Exhibition only." On hearing this they readily allowed our luggage to pass, and also asked me not to go out in the streets of London with such a profusion of jewellery on my person.

We went from here to a large Railway station. There were fruit and confectioner's stalls on the station at which pretty girls were employed as saleswomen; an interminable crowd of people kept coming and going at all the doors. I am extremely glad to record here that the name of Sir Jamsetjee Jeejeebhoy, the Parsee philanthropist, was well known out here too, and when I said that I was Parsee, I was at once identified as being of the same race as Sir Jamsetjee. During the whole journey and throughout my stay in England I wore my usual Parsee costume, without the least change. Five or six Parsee ladies had been in England before me, my own daughter amongst them, but none of them continued to wear their native dresses without making many changes and modifications even when at home, whilst in public they used only to appear in English dress, but I went everywhere in my Parsee dress and was in consequence much spoken of. Everybody was anxious to see me on account of the peculiarity of my dress and my appearance was evidently as novel and interesting to them as theirs was to me. We felt it, on our railway journey, as warm as in Bombay, the large tracts of verdant land and pleasant scenery were beautiful; wherever the train stopped crowds of people were to be seen; we passed well-built houses and tall smoky factory chimneys, away in the distance we saw hills overspread with eternal verdure—all so very new and pleasant to our eyes as to beggar description. The rugged gnarled trunks of great trees, like ivy-bound pillars, the leafy avenues, the open meadows, the rich velvety grass spun by Nature's hand, the cooling green foliage were all new sights to me. Excepting the slight smoke of the engine, we did not experience the least inconvenience either of dust or noise.

The neat snug little cottage enveloped in a profusion of flowering creepers was a novel, charming and picturesque sight; fine, large mansions may attract and impose us, but this quiet unpretending retreat endears itself to us by its simplicity. As we drew near the great metropolis rows of stately buildings came into view and soon the grand panoramic view of London with an immense wilderness of chimneys emitting black smoke, burst upon our astonished gaze. The network of railway lines intersecting and running into each other and the grand and majestic bridge over the Thames astonished us more than any other. Here, at the Waterloo Bridge station, I set my foot at last in London and the great aim of my life was realised.

XXV

In the Capital of the British Empire

Our train arrived at the Waterloo Bridge Station where I was much astonished to see an immense concourse of people, though nothing unusual was going on as far as I could make out. With mutual good wishes my son and I took leave of our fellow passengers who had accompanied us thus far, and entering a cab drove to Fitzroy Square to the house of Mr Dadabhoy, alias Dady, Solicitor. After waiting in vain for our telegram this gentleman had gone out, but we were welcomed by his wife and her maid, who came out to the cab and begged us to alight as Mr Dady was expected back shortly. Having partaken of refreshment we felt rested; shortly after Mr Dady came in and greeted us most cordially. He had not rented any lodgings for us beforehand as he thought it better for me to select one myself. Accordingly, I accompanied him in a cab and saw some apartments that were to be let, but did not find any to my taste. Thence we drove to Cavendish Street, Portland Place, where at No. 23 I found well-furnished apartments which were advantageously situated—just the thing I wanted.

The landlord, Mr Baker, was an old man, his grown-up daughter lived with him and managed the house. Mr Dady settled with them the rent, after which I returned with him and rested for the night at his house. The next morning after tea, I removed to the newly-hired lodgings, and Mrs Dady's maid took me to one of the grand public baths, situated at a distance of a mile or so from our lodgings; for in London all houses do not have this most necessary adjunct. These bathing places are splendid edifices and are divided into separate compartments; each compartment is furnished with a large tub, hot and cold water, towels, and a looking-glass; there are also maidservants there to assist the ladies. The charge for a bath is about a rupee and-a-half per head. Turkish baths can also be had here, but the charges comparatively are a little higher. After taking a bath, I returned to Mr Dady's and dined there after our Parsee fashion, as I was really tired with the English food which I had had during our long voyage. In the evening Mr Dady took us to Madame Tussaud's. We entered a large saloon fitted up like a palace and brilliantly illuminated. Here we saw arranged in groups wax-figures reclining on rich sofas or standing under a canopy representing in the most life-like manner the rulers of different nations surrounded respectively by their families and nobilities, all superbly clad in their respective costumes.

Art had so closely imitated nature that it was many times difficult to distinguish the living from the waxen figures. One waxen figure of an old man with a snuff-box in his hand who was offering continuously a pinch to the passers-by was such a clever imitation that many an onlooker was deceived. On the other hand visitors themselves are sometimes mistaken for the waxen exhibits.

When we were there, we were much attracted by the sight of an exceedingly stout lady seated on a divan in the midst of a group of waxen figures; her remarkable corpulence, her rigid attitude and her fixed stare of surprise drew towards her the attention of one of the young men who had accompanied us. Noticing that her eyelids moved, as he thought, by means of some clever mechanism, he approached, as he thought, the waxen figure with the intention of touching the eyeballs, when the supposed figure stood up in affright, to the wonder and merriment of us all.

Different rooms contained representations of different scenes from history or functions of State; one room for instance, contained an exact representation of a court of justice; another the death scene of a nihilist about to suffer on the scaffold; and the third showed how captive kings bewailed their cruel lot in such woe-begone attitudes and expressions that they excited our pity.

At the time of our visit Pope Pius IX had recently died and his death scene was portrayed with terrible realism. I was much pleased with all we saw here; it was past eleven ere we returned home. Hearing that a flower show of every known species of the rose, was to be held the next day at the Crystal Palace, I arranged with Mr Dady to go there, and so at nine on the following day Mrs Dady, her maid, myself and my son started by railway from the Victoria Station for this wonderfully beautiful place. So immense was the crowd there, that I being in my native dress and having several ornaments on, became much afraid. The railway here is so conveniently constructed as to lead right into the Crystal Palace Park, whence a flight of wooden stairs ushers the visitor into the main building.

Having been kindly warned that my dress and jewels would attract attention, I kept close to my son on the right and maidservant on the left. I heard someone remark in the crowd that the Rose Show being an annual affair was not so great an attraction as was my picturesque dress. Some of the gentlemen there were pleased to find me able to converse with them in their own tongue; and consequently I felt myself at home in their company. From my youth, I was an admirer of English society and used to mix with it in India; and I, therefore, felt no shyness when in the midst of it here.

A scene akin to one from fairyland burst upon my astonished sight when we had ascended the stairs. Standing on a balcony as broad as a public thoroughfare, I could see nothing but a continuous and most beautifully laid out garden in the midst of which stands the glittering palace on a rising ground. As its name indicates the Crystal Palace is a superb palace of glass, that is to say, its roof, ceiling and floors are constructed of solid glass. It must not be supposed, however, as I did before I saw the Crystal Palace, that it is made out of one single piece of glass; pieces of thick glass set in iron frames are used in building this most elegant and fantastic edifice.

The Crystal Place occupies a commanding position and is divided into a number of courts, picture galleries and a museum. I cannot adequately describe the wonderfully beautiful and interesting show of roses collected together in the spacious hall. Countless varieties of roses, all in the perfection of cultivation, were so artistically arranged that one was never tired of looking at them.

When fatigued with walking we entered one refreshment saloon about 1 p.m. and after partaking of some refreshments we felt a little refreshed and I then bent my course towards the picture gallery, as I was informed that it contained my daughter's portrait, done when she was in England in 1868. It is impossible fitly to praise this most excellent collection. The walls, throughout their whole length, are hung with pictures drawn by celebrated painters, representing, in life-like reality kings, queens, peasants, beggars, giants, fairies and scenes from nature. India cannot boast of possessing even one-sixteenth part of such a select and rare collection. All these pictures I saw with ever increasing wonder, some of them are so precious as to be valued at Rs 50,000 each. As the afternoon wore on, the crowd began to increase and at five the Lord Mayor of London and his retinue honoured the show with their presence. The Mayor was of a good and noble appearance and elicited marks of homage and respect from the people. We next visited the Egyptian and the other Courts and saw there the effigies of the various lands, but although the whole day had been spent in the Crystal Palace, there was much within left unseen while we had not visited the gardens at all. We therefore strolled out and the sight of this splendid garden at the still hour of dusk with its lovely flower beds and fountains was extremely pleasant, but as I was informed that there were many more splendid gardens in London, I did not linger here. There were athletic sports going on, which were to say the least, wonderful. From here we took leave of the beauteous Crystal Palace; on reaching home we had our pleasant supper and retired to rest, fatigued by the day's sight-seeing.

On the 1st of July I hired a cab and set out to see the public gardens, the principal one being the Hyde Park. My dress was the focus of attraction and many a high-born lady showed her approval of it by saying, "Such a beautiful and curious oriental costume never met my eyes before." My acquaintances recommended me not to wear jewellery, for mingling with the good harmless society there were many "light-fingered gentry" of both sexes, so well attired as to defy detection. From this place I returned home through Regent's Park and I resolved to pass all my leisure during my stay in London amidst the beautiful scenes of Hyde Park.

On 2nd July I went in the morning for a drive through Oxford and Regent Streets, Piccadilly and Bond Street. On returning to my lodging, I was gladdened by receiving letters from Bombay. In the afternoon, my son and I had a drive on the embankment of the Thames where a gentle breeze playing on the glass-like surface of the river, and the sight of several magnificent bridges soothed my mind. One of the characteristic features of London is its capacity for dispelling sadness and care; no one however careworn and oppressed can resist its joyous influence. In the evening we went to the Polytechnic where we saw diverse wonderful things worked by machinery. We saw a telephone and panoramic views of the Paris Exhibition and of several battlefields. My son this day visited Col. Sir O.T. Burne, who was much pleased at seeing him and gave him much useful information and advice.

On 3rd July at 3 p.m., I set out to purchase some fancy articles and then went in search of that jeweller who had seventeen years previously supplied me with ornaments and jewellery. His name was Webb, and I was not long in finding out his establishment. He was glad to see his own work again after so many years and which, he said, was still fashionable. He praised my refined taste and said he would be glad to execute further orders from me. I saw other jewellers' shops too; all of these shops appeared to me so rich and splendid that it made it difficult for me to give one the preference over the other. On learning that Parisian jewellery was of finer and more elaborate workmanship, I ordered a limited number of old ornaments to be merely remodelled according to the prevailing fashion and deferred my purchases till I went to France. Quitting the shops I drove past Buckingham Palace to Hyde Park, where I remained but a short time on account of the cold. The following day several jewellers called upon me and much of the day was spent in showing and drawing new patterns and designs. In the evening I went with Mr Dady to see his new residence in Kensington.

On 5th July I was engaged in writing letters to Bombay all day and in the evening went out for a walk. On seeing a number of beautiful girls alight from every omnibus that I saw, I asked them if they all were coming from school, when they replied that they were shop girls. In the large shops hundreds of girls are employed as saleswomen and seamstresses. To see these girls was to love them, so beautifully fair and young were they. I was forcibly reminded of those tales in which even kings were willing enough to be led in silken chains by girls of plebeian birth, and what to me at one time seemed only fiction, seemed now very likely to be the truth. While walking along, I met Mr Stevens, who, with his wife and daughter, was coming to pay me a visit. This gentleman was the senior partner in the well-known firm of Forbes & Co., and although he was well acquainted with the people of India, his wife and daughter, who had never been to India, were not, and they were therefore much interested in me and invited me to a tea-party at their place.

XXVI

More Glimpses of London's Greatness

The next days I passed in visiting the interesting places and objects in London and its neighbourhood. On 6th July I went see Westminster Hall and the Abbey. Passing through the Trafalgar Square, where there is a high monument erected to the great Naval Commander, Nelson, we came to a very large stately building. This building is divided into many departments, such as the Tower Court, the Parliament House and so on. Here I saw the splendid throne used by Queen Victoria when she came to open Parliament. To the left of this was the Price Consort's throne, which had unhappily been unoccupied for several years. After spending four hours in looking over these buildings we went to see the Westminster Abbey. Its spacious compound is used as a graveyard for the celebrated and worthy of the land. The priest in charge of this Abbey kindly explained to me all the rites and ceremonies of Christian burial and pointed out some very fine monuments with elaborate and costly sculpture. The colossal hall of this fine Abbey branches off like a public thoroughfare into four different sections and is capable of accommodating thousands at a time.

On 7th July I received visits from Col. Burne and other kind friends and in the afternoon I went with my son to Mrs Stevens' party at their residence in Upper Phillimore Gardens. In the course of our conversation I mentioned the disagreement between myself and my brother, and Mr Stevens was surprised and grieved to hear of this, remarking that it was at the recommendation of my husband, that he had taken my brother into his office when at Bombay. A visit to the Kensington Gardens terminated our rambles of the day, and on reaching home, I found to my great regret that in my absence Miss Manning had called upon me.

On 9th July my Parsee friends came to see me. These were Messrs Shapoorjee Jeewajee Dady, Manekjee Limjee Banajee, Bhicajee P. Dalal and Dorabjee Cursetjee Shroff. The next day my son-in-law's brother informed me that a Flower and Fruit Show was to be held, and at 3 p.m. I went to see it and found it well worth a visit. The Royal Family and many of the nobility had also come to see it. On the 11th I went to see the Royal Aquarium, but as I was there early I had to wait at the side of the Westminster Hospital. A gentleman came and politely requested me to take a seat in one of the rooms of the hospital. I gladly availed myself of this opportunity and was no sooner seated there than an elderly lady, who, I afterwards learnt, was the matron, came into the room and very kindly asked if I would not like to go over the hospital.

The arrangements inside were admirable and interested me extremely. The hospital was a large, many storeyed building, but I was so fatigued by the time I had looked over the first two floors that I was about to retire when the matron pressingly requested me to go over the whole building to satisfy the curiosity of its inmates; for she assured me that no foreign lady in such a costume as mine had ever been seen in the whole of England before; moreover, she added, the patients were also pleased with the kindness I showed them. I could not but comply with her request and was thanked by many for the trouble I took. Before leaving, the matron very kindly asked me to partake of some refreshments, which I thankfully declined as I had had my breakfast not long before.

My son and I now repaired to the aquarium, which from the very gates presented a novel and picturesque appearance. It appeared as if a river was dammed up by glass and parcelled out into different compartments, with glass all round. The bed of this artificial river was strewn with shells, sands and seaweed; swinging about darting hither and thither were fishes of all sizes and descriptions.

The aquarium was so large that the day did not suffice to see it all thoroughly. Thus England affords her people an unceasing round of refined and legitimate pleasures, even a tenth of which cannot be had in India. All this is due to our enlightened rulers who, by such unique and marvellous shows, render their country a fairyland full of wonder, beauty, skill and intelligence. The next day we visited the Tower of London. We had to pass through several smaller buildings, in one of which we saw the crown jewels and the valuable silver wrought ornaments of former kings. The crowns were richly ornamented with brilliant rubies and emeralds. Here is also to be seen an excellent imitation of the famous Kohinoor, the original being worn by our Queen Empress in her crown. Our guide gave us the particulars of all that we saw.

Our next visit was to St Paul's Cathedral, the largest of its kind in England. I cannot say enough in praise of its stately and imposing grandeur and chaste and elaborate decorations. Led on by a desire to see everything I climbed to the Golden Gallery, which is 350 feet from the ground, and was repaid for my exertions by the wonderful panorama spread out before me; from this height London looked much like a plaything.

Very much pleased with what we saw in this stately building we returned home and went at five o'clock to Miss Hill's party at Hampstead Heath to which I had received an invitation. About thirty persons had already assembled and were awaiting my arrival. They gave me a most hearty welcome and began to express their views of my dress and ornaments. I had been requested to bring with me the cap decorated with my family photographs and was much complimented by the assembly on my work and design. The two sisters, the hostesses of the day, had, out of filial love, undertaken to write a biography of their worthy father; on hearing of this I informed them that I also was engaged in writing my autobiography. The Misses Hill were under the impression that this was my first appearance in English society, but on my telling them that I had been accustomed even from my infancy to move in the English society in India, the guests remarked that my manners vouched for the truth of my statement.

On 14th July I visited my Parsee friends Mr and Mrs Framji Bomonji Cama and Dr Rustomji N. Khory. Hearing from them that Mr Dadabhoy Nowrojee Master* lived at Lad-brooke Grove at no great distance I went thither to visit him. On the 15th I went to Miss Manning's where I had the pleasure of meeting several Parsees, Mahomedans and Bengalees. On returning home I found that Mr Fitzgerald, son of the ex-Governor of Bombay, had called on me, and being most disappointed at having missed him I wrote to ask him when it would be convenient for him to see us, and the next day he invited us to come at 2 p.m. to his residence, Queen's Road, Kensington. We were late, and Mr Fitzgerald, waiting for a long time for our arrival, had gone and we were requested to follow him to the Charing Cross Station. The streets round the station were crowded with spectators, and though no other carriages were allowed to pass in so late, ours was at once admitted under Mr Fitzgerald's instructions.

The premier, Lord Beaconsfield, and Lord Salisbury were returning home victorious that day from the Berlin Congress, having established peace in Europe without bloodshed, and having reconciled two discordant nations, Russia and Turkey, with no other weapon than that of "moral suasion." To welcome back these great statesmen the crowds filled the streets, station and houses all along the route. The station was tastefully decorated with flowers and laurel leaves, and everyone seemed to vie with the other in the desire to show honour to England's great representatives.

The laurel is considered an emblem of victory. Inside the station a stand was erected for the accommodation of visitors, where in the front row seats were reserved for me and my son. We were, as usual, both in our native dress, which failed not in attracting general attention. At five o'clock the train steamed into the station, when the whole assemblage of spectators rose up to show their respect, and there was cheering, waving of hats and handkerchiefs as the two noblemen alighted. To my eyes both statesmen looked possessed of superior intelligence; they looked what they were—acute politicians and leaders of men. They acknowledged the honour done them by saluting the people in return, and entering their carriages, which had driven right

*This gentleman had contested the election for Holborn in 1887.

into the station, drove away. This was the first reception of this kind I had seen in England and it impressed me by its very heartiness. People made many a guess as to my nationality: some said I was a Parsee Queen, others an Indian Princess, and some went so far as to surmise that I was a Chinese lady. My carriage was literally hemmed in by the crowd from which it was extricated by two mounted policemen who came to my aid and conducted my carriage through the living mass until it was left behind.

On 17th July I went to a photographer's whose establishment seemed to be on a grand scale and largely patronised by the nobility. One of the saloons was reserved for the Royal family. The photographer requested me to return in a couple of days in one of my best costumes, when he would take my portrait and enlarge it to any size I liked; he further begged me to allow him to take a full-sized photograph for himself. This day, corresponding with the 1st day of the 11th month of the Parsees, was my son's birthday; we therefore spent the day in merriment in the company of our Parsee friends. In the afternoon we went for a drive, passed the evening in Hyde Park, and returned home for supper.

XXVII

Visits to the India Office and the Windsor Castle

On 18th July we went, by the kind recommendation of Col. Burne, to see the India Office. Dr (now Sir George) Birdwood received us cordially and showed us all over the premises. The India Office is a very costly and elegant building and of so big a size that we could not see more than half of it on that day. The elaborate masonry and the statues of Indian worthies with which the frontage is ornamented render this office one of the finest buildings in London, and a princely sum must have been spent on its construction. Every Indian visiting England should invariably visit this beautiful and magnificent building where business connected with India is transacted. Dr Birdwood asked me whether I knew Sir Cowasjee Jehangir Readymoney and was pleased to hear that I stood in near relationship to him.

We next drove to the house of Mrs Wester Phillips and afterwards visited the Zoological Garden which was not far off from there. On the 19th I went to see the Buckingham Palace, for which Mr Fitzgerald had kindly sent me a card of admission. The beauty of this palace can well be imagined from the fact that it is the residence of the Royal Family. The beautiful drawing-rooms, the furniture of exquisite workmanship, the rich curtains and carpets and the paintings executed by master hands all defy description. I need not say that I was much pleased at witnessing the royal splendour of this palace. No one, however morose and melancholy he might be, could see this palace without his spirit being enlivened.

On the 20th I visited Kensington Museum, and on entering the precincts of it I found the statue of my uncle, Cowasjee Jehangir Readymoney. I was very much interested in what I saw there. As soon as I reached home a man from Mr Dadabhoy came to enquire if I would in the evening go to the Covent Garden Theatre to hear the most famous singer of the world—Madame Patti. I agreed to this proposal and after supper drove to the theatre. It was a very large theatre, capable of holding seven thousand persons. Madame Patti played her part excellently. Her singing being in the Italian language elicited applause from those who were conversant with that language. I learnt with surprise that the nosegays thrown at the celebrated singer often contained bank notes, valuable rings and such other costly things concealed within the fragrant flowers. I noticed that bouquets came mostly from the boxes occupied by the nobility. The people of England care only for the higher sort of music and spend large sums of money upon it. Not only the wealthy but the middle classes too are the patrons. The next day I paid visits to Mr and Mrs Wesche and Mr Showell, ex-Magistrate of Bombay. Both these families lived there in a simple style compared with their mode of living in Bombay.

On the 22nd of July I received the sad tidings of the death of my worthy uncle, Sir Cowasjee Jehangir Readymoney, which had taken place on the 19th. Being very sorry I kept indoors all the day.

Mr Gladstone was to speak in the House of Commons against the infamous Press Act, which had been framed by Lord Lytton's Government. Mr Fitzgerald having very kindly sent me cards of admittance I went to the House of Commons. Mrs Gladstone, who was also one of the audience, enquired whether her husband's expected speech had drawn me there that day. I replied that as the topic was one relating to India, I was naturally very anxious to hear it discussed by statesmen like her husband Mr Gladstone. The scene was entirely novel to me, being the first political meeting I had attended. Here I had the satisfaction of making the acquaintance of Mr Fawcett, the philanthropist of India, and his wife. Who would not be touched at seeing this great man devoid of the blessings of sight? He wore green spectacles on his sightless eyes and a young boy at his side guided his footsteps. He shook hands with me and enquired if I had obtained a good place at the House. After returning from refreshments to the gallery a lady came up to me and took out a slip of paper whereon my name was written in full, but I could not guess how she had got it. The members who took part in the discussion spoke very impressively and were listened to with the gravest attention. After Mr Gladstone and some other members had spoken, Professor Fawcett stood up and, though deprived of sight, made a speech lasting over an hour and a half. The sight of this blind champion of India's rights and liberties as he stood there, giving utterance to his hopes and aspirations, was most inspiring to me, one of India's daughters. I was leaving my place at 3 p.m. when Mrs Gladstone had the kindness to shake hands with me. I enquired of an official the name of the lady who had got my name so correctly and was told that it was Mrs Cavendish Bentinck.

On the following day I paid a visit to Mrs Fawcett and in the evening dined at Mr Wesche's. On the 27th I started for Brighton to see the aquarium there. The climate of Brighton is more temperate than that of London. Having heard that Sir Albert Sassoon had a house at this place I went there to see if I could see some member of the family, but to my regret I found that Sir Albert had gone to Paris and his daughter Mrs Gubbay had left for Vienna. I found that the splendid residence vied with even the Buckingham Palace. After seeing the aquarium I took train from Addison Road Station to Richmond where the mother and children of my kind friend Colonel Baker, R.E., were living. Before leaving Bombay, Col. Baker had given me a letter of introduction to his mother who had written to me requesting me to come and see her at Richmond, as she was unable to come up to London. After returning home I drove to Mrs Bentinck's, Grafton Street, and found her house to be a splendid mansion. Mrs Bentinck inquired if I had been fortunate enough to see Her Most Gracious Majesty the Queen-Empress, and on my replying in the negative she most kindly offered to present me if I would, after visiting Paris, come to Scotland where she would be in October. To this kind proposal I could not accede on account of the severity of the weather of Scotland.

Having through the kindness of Mr Fitzgerald got a card of

admission to see Windsor Castle, my son and I took train for that place. A guide was waiting to show us over and he gave us particulars of the various kings and queens who had lived and died in this magnificent castle. The castle has a fine situation on a slight eminence and is surrounded by a grand and extensive park. This palace has a far nobler appearance than that of the Buckingham Palace. The apartments occupied by the members of the Royal Family are very handsomely furnished. These private apartments are not usually open to visitors, but the card of admission with which I was furnished allowed me this privilege. Adjoining the castle stands the small but handsomely built Royal Chapel. Here I saw a fine marble group representing a beautiful female with four sweet children clinging to her. This group, I afterwards learnt, was meant to represent Virgin Mary and the four deceased children of the Royal Family, one of these being the little son of the Princess Alice of Hesse, who had the misfortune to fall from a window and be killed. I next visited the stables and left the castle at 5 p.m. Just as I was leaving, Prince Leopold, the youngest of our Queen's sons was seen driving with his companions. Afterwards I visited the Virginia Water, a picturesque lake, and the Deer Park. On the 31st I went to see Mrs Bentinck in the afternoon and on my return received a visit from Miss Manning. This lady put herself to much trouble on my account. Having spent the following few days in miscellaneous visits, I went on the 4th again to see Mrs Baker at Richmond. On my way home I saw the Kew Garden. Reaching home at seven o'clock, I found a note from my valued friend, Mrs Cavendish Bentinck, enclosing a ticket for a box at the theatre. I felt myself to be under the greatest of obligations to her and take this opportunity of again expressing my grateful sentiments for many a favour shown to me by her during my brief stay in England.

XXVIII

At the Paris Exhibition

On 9th August, after breakfast at seven o'clock, I bade adieu to the place where I had put up for the last six weeks. Starting from Charing Cross Station we reached Dover pier at 9.30 a.m. and going on board the twin-deck mail steamer left the shores of England. The English Channel is said to be very rough, but we found it calm; the atmosphere was sultry, but the passage of about two hours' duration was very smooth and enjoyable.

Amongst the passengers was a lady, named Mrs Lyons, with whom I had a long talk; she knew several of the Parsee residents of London and Paris, of whom she gave me a very good report. One of these, Mr Perojshaw Ruttonjee Cama, had left his family and was leading the life of a recluse in Europe. Previous to my departure from Bombay, his mother had earnestly requested me to find out her son's whereabouts and to write to her full particulars about him; this even then I hoped to be able to do.

At noon we landed at Calais and immediately took the train for Paris, which we reached in the evening. The station—the Gare du Nord—was so excessively crowded that I would have found it extremely difficult to get out of it at all, had not Mr Lyons kindly assisted us in getting our luggage examined and escorted us to a cab. This gentleman recommended us to go to the Hotel Mirabeau where he assured us we would be comfortable and where we would find several Parsee gentlemen lodged. We accordingly drove thither and after supper there came several Parsee gentlemen of my acquaintance to see me.

During our conversation when I enquired after Mr Cama, they told me that it would be next to impossible to see young Mr Perojshaw, for were he to hear that anyone from Bombay had been enquiring after him, he would at once change his quarters and go no one knew whither, but I resolved to try to see him early in the next morning. Accordingly after breakfast in the next morning I set out in quest of Mr Perojshaw Cama, but I found to my regret and surprise that he had left his lodgings the night before and gone, nobody knew where. I next went, provided with a note from Mrs Cavendish Bentinck, to find out some lodgings which that lady had highly recommended to me.

It was past two o'clock ere I succeeded in reaching my destination. The landlady was pleased on reading Mrs Bentinck's note, but she showed her disappointment at being unable to accommodate me as all her rooms were occupied. She recommended the new Continental Hotel to me and I accordingly ordered the coachman to drive to that place.

On the way I met one of my countrymen, Mr Jamsetjee Dastoor, who kindly accompanied us to the hotel. I engaged a couple of rooms on the third floor at a cost of Rs 15 a day, which was reasonable enough; these rooms were, of course, smaller in size than some others whose rent was exorbitant, but they were equally well provided with the necessaries and comforts of life. Indeed what I had been allowed to view and admire at a distance in London was in reality all round myself here.

On the day of my arrival, I went and sat down in the drawing-room and no sooner had I done so than the other occupants of the room became interested in me. Some began to walk about me and scan my dress, and some addressed me, but as I could not understand French, conversation was impossible between us till an American girl asked me if I knew English, and upon my answering in the affirmative she very gladly became my interpreter.

While we were chatting the dinner bell rang; my son and I took the seats which had been reserved for us at a table capable of accommodating from a hundred and fifty to two hundred persons or even more. I found the French dishes very much to my liking, for they closely resembled our own. Besides poultry and mutton, there were dishes prepared of ham and beef, neither of which I touched on account of the restrictions placed on them by the Parsee religion. At this my two neighbours manifested much curiosity. After a sumptuous repast I adjourned to the drawing room and entered into conversation with the ladies assembled there with whom I soon became familiar.

On the 11th, descending to the dining room, in the morning, I found groups of persons seated round small tables taking breakfast. I ordered my simple meal of bread and coffee; both these I found excellent. Mr Jamsetjee came to escort us to the Exhibition and on seeing him my mind was set at rest, for he could speak French as fluently as a Parisian. After an hour's drive, we reached the Exhibition; from afar we had seen the large dome with which the building is surmounted.

Even at that early hour, there were no fewer than ten thousand persons assembled there; I was afraid of mingling in such an immense crowd. However, I took my ticket and entered the garden from which one could go to the various amusements at the Exhibition. Having, with my companion and son, entered the Exhibition grounds, I found myself speedily hemmed on all sides by the mass of people whom my Parsee attire had attracted towards me; however, by God's protecting care and the tact of Mr Jamsetjee, who replied in different languages to all who were curious enough to question him about me, I felt no inconvenience or difficulty. The police were on the alert too, and as I had on my person all the jewellery and ornaments customary amongst the Parsees, the well-meaning out of the crowd advised me to be very careful. I subsequently found this was really the case, and that gave me confidence and prompted me to go on further and further. With great courtesy the people used to make way for me, politeness being one of the French characteristics.

The area of the ground of the Grand Exhibition was equal to that of a good-sized town and it was divided into about thirty distinct courts, as each country of the world was represented by a court specially set apart for it; for example, the arts, industries and products of India were shown in one, in another those of England, in a third those of China, and so on; each of these so called "courts" was somewhat like a street with shops on either side. Besides the countless articles exhibited there such as jewellery, piece-goods, metal work, articles of wood, stone and china, there was machinery at work demonstrating how all these things were made from raw material.

We saw how the diamond is polished, how steel pens, pins and needles are made, how porcelain crockery and glass is moulded, how chintz-printing is done, and most interesting of all, how is most intricate lace woven. We also saw instantaneous photography, painting at sight, machine-made jewellery, imitation jewellery in glass, stone and metals and some pieces of jewellery artistically worked in filigree. Pretty young girls were to be seen blowing glass into a thousand and one nicknacks [sic] with astonishing skill. It is better to incur fatigue and danger and see the wonders of the world than to live a long life of continued idleness and luxury.

When I was in London, I wanted to visit Liverpool, Birmingham, Manchester and such other well-known seats of industry, but my friends dissuaded me from doing so and advised me to see the great Exhibition, saying that it was a compendium of all the curious, notable and elegant productions and sights of the world that the age could produce; these words I found fully verified and was therefore very grateful to my kind advisers. Led on by an eager impulse to see everything, I never halted till two o'clock, when I felt rather tired, so we went and had tiffin in one of the many restaurants in the Exhibition grounds; and as this was the usual hour for that the meal, the crowd of hungry visitors was enormous, and the hurry and bustle brought into my mind a public dinner in Bombay. We turned again to see the Exhibition, for we had seen till then but an infinitesimal part of it; wherever I turned my eyes I saw such novelties that had my means permitted, I would have made many purchases.

To enumerate all these countless curiosities would require four books of the size that I am writing, but even then I am afraid the list would be an incomplete one. During my stay in London I had not seen anything that would bear comparison with what I saw in Paris in so short a time; in fact, this marvellous Exhibition had culled the choicest products of more than thirty countries, and we thanked God for having allowed us the privilege of seeing it. My utmost ambition was to visit England, but God not only had gratified that ambition of mine, but had graciously crowned my utmost hopes by bringing me to see this grand Exhibition teeming with thousands of wonders. I do not know how to show my gratitude to the Almighty for all these favours except by doing whatever may be pleasing to the Disposer of all events. At 6 p.m. we returned to our hotel.

On the 12th I started with my son to see the city. I will not attempt any detailed description of the buildings in these big cities of Europe, as almost all the Government buildings constructed in Bombay are built on the plan of the houses in these cities, nay in some cases even with some improvements. Delhi, Lucknow and other ancient cities in India have their fine buildings too, some of which are equal, if not superior, in elegance, to those of London and Paris. The Taj Mahal, at any rate, is unrivalled. It must, however, be said in justice to Paris, the Queen of Fair Cities, that it would require a poetic fancy and an eloquent pen to praise or describe it aptly.

The next day I visited the Exhibition again. The fee for admission was only one franc, and yet what a large amount must have been realised by the daily receipts, the average number of visitors being 50,000 per day, since the opening of the Exhibition three months ago. This fact alone many convince my readers of the universal interest and attraction of the Exhibition. With true feminine curiosity, my mind was set upon seeing the jewellery, and I saw among other articles a pair of large pearls—the size of a sparrow egg—which in my opinion, was the best of the whole collection. Much pleased with what we saw, we left the Exhibition in the evening and crossed the river in a steam launch from which we enjoyed the views of the beautiful city.

On the following day I went to make arrangements for the despatch of my luggage and to secure passage from Brindisi to Bombay and also visited the Exhibition. Returning to our hotel in the evening, I had a talk with the other visitors, amongst whom were the American Consul, Mr B. J. Beiscotto, and a Mr and Mrs Kirby, who, like myself, had left their native country to come and see the Exhibition; they intended to stay a considerable time in Paris and wished me to do likewise and then go with them to America. I found the American people frank, polite and independent, and, what is still better, without pride, so that the rich and poor associated together without any reserve.

XXIX

My Ascent in a Balloon

Next morning I heard that a balloon was to ascend from the Trocadéro (the Exhibition), and that anyone who liked could enjoy the novel pleasure of an aerial sail. My hotel friends were surprised to hear that I ardently longed to go up in the balloon and asked me, whether all the Parsee women were [of] a bold, intrepid nature like myself. I had to dispel this very erroneous idea by telling them that a few years ago Parsee women and even a few of the men were frightened at Europeans, and would run away if they saw any approaching them. I, however, by my early associations with Europeans had imbibed their tastes and some of their courage. These remarks pleased my American friends, who again urged me to visit New York, most hospitably extracting from me a promise that, when I did so I should go to no hotel or boarding house but stay with them.

Dressing myself in warm clothing and carrying with me in a handbag some note paper, wine, biscuits and a piece of iron to which to attach any missive I might wish to send down to the people below, I set out for the place from which the ascent was to take place. Here there was an immense crowd, whose amazement at seeing me amongst the aeronauts was most amusing to behold. On payment of a sum of Rs 10, I took my seat.

This balloon, being merely intended for pleasure excursions, was attached to the earth by a long rope. There were in all fifteen passengers, three of whom were ladies. I did not allow my son to accompany me for fear of an accident. At 5 p.m. we began gently to ascend, and I saw the earth receding from beneath us. Presently the panorama that spread itself out before us, as we hovered over the splendid city was most strange and fantastic; the people whom we had left below might have been taken for a swarm of bees, the river Seine with its stately bridges, the gardens with their flowers and ancient trees, the fountains with their feeble jets of water vainly trying to reach us, the proud monuments, the magnificent buildings and their tall spires, the majestic Opera House, the thousands of boats darting like fishes hither and thither on the water, the Exhibition from which hundreds of flags were gaily waving, and the innumerable other places of interest in this wonderful city formed a scene which bore resemblance more to the fabled abodes of genii than to anything sublunary; indeed, might we not say that it seemed a faint reflex of the unfading lustre and undying joy of Paradise itself!

How long will my wealthy sisters shut themselves up in their old habits and prejudices, shunning the healthy and ennobling pleasures which lie alluringly at their very door! Why do they cling so tenaciously to their idle crude custom, and know no higher ambition than to glide along in the same groove as their ancestors, instead of proving themselves worthy of the times they live in by basking in the free air of enlightenment! Awake, dear sisters, ere the stealthy hand of Time rob you of youth and opportunity to learn wisdom! To die in the hope of entering Paradise is blessed, but thrice blessed is he who, living a life of piety and virtue, learns something of the world he lives in, and of the other races of mankind who share it with him.

But to return to the point—as the balloon rose higher and higher, the cold became more intense, and as I began to shiver, I had to take a good draught of the wine I had brought with me. I offered some to a lady who looked very delicate and who felt grateful for the offer. We had now risen to the full height allowed by the rope, namely 700 metres, and I experienced an exhilarating sensation of pleasure in soaring like a bird above the earth—a pleasure enhanced by the knowledge that we were securely tied to mother earth and that all precautions were taken to preserve the balloon in its upright position. As we began to descend, Paris which had dwindled into an insignificant speck, gradually assumed her own graceful dimensions and we were soon deposited again on *terra firma*, after an aerial flight of forty-five minutes.

A medal commemorating our ascent was presented to each passenger. Oh! for words to describe this exciting adventure. As the gardens of the Tuileries had attracted my notice from the balloon, we went there and found much to admire. It covers a large area and is rich in flowers, lawns, avenues, trees, statues and fountains; an old-fashioned stately atmosphere pervades the place. The palace has been in a state of dilapidation since the Franco-German war but is imposing in its very ruins.

On 16th August, after writing letters to Bombay, London and Germany, we went to the Exhibition and spent the whole day in looking at the fine collection of pictures, but it would have needed a full month to see them all thoroughly, so immense was the number, some of the pictures were valued at from a lac to a lac and a half of rupees—almost incredible to our Indian mind. On the 17th I went to a jeweller's and ordered some ornaments to be sent out to me to India and returning heard from my son of his having accidentally met a gentleman of the firm of Messrs Fallek, after we had given up all hopes of seeing anyone of that firm. Messrs Fallek, while in Bombay ten years before, were in the habit of coming to our place to negotiate, through my husband, for the purchase of pearls. The gentleman was much pleased at our being in Paris, and invited us to spend the evening at his house. Then we went to a photographer's and had ourselves photographed.

On the 18th, after breakfast, I started by train for Versailles, which was reached in half an hour. This was a national fête-day, an anniversary on which the fountains play and crowds of people flock to see them. Within an enclosure, the beautifully designed garden lay in its smiling beauty, interspersed with alabaster equestrian statues. Proceeding along the avenue, we came in sight of the celebrated palace—a building worthy of such surroundings. As I was entering the spacious hall, an Englishman, named, as I afterwards learnt, Mr Cuthbert, politely enquired if I had been there before and as it was difficult to see all the places of interest in the palace without guidance, he most kindly offered assistance and I most gladly availed myself of it, thanking God, who in every emergency, anticipated and even exceeded my wants.

The palace is divided into many suites of apartments, each in the charge of an official, who conducted the visitors through the suite and gave an account of everything contained therein, Mr Cuthbert kindly translating to me as we went on. The ancient furniture was so beautifully polished that it looked quite new. There were splendid old pictures in all the rooms, and the entire walls of several others were hung with tapestry, representing battle scene [sic]. The palace itself is a noble building, and contains so many interesting objects that we were worn out with the very looking at them. The ceiling of the dining hall is exquisitely painted with figures of fairies in gold and silver.

There were four other equally splendid palaces standing at a mile distance from each other in the garden. The extent of the garden can be judged from this fact, but its beauty must be seen to be believed. It is a terrestrial Eden and has a number of cool retreats and shady arbours. There are also undulating pieces of ground covered over with luxuriant grass, romantic lakes lying at the foot of hills and swiftly flowing streams meandering through the lovely landscape. In short, nature and art have combined to produce a masterpiece.

We saw a number of carriages here which had belonged to Louis XIV and Napoleon Bonaparte; they were richly gilded and painted with birds, the seats were covered with velvet and hung with gold and silver tassels. Each carriage was valued at 100,000 francs. Proceeding further, Mr Cuthbert exclaimed: "Here is the centre of attraction!" And so it was truly.

We stood before a large pond or reservoir of water in which about a hundred fountains were playing in the most fantastic forms. Some represented a tree with its trunk, branches, twigs and leaves. Others assumed a thousand fanciful shapes as they rose and fell, while the largest, which only plays once a year on this day, represented Neptune, the God of Water. In this one figure, there must have been at least a thousand jets at play, the air around was thereby rendered as moist as in the rainy season. There were seats arranged as in a theatre down to the very margin of the lake for the convenience of the numerous spectators. It is impossible to convey to my readers an idea of the marvellous beauty of this enchanting scene. Taking leave of Mr Cuthbert, we hired a carriage and returned to our hotel at 6 p.m.

On the next day I saw Sir Albert Sassoon after a lapse of six years and found little or no change in him. We had a pleasant conversation on the past. Afterwards Messieurs Fallek came and took me to see their house where we had a pleasant tiffin and a merry chat. They afterwards took me to see the Grand Hotel which was considered the best till the Continental was built.

The 22nd of August being my birthday, I rose early to pour out my thanks to God for His mercy in having granted me the fulfilment of my long-cherished desire, namely, the visit to England, and for having, in addition, enabled me to see the great Exhibition and be a lodger in the best, though none the less expensive, hotel in Paris. After breakfast I went with Mr and Mrs Kirby and their daughters to the Bon Marché, one of the most fashionable shops in Paris, in size and magnificence a veritable palace. It was difficult in the midst of so many beautiful things in the shop to make a choice, but at last I selected some silks, fans, handkerchiefs and woollen fabrics. One of the superintendents kindly showed me over the entire establishment, saying that their shop was never before graced by the presence of a lady of my race and dress, and the entire staff therefore had stopped work to have a look at me. Again on the 23rd and 24th I visited this shop and made some more purchases.

Two days were spent in leave-taking and making preparations for our departure, and on the 28th I went and bought Cook's Tickets for myself and son, and then went to have a last look at the Exhibition and saw what I had seen hurriedly before. Returned again after dinner to the Trocadéro and took a sorrowful farewell of this unparalleled Exhibition, which had been the main incentive to my crossing the ocean.

The last evening at the hotel was spent in the company of my friends; we pledged each other's health and spoke of meeting again. I received visits from M. Phalampin, the Messieurs Fallek and other friends, as also letters from my friends in Germany, who were on the tiptoe of expectation regarding my intended visit to them. Glad as I was on the one hand, I was sorely aggrieved on the other, at hearing from Bombay that my dear husband was involved in some pecuniary troubles. Although this news occasioned me great chagrin I did not give way to despair, but confined my travels on the Continent to

Germany, Italy and Switzerland only, and relinquished now the half-formed plan of returning to London and seeing Scotland.

On the 29th I was engaged all morning in packing up my luggage and in settling accounts with the jewellers and the hotel and giving gratuities to the attendants. The general manager of the hotel, who had obliged me in a variety of ways, only asked for my photograph which I willingly gave him. Parting is always attended with pain. This I felt when bidding a temporary farewell to my native place, Bombay. The great regret that my husband, whose kind indulgence procured me all these enjoyments, did not share them with me, was never for a moment absent from my mind, but I never ceased entertaining hopes that God Almighty would one day permit us to revisit Europe together, which hope alas was never realised.

From the Hotel we went to the Gare du Nord and took train for Cologne.

XXX

Meeting Mrs Ahlers at Bonn

We reached the station of Cologne at daybreak on 30th August where my most intimate friend, towards whom I felt the affection and confidence of a sister, was awaiting our arrival. This lady was Mrs Ahlers, widow of Rudolph Ahlers, Esq., late partner of Messrs Volkart Bros. The closest friendship had long subsisted between my family and this amiable pair.

Mr and Mrs Ahlers left Bombay in 1869 and were leading a very happy life in London till the untimely death of Mr Ahlers in 1876 plunged his poor wife and his numerous friends into profound grief. Mr Ahlers, by his diligence, integrity and extraordinary intelligence had, while still a young man, risen to the position of a partner in the firm of Messrs Volkart Brothers, and had God spared him, he would, as a chief partner, have made a great name in the world and my husband would not have been separated from the business of that firm after a connection of seventeen years. Mr Ahlers' aged father still lived to bemoan the loss of his only child cut off in the prime of life from happiness and usefulness.

The grief which I shared with Mrs Ahlers impelled me to go to her and be comforted by seeing a reflex of my honoured friend Mr Ahlers in the children he had left behind. Ten long years had passed since we had seen each other. Mrs Ahlers, recognising me from my Parsee dress, ran up and embraced me, but grief had wrought such a dire change in her that I would never have known her again. She was dressed in deep mourning and a deep shade of melancholy had settled on her once joyful face. "Since I lost my husband three years ago," she said with a heavy sigh, "the world has been a blank wilderness to me, but now I have some cause to rejoice in meeting my old friend." After breakfast, which Mrs Ahlers had got ready for us at the station, we entered the train again and reached Bonn at 11 a.m. I took up my abode at my friend's house and found her love and regard for me as warm and sisterly as ever. We embraced each other, and our tears mingled, though we could not yet speak of the dearest wish of my heart, *viz.*, to see her dear children, but they were in the country, their mother having left them hurriedly the previous day to come and meet me at Cologne; they were to arrive more leisurely the next day.

A friend and neighbour of Mrs Ahlers, a German Professor, a man advanced in years as well as in learning, came in to see and invite us to dinner. He was much amazed at the Parsee costume worn by my son and myself and seemed pleased at making our acquaintance. His wife and children were spending the vacation in England but he said he would summon them home as he knew that they would like to see me and he was disappointed to hear that my stay would only last for a few days. He was of a jovial disposition, and though he could only converse with me through Mrs Ahlers as interpreter, we soon became fast friends.

Returning from the Professor's house at three o'clock, I took a little rest, after which my friends took me for a drive to see the town. Bonn, situated on the beautiful river Rhine, its pretty villas surrounded by lovely gardens, its many trees and the view of the Seven Mountains in the vicinity all combine to give it a cool and pleasant appearance. It is the seat of a celebrated university to which students come from all parts of the world; the climate is salubrious and living is cheaper than in England, for which reason my friend had chosen it for the education of her young children. The roads and houses are much like those of Bombay. We were all tired, and after an early supper retired to rest.

When I got up in the morning, I found that my friend had got breakfast ready, so after a sisterly kiss we sat down to table. The professor dropped in and joined us, and afterwards a lady from Bombay, who had known me when she held the post of Superintendent of the Alexandra Native Girls' English Institute, came in too and we had a great deal of interesting conversation. In the evening we took a drive through the town.

When we got home I found to my great joy that the children had arrived. They had been given to understand that their mother's brother and sister had come to see them, and in this expectation they came bouncing up to us, but stopped abruptly on seeing my strange dress. Their mother reassured them, and they then embraced and affectionately kissed me, so that I felt almost as much satisfied as if their lamented father, our esteemed friend, stood before us. We all sat down together to dinner and in one hour these sweet children, a boy and two girls of tender years, had become so familiar with me that we could scarcely separate when bedtime came.

The whole of the next day was spent in the children's company, and in the evening we dined at the Professor's where I made the acquaintance of the Misses Allan-Olney, who were much interested in my nationality. Next day these ladies called and received my photograph. At the happy suggestion of my dearest friend, she and her children, my son and I went and had ourselves photographed in a group, as a souvenir of my visit. I had with me a set of Delhi ornaments which Mrs Ahlers accepted and wore on this occasion. This day being the anniversary of the battle of Sédan, the town was gaily decorated and everybody kept a holiday. In the evening I went with my friend to a small party. On the 4th we had a delightful excursion to the Drachenfels or Dragonrock, one of the Seven Mountains, about half an hour's journey from Bonn, and on the 5th after breakfast, I went to have my photograph taken. The photographer here, like his brethren of London and Paris, begged to be allowed to take a life-size portrait for himself, the singularity of my dress making me an interesting subject to him and his fraternity.

The next day we were ready for departure. As the time for parting drew nigh, we grew very sad; and I was loath to leave the congenial company of my friend and her children, but I drew consolation from the resolve that, if God were to spare my life, I would return and make her house my home.

XXXI

From Tardeo to Bhandoop in Europe!

On the morning of 7th September, we all sat down together for the last time to an early breakfast, the children pressing round me and crying, "Aunty, don't go to your own country and leave us." I felt parting from them as keenly as if I were tearing myself away from my own family. Afterwards we went to the station accompanied by the good old Professor, whom I warmly thanked for his kindness and hospitality. Taking a tender farewell of my friend and her children, my son and I entered the train and were carried away from the good town of Bonn, the little friendly group standing on the platform waving caps and handkerchiefs to us till we were out of sight.

At Mayence we were met by a servant of Monsieur Knoop's and a couple of landaus had been sent to convey us and our luggage to that gentleman's house at Wiesbaden, about an hour's distance. The roads and two-storeyed houses here bore a strong resemblance to those of Bombay, the whole drive reminding me strongly of my trip from Tardeo to Bhandoop! At about 11 a.m. the carriage drew up under the portico of a handsome bungalow, very similar to Sir Albert Sassoon's "Sans Souci" at Bombay. I was received by Mme. Knoop's daughter-in-law. Presently Mme. Knoop herself came and shaking me warmly by the hand, expressed her pleasure at seeing me, led me to the saloon and presented to me her husband, a venerable looking gentleman, their only daughter and their three sons. After a few kind inquiries about my health and the journey, Mme. Knoop took me to select for myself whatever suite of rooms I preferred; but I told her that my stay would only be of a few hours' duration. I had seen enough of the grandeur of Europe, and it was only for the purpose of making their acquaintance and of conversing on some business matters that I had intruded upon their hospitality. When tiffin was announced, Monseiur Knoop led me in on his arm, and I had the pleasure of seeing at the table, Mr Muller, late partner of Messrs Knoop & Co., who had, in company with Mr Ahlers, often visited me at my house in Bombay. After an interval of twelve years we met here quite unexpectedly and we mutually expressed joy at seeing each other again. Mr Muller said: "You have not changed in the least, except that you have not got the large nose-ring pendant from your nose which I used to see before." He had been a guest at my children's weddings, where he had observed me wear this ornament, then in general use amongst Parsee women but now brought into disuse by time and fashion. After tiffin Madame Knoop took me over the whole house, furnished with regal splendour. Monsieur Knoop is an influential and highly-respected citizen of Wiesbaden, and it is said that the Emperor William once honoured this palatial residence with his presence.

At five o'clock we took a drive. As we drove along, the people betrayed by their looks their astonishment and curiosity at my appearance. After looking at everything and enjoying the scenery we got back to M. Knoop's. I sat down to talk about my husband's connection with M. Knoop's firm in Bombay. After a patient hearing of what I had to say, the kind-hearted M. Knoop said: "If that is all, I will direct my son to write to our Bombay house advising them to accept your guarantee in place of your brother's." After supper we took our leave of his charming family with whom in the space of a few hours a most friendly footing had been established. In parting they all presented me with their photographs, and Monsieur and Madame Knoop instructed their servants to assist us at the station and see us safely off. I, in return, blessed them for their kindness and hospitality and bade them farewell. The long drive back to Mayence was most enjoyable, the beautiful verdant landscape being illumined by a flood of argent moonlight. We left Mayence at 10 p.m. and reached Bâle at daybreak.

We found that we had missed the early train, so, to turn the time to account, we hired a carriage and drove off to view the town. It is simply a pretty place of ordinary type, nothing grand or striking about it. At 10 a.m., we again seated ourselves in the train and at 3 p.m., arrived at Constance, where I found my old friend, first known as Mrs Geo Volkart, now Mme. Amman with her step-son, waiting for me at the station. Eighteen years had elapsed since we last met, but she had the same handsome healthy appearance as of old, and I was rejoiced at seeing her again, and in good circumstances. We drove in her carriage to a villa on the lake.

This lake, in extent like a sea, is very beautiful, with the cool breezes fanning its bosom, and the verdure all around backed by the hoary mountains. We—Mme. Amman and I—had much to say to each other of all that had happened to us since we had last chatted together. Her husband had gone to Winterthur and was to return in a week and she looked forward with pleasure to my meeting him; however, I informed her that I could only be her guest for one day. In the evening we sat on the balcony enjoying the scenery, the villa being built on the very margin of the lake. As this was a national holiday the lake was covered with pleasure boats and delicious strains of music were wafted to our ears over the glassy surface of the waters.

Fatigued with travel and pleasure, I retired early to rest, my good friend having prepared special accommodation for my comfort. When I rose next morning and looked out the house appeared as it were to be standing in the middle of a sea; indeed, the different aspect of the lake at different times was curious and interesting.

After breakfast I narrated to Mme. Amman my travels in India and Europe; she listened to them with unfeigned surprise, for she had remained sufficiently long in Bombay to know the timidity of the Parsees and their retiring disposition, and though she had often met me in English society, she had never heard from my lips how ardently I desired to visit England. We went into the town of Constance to see Mme. Amman's winter residence, a spacious, handsomely furnished house with all the studied comforts and luxuries I had seen at M. Knoop's. Returning to the villa we sat down to dinner, after which young Mr Amman took his leave as he was going to Winterthur to join his father. He begged me and my son to accompany him, assuring me that the Volkart family at Winterthur would bitterly regret not seeing me, but as my time was limited and I had a longing to see Rome, I resolved to prosecute my journey without further delay.

I should have liked to see the original of the large oil painting presented to us in 1867 by Mr Volkart which hangs in my drawing-room at Bombay and which is said to be a faithful portrait of the worthy gentleman and I regretted having lost the opportunity, but my regret was the less as I looked forward to the day when I would start on a tour through Europe accompanied by my dear partner in life and together visit the people and places we had, all our lives, felt interested in. In the afternoon my son and I started on a return journey to Bâle—both in going and returning we had a glimpse from the train of the falls of the Rhine at Schaffhausen.

The scenery of Lake Constance and the River Rhine was romantic in the extreme. I was particularly struck with the abundance and luxuriant growth of the Aracaria trees, so rare and scanty in Bombay as to fetch fancy prices; their verdant appearance on both sides of the Rhine still lives in my memory. We reached Bâle again at 9 p.m., and crossing a beautiful bridge over the Rhine, arrived at the Hotel Schweizerhof, where we got pleasant rooms on the first floor.

Next morning we took train for Geneva. The entire journey was through romantic mountain scenery, the railway verging on the mountain base and sometimes winding in a serpentine course over it, appeared to us much like the line over the Bhore Ghauts. We reached Geneva, the most beautiful city of Switzerland, the land of beauty, at 2 p.m. and after depositing our luggage at Pension Windsor, hired a conveyance for a drive through the city. Having seen all the interesting places and objects we left Geneva at 10 p.m.

The great comfort of travelling in first class is that you generally have the whole compartment to yourself. On this occasion, however, a male passenger entered our carriage and he was so intoxicated that we feared a disturbance, for, notwithstanding the remonstrances of my son, he persisted in sitting close to us. At the next station we complained of him and the station master had him removed. During all my travels I was not a day sick or indisposed, for which I offer silent but heartfelt thanks to God the Giver of all mercies. We reached Modena early in the next morning, having passed through what was then the largest tunnel in the world—the Mont Cenis Tunnel—which took half an hour to traverse; we saw thousands of workmen working here by torchlight. From here we took another train and reached Turin at nine o'clock where there was a stoppage of an hour and where we had our breakfast. We passed in the course of the day many cities of note and antiquity, such as Parma, Bologna (the oldest Italian university), Ravenna, etc.; the bird's-eye-view got from the train was enchanting and made me long to see this land better. At 9 p.m. we reached Florence—"the Beautiful"—the station was splendid and filled with a concourse of people. We had our supper in the refreshment room, which was as large and as brilliantly lighted as a palace or the best Parisian hotel. Then stepping into the train again, we resumed our journey to Rome.

XXXII

Rome—The Mistress of the Ancient World

At day-break of 12th September we reached Rome, the capital of Italy, immortalised in the history of the ancient world. Seeing crowds of people at the station, I apprehended much difficulty, as I was in a strange land, not conversant with its language and without a friend to help me, but everyone was polite and I showed my card of recommendation for the Anglo-American Hotel, with which I had been provided in London, and drove thither. Here I was well received by the manager, and a handsome well-furnished apartment on the first floor, for which the terms were extremely moderate, was allotted me. After a refreshing bath and a good breakfast my son and I were setting off to view the city when the manager of the hotel advised me to hire a guide, and that too one who could speak English, as otherwise I might miss the most notable sights. This I accordingly did, and at nine o'clock we started with our guide whose charge was at the rate of Rs 5 a day. I gazed with awe and admiration on the architectural glories of a former age now crumbling to decay but magnificent even in their ruins.

Our guide took us from one celebrated pile to another, giving us an outline of the history of each which I noted down in pencil. Thus we saw the walls and gates of Rome, the Arch of Titus, the Arch of Constantine, the Pantheon, the Basilica of St Lateran, the Museum, the Colosseum, the Temple of Venus, the Theatre of Marcellus, the Forum, the Sancta Scala, St Pietro Vinculi, the Column of Constantine, the Palace of the Caesars, Trajan's column, and many statues, arches and fountains. The gardens are in many instances now rank wildernesses overgrown with weeds. Proceeding beyond the fort we approached the church of St Paul, which, as seen from outside, presents no special feature except that of its height and solitary position. On alighting from our carriage, I noticed a great many poor people about the doors, asking alms, just as our Parsee poor do around our Fire-temples. Further along we were met by officious priests who saluted and made way for us, but on receiving a friendly hint from my guide that these civilities would have to be paid for, we thanked them and went on by ourselves. Entering the noble doorway what a splendid sight burst upon my gaze! The whole of the grand hall was paved with highly polished blocks of marble, some thousands in number, and each of them larger than could be procured elsewhere; these slabs of marble were either painted or arranged so as to represent the white billows of the ocean. Lifting our eyes to the ceiling we were again lost in admiration, for there the limner's art had produced a masterpiece, representing a crown, supported by aerial creatures of wondrous beauty and grace. High up in niches in the wall, life-sized statues of the Popes stood, giving evidence of the perfection to which the art of sculpture was brought in remote ages.

As in our Fire-temples, large recesses in the walls were provided with candles, so huge as to resemble small pillars of marble. We have been so fortunate as to have seen many noble buildings, but none at all comparable to this magnificent church—all others pale before it as the moon before the sun, and it is no exaggeration to say that if anything on earth can illustrate the sublime beauty of Paradise it surely must be this wonderful place. It has, however, been so frequently described by abler pens than mine, that any further praise would be like gilding gold or painting the lily: sufficient it is for me to say that this edifice is in my estimation the acme of architectural perfection.

Returning homewards, I saw the ruins of a mighty amphitheatre built by the Romans about 2,500 years ago and known as the theatre of Marcellus. After seeing other interesting memorials of past ages we threaded our way back to the hotel through narrow streets like those in the villages around Bombay. After an hour's rest we started again with our guide. We were now to see St Peter's Cathedral, the most famous church in the world. I found that in grandeur and sublimity St Peter's was equal to St Paul's. As with us there are small Fire-temples, called "agiaries," within the principal temple or Atashbehram, so there were many subsidiary chapels in St Peter's Cathedral. The enormous dome took many years in building; its dimensions though large are elegant. If I might be allowed a comparison between what is humble and insignificant and what is unparalleled, my readers might glean an idea of this celebrated church by imagining the Town Hall of Bombay magnified a thousand times and the whole Elphinstone Circle and the Garden stretching around it converted into a marble pavement. We next went to see the Vatican, the palace of the Pope, which adjoins the Cathedral. The picture-gallery is the most celebrated in the world, as it contains the masterpieces of the ancient Roman painters, the models from which artists of all future ages have studied their art. While walking here, we were met by Cardinal Macchi who entered into conversation with me, asking about my parentage, caste and religion. He spoke in favour of the Zoroastrian faith.

I expressed my ardent desire to see His Holiness the Pope, whereupon he said that the Holy Father could be seen every fortnight when presiding at a congregation, but as the last one had taken place only the day before, it would be thirteen days before the next opportunity of seeing him would occur.

"My stay here," I replied, "will not be more than two days as I have merely come to see the most celebrated city and the finest churches in the world."

The Cardinal seemed pleased at this and asked if I was really very anxious to see the Holy Father, to which I replied in the affirmative. We then parted and my son and I went to the summit of the hill Janiculum which commands a panoramic view of the city and the surrounding country. Rome is enclosed by a wall and well-fortified. From thence we strolled through the extensive Borghese Gardens, then along the banks of the Tiber and through the public thoroughfares, reaching our hotel at 7 p.m.

XXXIII

My Visit to His Holiness The Pope

Returning to the Hotel from my morning drive, I found a note waiting for me. My guide read it, as it was in Italian, and expressed his astonishment, for it was from Pope Leo XIII himself who, hearing from Cardinal Macchi of my very great desire to see him, asked me to come at four o'clock that afternoon, when he would grant me an interview and give me his blessing. My acquaintances at the Hotel congratulated me on this unexpected honour, as it was known that His Holiness only accorded an audience to those who made a written application for it, which, however, was at the option of the Pope to grant or refuse. This gracious invitation threw me into a dilemma, as all my best suits were packed up and sent to Brindisi and I was here with only ordinary things suitable for travelling.

To appear before a personage more eminent even than an Emperor in such everyday clothes would be humiliating, and I therefore directed my guide to go to Cardinal Macchi and ask whether it would not be deemed an insult to appear at the audience in such a dress as he had seen me in yesterday, but his reply dispelled all my fears. I put on all my ornaments, for I carried them about with me wherever I went, and carefully concealed them under my saree, so that even the guide who went with us could not have guessed that I wore them.

When we drove to the Vatican, we were conducted up a noble flight of stairs to the first landing where two sentinels in full military uniform were stationed. Here I was met by a priest, who spoke English, and who after congratulating me on the distinguished honour conferred upon me by His Holiness, began to initiate me into the etiquette to be observed at the interview. On hearing that I should have to kiss the Pope's toe I expressed my objection, for though right and fitting to pay due homage to one whom God has raised to such a high position, such an act as kissing one's toe would be considered sinful by the Parsees, one of our rules being that "if the hand comes inadvertently in contact with the toes it is polluted and must be washed clean." I told this to the priest and added—"Very minute are the observances enjoined by my religion and I always hold them in high esteem," and approving of what I said in justification of my objections he led me through the palace.

Every room or landing was guarded by two soldiers, and after passing through six or seven we reached a magnificent hall where I was told to sit down. This room and the furniture it contained were all of uniform colour—bright red—and the guards who patrolled here were dressed even to their boots in the same flaming hue.

Presently the priest returned, and requested me to kneel down on receiving the Pope's benediction and to kiss the fingers of his hand which he would extend to me instead of his foot. He then brought me to another hall painted and furnished entirely in milk-white colour; here I saw a venerable person of angelic appearance coming towards us at a slow measured pace. At sight of this thrice holy man we dropped on our knees and made humble obeisance which he graciously acknowledged. At that moment I felt such ecstatic joy as could not be described—what I suppose one would experience in converse with a prophet or being of another world.

The Holy Father had the majesty and winning mildness of aspect which we attribute to angels, surely beloved of God must he be to be exalted so high above his fellow-men! He wore white robes and had a white cap upon his head. His dress exactly resembled that which we Parsees prepare on a death anniversary for our departed, and for the first time I saw it on the person of a living man. The Pope wore no flowing beard to enhance the majesty of his well-proportioned form.

In a clear melodious voice he poured his benedictions upon me and my son, after which he condescended to converse with me.

Our conversation was carried on by the Cardinal interpreting for us, and the following is the substance of it. After placing his blessed hand on my head he said: "May you live long and be firm in your faith whereby all your best aspirations will be fulfilled." I humbly requested him to transfer the first part of his blessing—the long life—to my son who was with me and whom he had mistaken for my husband. Taking out my watch and showing him the beautifully enamelled portraits of my dear husband and daughter on its lids I besought him to bless them with long life and vouchsafe to me the blessing of closing my eyes while these—my all-in-all—should be in the full enjoyment of health and happiness. With a smile beaming on his heavenly countenance he blessed me in these words: "May God fulfil your best wishes and may you reap manifold advantages from your long and arduous travels when you shall have reached your own shores in peace and safety."

"Pray hand me your card," he said, "that I may remember you in my prayers and invoke the assistance of God on your every laudable undertaking." He continued: "You must assuredly have been much pleased with the beautiful churches of St Peter and St Paul," whereupon I respectfully informed him of my having seen both these celebrated buildings of which the imposing appearance would ever live fresh in my memory and the few days spent in Rome would rank amongst the happiest of my life. He then asked me to stay for a month when his Cardinal would introduce me to the reigning Sovereign of Italy. Gratifying as this gracious proposal was, I had to decline it as my stay in the Eternal City could not be prolonged.

"The great honour you have done me," I supplicatingly said, "by this interview has made such a deep and grave impression on my mind, akin to what we mortals feel when holding discourse with an angel that I am under a debt of the greatest gratitude to Your Holiness. Believing you to be an emissary of God, I invoke your blessing on me."

On hearing this, the Holy man said: "God always helps the righteous. My heartfelt benedictions be ever on your head." I further informed His Holiness that I had at first only intended to stay but two days in that imperial city, but having been favoured by an interview with such an exalted, estimable and worthy potentate as His Holiness,

I had resolved to stay a few days longer, though all my luggage having been sent off to Brindisi, I had taken the liberty to appear in his august and holy presence in my ordinary garb.

"Is there then any other sort of dress in use among you than what I see?" Hereupon I produced my photograph and explained to him that though the fashion of the dress always remains the same, we wear a more elaborate and costly dress on festive occasions or when paying a visit. I then asked if His Holiness would be pleased to keep the photograph in his majestic palace and he, with much pleasure, ordered his Cardinal to take the picture, as the Pope never accepts anything but through one of his Cardinals. Our conversation lasted for about an hour, then I took my leave enriched by his many benedictions.

On the 14th after tiffin we went to see the King's palace. As King Victor Emmanuel was away on a tour through his dominions, I was permitted to enter without much ado.

Leaving Rome at 11 p.m., at daybreak we reached Cazerta, which is at an hour's journey from Naples, but to see this city, second only to Rome I should have had to cancel my through ticket to Brindisi. This I did not feel inclined to do and therefore continued my journey through the fruit-growing district of Italy and reached Brindisi the following morning. Here I found young Mr Amman waiting for me, as he also was going to India by the mail.

My tour in Europe was now brought to a close and I longed to see my dear husband, daughter and son in Bombay, but I was grieved to part from my eldest son who had been my constant companion in my journeys and who was now going back to London to complete his professional studies. I had to silence my scruples and solicitude by the thought that the separation was necessary for his future welfare in life.

I embarked on board the P&O Steamer *Ceylon*, and passed the first two days in melancholy loneliness, but after that, I began to mix with my fellow-passengers who were very agreeable and jovial. On the 4th day we reached Alexandria at an early hour of the morning, and I went ashore with Mr Amman and two other young gentlemen. The town bears a euphonious high-sounding name reminding us of the great conqueror who, in ages gone by governed the whole known world, but yet squalor and dirt prevail here. In the evening we started from the

Alexandria Railway Station, and the next morning reached Suez where the steamer *Geelong* was waiting for us.

The 20th of September was an auspicious day—the New Year's Day of the Parsees. Our steamer left Suez as soon as the passengers were on board. The weather in the Red Sea was extremely sultry, in consequence of which the passengers slept on deck. I could not do so and was nearly roasted alive in my cabin much to the detriment of my health. However, the company on board was refined and agreeable, and as some of the passengers were good vocalists the time passed smoothly along. A lottery was started to which each subscriber contributed Rs 5. About Rs 125 were collected, and much to the surprise of myself and everybody else, this sum fell to my lot. During all my travels I had not lost anything, save a small diamond from an ear-ring worth about fifty rupees, which I had lost a few days before in this steamer. Although I did not care much for the paltry loss, I was uneasy as it took place at the termination of my journey, and as I thought that it prognosticated evil, but the loss of the diamond was made up, over and above, by this fortunate windfall for which my grateful thanks are due to Him who cares for us all. We reached Aden on the 25th, but I did not go on shore.

On 3rd October about 3 p.m. the steamer anchored in Bombay harbour. My husband, whom I had apprised of my arrival by telegram from Aden, had been most uneasy at the protracted delay caused by an accident on our way from Aden to Bombay and now he with my second son came on board and heartfelt was our joy at meeting again and finding each other safe and well. Shaking hands with the Captain and all our fellow-passengers, I bade adieu to the *Geelong* and drove to my residence at Tardeo, where alas! sorrows and apprehensions awaited me instead of the peace and joy which had till now reigned there.

XXXIV

Some Vicissitudes of Indian Life

While in Paris I had heard much from the friendly and hospitable Americans sojourning in the Hotel about the grandeur of their country and had resolved to go home and settle my husband's business matters and then start for America. With this in view I had written asking my husband to seek out a tenant for our bungalow, and on my arrival I found that Mr Vincent, the Deputy Commissioner of Police, was in treaty for it, and wished to take it upon a long lease. I next desired my husband to relinquish his business, to pay off whatever he might be owing, and to collect any money due to himself.

On the day after my arrival Mr Vincent came over to our place to settle about the bungalow. He even consented to our retaining possession of a small bungalow within the compound, into which we accordingly moved.

On setting out from Bombay I had not been able to see my good friend, Lady Staveley, wife of the Commander-in-Chief, as she was then at Matheran, but when I returned to Bombay she kindly came to pay me a visit as she was about to start by the mail of 8th October. I was unfortunately not at home. The cause of my absence was that one of my cousins had just died in England, and the sad news had just been telegraphed to his relatives to whom I had gone on a visit of condolence. I could not see this cousin of mine when in England, although he had written expressing his earnest desire that I should do so, and now I was doubly grieved at my neglect. On returning I learnt of Lady Staveley's visit which I returned next day when we were mutually pleased to meet again. Through Lady Staveley I had formed the friendship of Admiral and Mrs Corbett, whose guest I was at the ball on the man-of-war "Euryalus."

As soon as we were settled in the small bungalow, I urged my husband to expedite the closing of all his accounts so that we might start for America at an early date—but "man proposes and God disposes"—I was not able to start for many years.

My mother, who had been suffering for ten years from a chronic malady, became very ill at this time, but I never thought that this illness might prove her last. But so, alas, it was, and she died without my either going to see her or having her removed to my place. My grief at the sad death of my mother was mingled with vain regrets; for two months following her death I did not stir out.

Preparatory to our departure for America I resolved to sell off the entire household effects including carriages, horses and even clothing, and to let the two bungalows. As on the former occasion when I was going to Delhi, my friends were again put on a wrong scent by our giving out that we were going to the Nilgiris for four years. Natives of India are opposed to the idea of selling household furniture, regarding it as an ill-omen, but I had no hesitation in disposing of our old wares to substitute new ones when required. After this I had to go through a series of domestic troubles brought about by the hostile conduct of my brother, and I for a time kept aloof from all social pleasure. About this time my daughter's only daughter was invested with the sacred girdle and thread, but grief lay heavy at my heart, and so I was not present at the interesting ceremony. For the same reason I declined an invitation to the opening ceremony of the new Prince's Dock and another to an evening party at Government House. Shortly afterwards Lord Ripon arrived in Bombay as Governor-General of India and his arrival was the occasion of another gay time. Lord and Lady Lytton also soon arrived in Bombay en route to England, and I was favoured by a card of admittance to the Dockyard to see their Excellencies embark and wish them "God-speed." On seeing me there Lord and Lady Lytton came up, and with great cordiality shook hands expressing their pleasure at seeing me again. I asked permission to introduce my husband to his Lordship, to which he warmly assented.

From the year 1879, I went on gradually liquidating my husband's debts, and in so doing, though it cost me the large sum of one hundred thousand rupees, I felt much satisfaction. To do this I had to refrain from every luxury and amusement, but this caused me no pangs and I was recompensed by the fact that my husband's credit amongst his commercial friends suffered not the least diminution. Thus out of my own private property I purchased my husband's freedom, and I was loath to allow him to embark on any business again. I could not, however, have entire control so as to prevent him now and again from seeing his friends and old business colleagues.

Having been all his life accustomed to activity he could not endure being thus cooped up, so one day without a word of intimation to me or anyone else (as I thought) he disappeared from Bombay. I leave my readers to judge of the uneasiness I felt when I did not find him at home as usual in the evening. He had gone to Rawal Pindee, a journey of six days by rail and tonga. I at once started for Rawal Pindee with but one attendant, and after a long and perilous journey reached my destination, where to my great satisfaction I at last found my husband.

The first thing I asked him was whether he intended to return home with me to Bombay or remain where he was, to which he replied that his desire was to open fresh negotiation with his old acquaintances, the merchants of Peshawar, Kabul and Cashmere, and that I could stay with him for some months. Thereupon I expressed my fixed resolution never to allow him to enter into any sort of business in my life-time. Old Mr Dossabhoy, the Chief Manager of my late father-in law's firm and a man full of the experience of seventy-five years, concurred with me fully and persuaded my husband to go back with me, and finding that I had no wish to stay another hour at Rawal Pindee, he prepared for starting and expressed regret at my having undergone so much trouble for his sake. Thus my husband returned with me to Bombay and I little felt the fatigue of the journey when the object with which it was undertaken was fully attained.

Thus once more restored to ease I resumed my social pleasures and was present at several balls and parties at Government House. I was also present with my husband and son at the ball given by General Warre at his residence where I had the honour of being presented by our host to Lord Ripon who shook hands with me and expressed his pleasure at seeing us there. I had again the good fortune of meeting Lord Ripon at the Government House the very next day when that noble personage at once recognising me shook hands with me. Those who are truly noble, by their considerate kindness, add grace to the title they bear. At this moment, I recalled the blessings poured upon me by His Holiness the Pope: they were now partly fulfilled.

The Rajah of Chota Udepur wanted to receive Sir James Fergusson, and for this purpose he requested me to place the hall of our bungalow at his disposal for two hours, and I most readily complied with the request. The reception took place at 4 p.m. The Rajah did not understand English and thus the necessity of an interpreter having arisen I was requested to act as one, which I willingly did. In the meantime, my husband arrived and I craved permission to present him to Sir James, which he kindly accorded. After the reception was over, the Rajah and his wives, who had also come there, heartily thanked me for the convenience I had afforded them and went away pleased with me.

Some months after this I was present at an Evening Party at the Government House, when the late Lady Fergusson, who sat beside me, much admired the border of my saree. I told her it was my own work, and requested permission to embroider a cap for her little son. She kindly granted the permission and I forthwith commenced the work and presented the cap with my own hands, and Lady Fergusson accepted it with great pleasure.

This interesting episode had an unpleasant sequel. My progressive attitude and social successes had created many enemies. Such is unfortunately the tendency of jealous human nature. Those most against me were my own relatives. To them and to their coterie I was a *bête-noire* to be put down by any means. My brothers, with whom I had heavy litigation, took a leading part in the misrepresentations that followed. The cap was returned by the Private Secretary to H.E. the Governor. In his forwarding letter, dated 15th July 1881, he stated that Lady Fergusson, while sensible of my intended kindness in making this friendly present, regretted that, as she had since the presentation ascertained from experts that the article was one of considerable value, she was precluded from retaining it, as being contrary to established usage. Much as I felt the incident, I have under God's grace lived to the discomfiture of my illwishers, to be honoured in a much higher sphere, *viz.*, at the hands of our late Sovereign himself, and his consort the queen-mother Alexandra.

Thus I was leading an easy life after clearing off my husband's liabilities and was fully enjoying social pleasures. But this easy life was not to run long. Very soon I had the misfortune of finding myself entangled in law suits of the most complicated nature, my opponent being none else than my own brothers, who had on several occasions been the cause of my uneasiness. It is impossible to describe the worry and expense I was put to in this protracted litigation. Suffice it to say that no man of ordinary courage would have survived it, much less one of the weaker sex. In such suits attorney's bills run to large figures, and I would warn my readers against placing themselves implicitly in the hands of attorneys whose bills in many cases far exceed the expectation of their clients.

It has several times been my good fortune to recover lost jewels after all hope for their recovery was given up. Such things are but of rare occurrence, and can only be attributed to special Divine favour, of which I have very often been a recipient. The misfortunes of persons walking in the right path and doing what is most welcome to the Giver of all mercies, are shortlived and are very soon followed by circumstances which not only make one forget the pain of unfavourable times, but prove productive of greater pleasure than what would be otherwise experienced. I would not have felt that happiness in getting new jewels without any cost which I felt when I recovered my lost jewels, which not only brought with them their secular value but also a part of Divine mercy which gives us all the greater pleasure and inspires us all the more to admire the unfathomable actions of that Supreme Being. I always think it my first duty to offer my humble prayers to Him and do what would best please Him.

Were the pleasures of human life unmingled with sorrows and calamities the existence of that Omnipotent Power would have remained in obscurity. But His ruthless and at the same time merciful hand works without intermission to keep the frail creatures of this mortal world alive to the sense of their duty. For a time I had to shut myself from all social pleasures owing to the pecuniary embarrassments of my husband, and I gradually found my way to relieve him from all his liabilities and began again to go my old ways, hardly knowing that difficulties were awaiting me at no great distance. My daughter, who had all the time been most obedient and respectful to me, began under evil influence to assume a most supercilious attitude towards me. She being my only daughter I had allowed her every indulgence which a fond mother could be supposed to bestow on her children, and had loved her more than I loved my sons. I therefore felt extreme grief at heart when she turned a deaf ear to my good advice and openly offered me insult. Soon after this unhappy breach between us, her husband went to England to carry on business once again and there he opened the firm of Messrs Cama Bros. After some months she also left for England with her children, but after a few months returned to Bombay under medical advice. During her stay in Bombay she lived at her friend's house against our wish. After four months she returned to her husband without even seeing me or listening to my advice.

After my daughter's departure for England, my mind was not quite at rest for many months. The crow is supposed by the Indians to be a bird of ill-omen, and I was not long in realising that the belief was not quite unfounded. Once I was actually scared out of my wits by the terrible screech of a crow, and I expected to hear some very bad news. The whole of my body began to shake through vague undefined fears and alas! I soon found the prophecy fulfilled. I had the misfortune to receive the sad news of my dear son-in-law's death at Devos-Platz in Switzerland, on 2nd January 1884, separated from his friends and relatives. I deeply felt this bereavement, for to me my dear departed son-in-law was far more beloved than my own daughter. What grieved me more was that he died in a place where there was no one to perform the necessary funeral rites enjoined by our religion. After some time my daughter returned to Bombay with her three grown-up children and I went to the Apollo Bunder to receive her, but even after the sad bereavement she had undergone she bore the same stubborn attitude towards me as before. What could a mother do under such circumstances but pray for her health and happiness.

My daughter also bade adieu to this world at Bandra on 26th

January 1890. It is needless to add that her death was another heavy blow to me. In her last illness I went to Bandra only to find her unconscious and after a few hours she breathed her last. Her remains were brought to Bombay at her dwelling house at Cumballa Hill where her funeral ceremony was performed with all religious formalities.

XXXV

My Husband's Life and Career

Much of the remaining portion of this work will be devoted to an account of my tour round the world. With what spiritual gratification would I have penned it had Providence fulfilled my long cherished desire to make that tour in the company of the beloved partner of my life! While enjoying the beauties of nature in Europe during my visit to that Continent on the occasion of the Paris Exhibition, the thought of my husband not sharing my intellectual pleasures often troubled my mind, but I drew consolation from the prospect of my desire being realised at a future date. That consummation, alas! was not to be fulfilled. Difficulties of an insuperable nature intervened, and years passed before I could find myself in a position to undertake that expensive and enterprising journey. Before the achievement was made, my dear husband had bidden farewell to this mortal world. Posterity may do further justice to his noble memory, but I deem it my sacred duty to preserve in these pages a brief record of his life, in which the young generations of my community will find many useful hints that will prove of value in shaping their own careers.

Mr Cowasjee Jehangir Jessawalla was born on 15th May 1819, immediately after the establishment of British Rule in this part of the country. Even in those early days, he had received an English education which proved of the greatest use to him in the management of his father's firms, known in Northern India and Kabul, under the name of Messrs Jehangir & Co., which he was called upon to undertake as soon as he came of age. Travelling in those days was so very unsafe, troublesome and perilous that only a few could carry on and succeed in a business such as my husband conducted. But he did his duty with assiduity and intelligence which ensured the prosperity of the firms entrusted to his charge, and won for him the confidence of his father, who entrusted to him the sole management of the business. As already noticed, he was present at the Kabul war in 1839. He was instrumental in the establishment of several firms in Northern India, *viz.*, Peshawar, Rawal Pindee, Murree Hill, Sukkar, Mooltan, Lahore and last though not least in Kabul itself, for the purpose of providing the British Army with supplies. He was held in high respect by many British officers of the Army, and was on one occasion so far back as 1848 presented with a "Khillat" in the court of the Nawab of Bhawalpore. He was a thorough businessman, and played a most important part and enjoyed the widest confidence in the commercial sphere of Bombay. He was for several years closely connected with the leading paper of Bombay, *viz.*, *The Times of India*, and worked as a guarantee broker of the well-known European firm of Messrs Volkart Brothers for nearly 20 years, during which period he took a very active part in establishing many public companies such as the Bombay Native Insurance Company, the Bombay Oil Press Company, etc. He also had his own steamers running between Bombay and Kathiawar.

It is sad to notice that the Parsees of today do not pursue with the same vigour those maritime activities which my husband and other leaders of trade evinced in the early years of the nineteenth century. After leaving Messrs Volkart Brothers' firm, he was employed as a broker in the firm of Messrs Knoop & Company. About the year 1875 he was engaged with Mr Nolke, ex-manager of Messrs Volkart's firm in Bombay, in establishing a large cotton mill at Oomrawuttee—a scheme which did not, unfortunately, meet with success. His over-liberal nature often exposed him to be duped by self-interested persons, and had I not taken an active interest in his business affairs and helped him from time to time he would have been involved in endless difficulties.

For many years after my return from Europe our life was far

from happy. We had to grapple courageously with numerous serious difficulties. My husband had incurred heavy liabilities, and I had to clear them off with no other object in view than to see him happy. After this I had to defend myself and my husband against spurious claims in the courts of law, all of which I contested successfully. Finally my daughter's unfilial and wayward behaviour vitally wounded my peace of mind as well as that of my husband whilst her own death plunged us into indescribable grief. These misfortunes I patiently bore, never allowing outward appearance to betray the internal commotion lest my dear husband should give way in his declining age. But there is a limit to human life, and the hand of death works inexorably on the rich and the poor, the fallen and the righteous alike.

On the 4th of December 1900, at the patriarchal age of eighty-one, my husband left the busy scene of this life, leaving me, my sons and numerous other relatives to bemoan his loss. The extreme grief that I felt at heart can be better imagined than described. To an Indian wife there is no greater bereavement than that of losing her husband, and it was difficult to console my mind now that my beloved husband had passed into eternity never again to be seen by physical eyes. His soul left the terrestrial abode to choose a celestial residence, but the noble qualities of head and heart which had endeared him to all will never be obliterated from the minds of those who knew him.

To me he was a model of virtue and the personality of simplicity and artlessness, combined with complaisance and modesty of nature which made me love him all the more, and to look upon him as the inspirer of all that is good, noble and beautiful. It was through my having been gifted by the Almighty with the partnership of such an ideal husband that I was enabled to translate into action those great lessons which I had learnt at my mother's knees.

My reader will have seen that I was not long in realising the ideals of my girlhood. When I take a retrospective view of my life, I cannot but offer fervent prayers to God for having united me to a partner, who far from discouraging me in the least, paved the way for my doing what with the greatest satisfaction I am today putting before the world. But for all the facilities he gave me I could not have achieved the record of my life. What wife would not deeply feel the loss of such a partner even though he might have died a happy, natural death. My dear husband was all that could be desired, and it was no wonder that sorrow lay heavy at my heart.

The intensity of grief at last began to tell on my health, and I was advised to remove to a temperate climate for a change. I therefore went first to Cashmere and then to South India and although the beauties of nature and change of air had their effect in enlivening my depressed spirits for a time, that venerable image of purity and nobility was never for a moment absent from my heart, causing occasionally a renewal of grief which could not be mitigated except by the lapse of time. What else should I ask of the Giver of all mercies, but that eternal blessings should crown my beloved husband in heaven, and that he should inspire succeeding generations to tread in the virtuous path laid out by him, which alone will elevate their minds to nobler ends, and make them endure without regret the absence of the transitory pleasures of this world which are like gold-lacquer or their veneer superimposed upon the real aims and objects of life.

XXXVI

In Cashmere—The Venice of India

As I have already said, the loss of my dear husband was deeply felt by me and my dear sons, and the sudden bereavement so told upon my health that I was strongly advised to seek a change. On hearing of this my youngest step-son Dorabjee who had his business in Shrinagar (Cashmere) asked me to take a change to its salubrious climate.

In the company of my younger son, I left in the beginning of May for Rawal Pindee, where my step-son Dorabjee was staying with his family. It is a far cry from Bombay to Pindee, a distance of 1,500 miles and we were five consecutive nights in the train and four long weary days.

During my stay here for a week with my son and his family, I was visited by Khan Bahadur D.F. Commodore and his family as well as by several other Parsee families. I was gratified to see Mr Commodore in such affluent and prosperous circumstances. It was through his indefatigable zeal and industry that he rose to such a position. He went to Punjab first in our family's firm of Jehangir & Co. It was a source of satisfaction to me that he and his relations had full respect for members of his former master's family.

From Pindee I, in the company of my sons, proceeded by tonga to

Shrinagar, a drive of 200 miles, halting at Dak Bangalows at Murree, Baramulla, Dulai, Uri and other places. It was prohibited to travel by night after sunset. Though the journey was tiring, yet it was after all a pleasant drive through mountainous regions surrounded by lofty hills, and the wonderful riches of the gloriously coloured foliage and groves and avenues upon the banks of the vale of Cashmere.

The scenery is indescribable. The romances of Moore in the Lalla Rookh may be extravagant but after all few will deny that fiction is not surpassed by fact. Shrinagar is on an elevation of nearly 6,000 feet above sea-level, and our last day's drive opened fantastic views before our eyes. Before reaching Shrinagar we entered Poplar Avenue which was an [sic] unique sight to observe, as it resembled the long avenue of high-grown trees I saw at Windsor when going to the Mausoleum. Thank God we reached our destination safe and in good health. The place where I put up was a large building containing the business and residential quarters of my son and his partners carrying on their trade under the style and firm of Messrs Pestonjee & Son. It is situated on the river bank in the midst of the commercial part of the city. For a few days the weather was rainy, and we felt bitter cold and confined ourselves to our quarters. The change brought me and my sons great relief, and the climatic influences considerably improved my health. It is a pity that the cherished desire of my life to visit Cashmere was attained under such sad circumstances.

Shrinagar is called the Venice of India. I noticed that people for the most part were living in boats, and all the buildings were surrounded by water. Cashmere is under the benign reign of Maharajah Partap Singh, assisted by his able and learned Councillors. It is gratifying to observe that my own step-son as well as many other Parsees are flourishing as merchants, doing business under the special patronage of His Highness. As I came specially to recoup my health after my last bereavement, I did not feel inclined to move about freely as I wished to do. My sons, however, tried their utmost to appease my mind by taking me round the town now and then. Khan Bahadur Commodore's good-natured daughter Mrs Cama was so kind as to bring her own boat, and induce me often and often to accompany her to see the interesting sights of nature. It was so refreshing and tempting to move about in the various camping grounds—the Chenar Bagh, Shalimar

Bagh, the Munshi Bagh, etc., and also the well-known large lake, the Dal.

Days passed more quickly than might be expected. Visitors to Shrinagar used to frequent my son's firm, as he was doing the business of general merchants, and I had occasion to make acquaintances which enabled us to pass our time pleasantly. Here I had the good fortune to see the son of my friend Mr David Ezra, Mrs Ezra's grown up son, and he became so friendly with us, that we used to see each other very often and passed our time merrily by talking about the old customs of our respective nationalities. He was, indeed, so kind to me and my son, that he asked us to lunch and tea, and kept up his family's ties of friendship with us. I also had the pleasure of meeting here another good friend Mrs Solomon Sassoon of Bombay who came here with her children.

Although, education has been so freely introduced amongst the male sex in Cashmere that almost all the high officials from the Prime Minister downwards are men of great culture, yet it was disappointing to notice that education amongst the gentler sex had not made any advancement in such a well-refined State. This being the case I had not the opportunity of making the personal friendship of Cashmere ladies of the upper circle.

My son being familiar with the Royal Household expressed my wish to the Maharajah to pay our respects to His Highness and his Royal Ladies. But to my great surprise I was informed that the Royal Ladies had not returned from Jammu to Shrinagar. His Highness himself expressed his own willingness to see us at his Palace, and sent his own boat to escort us. On arriving at the Palace I was met by a Secretary who took us up by a flight of stairs from the landing place into the Grand Hall in the presence of His Highness. We found him seated on a white sheet of cloth spread out there. On seeing us he at once got up, and graciously receiving us, warmly shook hands with us, and ordered chairs to be brought for us, but paying due homage to his exalted position, we humbly declined to sit on chairs and asked to be allowed to take our seats on the same cloth where His Highness was sitting. He was dressed so plainly in white that it reminded me of His Holiness Pope Leo XIII, who was all simplicity and preferred not to display his high position. We were introduced to the high officials, amongst whom was his own brother, to whom also we subsequently paid a visit at his own palatial residence as he showed an inclination to see us.

During our conversation His Highness touched on many aspects of my career, since he had come to know about it from his Secretary. The first and foremost of his questions was what made me put on a black saree on such an occasion, whereupon I explained to him that since I became a widow I wore it as a sign of mourning out of respect for the memory of my dear departed husband, and His Highness and all his officials were highly gratified to find how devotedly I was following a time-honoured custom. The conversation then turned to my education, my travels and last but not least, on my ascent in the balloon. Then he enquired of me whether I had the same pluck and courage to repeat the feat again if he prepared a balloon at his own expense, to which I had to answer negatively with great reluctance on account of my old age. Then he referred to the autobiography I intended to publish which he said would greatly please him to read. My interview was, indeed, a very happy one and it lasted for more than an hour. I earnestly thanked His Highness for all his kindness, and on my leaving he offered a tray of leaves and betelnuts, etc., as the formal parting ceremony observed by the host to his guests. The Palace of the Maharajah looked very attractive and imposing from the river side.

Cashmere is celebrated for its costly and beautiful shawls. It is said that a few years ago nearly half the people of Shrinagar were shawl weavers. Shawl merchants, hearing of our arrival, visited our camp with specimens of their wares from which we purchased some shawls in memory of our visit to Cashmere.

Prices varied from ten rupees to a thousand rupees, such was the work we had the opportunity of witnessing on the spot where they were manufactured. Other shops worth visiting were of lacquer work, silverware, silk garments and ornamental painted woodwork. We ordered out silver tea-sets, bowls, frames, etc., and from a vast selection we bought various articles which we had packed and sent direct to Bombay.

We generally spent our evenings in boats across the Dal Lake, an immense stretch of water, covered in many places with great lotus leaves and pink blossoms. Cashmere is not a poor country for fruits and vegetables. Big baskets of yellow pears, peaches and grapes as well as cauliflowers, tomatoes and many other vegetables were brought to us at all times of the day for a few coppers. It is no doubt a land of ideal climate and of ideal scenery, where one might enjoy one's life upon a mere nothing in roaming over the Vale of Cashmere and its glorious mountains from April to November.

Another interesting sight well-worth visiting was the hill known as Solomon's Throne or "Takht-i-Suleman" wherefrom a beautiful panoramic view of the city can be had. The city is a somewhat confused mass of houses, overhanging either side of the river and the smaller canals, which in many places form the only streets. The wooden houses stained and weathered into rich tones of grey and brown, look remarkably picturesque with their balconies and carved windows. There are six or seven bridges across the river, built of beams laid on timber and stone piers. If Shrinagar had a little more gorgeous colouring it would be a second Venice. The beauty of women in Cashmere is none the less noticeable than that of the women of any European nation. One can compare it with Circassian beauty. The women are very simple in their dress, those of the middle class wearing only a white robe.

Another interesting place we were advised to visit here was "Islamabad." To proceed there we engaged one of those houseboats called "doongas" or "Kishtie" which we found in numbers in Cashmere. We left Shrinagar in the morning and were soon gliding between banks covered with evergreen trees. Our "doonga" was something like a house-boat, but too rough to be dignified by such a name. When it grew dark we passed several other doongas, the crew of some of them singing weird chants, of which they seemed to be very fond. Next morning we were at "Islamabad." Here we went to see two water-falls, and rowing in the river was, indeed, very delightful. The surrounding scenery surpassed many aspects we had come across, during our extensive travels in the East and West. We spent a week in the "doonga" and returned to Shrinagar after a pleasant change. One might easily spend a whole summer in this way on the Jhelum and its tributaries under the hospitable shade of a "doonga," making as many expeditions as one might fancy.

His Highness the Maharajah has founded a Charitable Hospital free to all comers, which was under the management of an able physician, Dr Mitra of Calcutta. The institution is worth visiting. During our stay here Dr Mitra and his family were very kind to us and often exchanged visits and invited us to tea now and again. The European quarters of Shrinagar are also very delightful. They are resorted to by a large number of visitors during the season.

After a stay of more than three months I left on 22nd August, bidding goodbye to my son Dorabjee, who had made my stay as comfortable in every way as a dutiful son should do, to his partners and to many other kind friends in Cashmere. We returned by the same route to Rawal Pindee *via* Baramulla and Murree Hill. We halted at Dulai and Uri on our way back. In my opinion no traveller in India should miss a visit to Cashmere and its environments. It is one of the most fascinating and beautiful places of resort, and the longer one stays there, the harder it is to leave, and the dearer it becomes to live in.

The drive was an uneventful one. As we were going down, the scenery, which was grander while coming to Baramulla, became less interesting. As we neared Rawal Pindee, we were hearing the last of the horn of the tonga-driver. On arriving at Rawal Pindee we were received by Khan Bahadur Dhunjibhoy and his family, and treated most hospitably. We spent a whole day in their company. He is a great mail as well as Government contractor. The establishment of his mail and passenger tongas with hundreds of ponies was shown over to us; the management was excellent and everything gave the appearance of perfect order.

Our host is a great landed proprietor, and I was taken to see a new bungalow which he had built for hire. It was a fine piece of architecture; I think the only one of its kind then in Pindee.

From Pindee I took train for Lahore where I halted at the residence of my husband's cousin, Mr Eduljee of Jamsetjee Son. It was no doubt a happy meeting after the first Delhi Durbar, on which occasion he had been good enough to give us every help and assistance. From Lahore I started after a day's rest for Agra, where I stayed for a day, as my son had not had a chance of seeing the Taj Mahal. I went with him once more after many years to see the fascinating Taj. As Lord Roberts wrote, "Go to Agra: the Taj alone is worth the journey."

Returning from the Taj, I took train and arrived in Bombay with my health improved and the grief caused by the loss of my husband somewhat soothed. Such are the vicissitudes of human life. I might have stayed away one or two months more, but this being the first year of my husband's death I had to perform the Muktad ceremony lasting for eighteen consecutive days. It has been thought that by performing this ceremony, the departed soul revisited this world and made home with the nearest and dearest ones.

XXXVII

My Travels in South India

In the year 1904 I had the misfortune to lose my only beloved granddaughter, Mrs J. R. Patell, who died of plague at the age of thirty-three years, leaving behind her one son and daughter to bemoan her loss. The calamity told so seriously upon my health that I was compelled to leave my home for a long change. Having been advised to avail myself of a cold climate I resolved to go to Ootacamund and the Nilgiri Hills. I started in the middle of October with my younger son and a servant for Madras.

After arriving at Raichur, the junction for the Madras Railway, we proceeded to Madras, which we reached in the early morning on the fourth day after sixty hours' travel by rail, a distance of about 800 miles from Bombay. On arriving at the Madras Station we were taken by a guide to a hotel which was close to the Municipal Office, where we stayed for two days, and then we shifted to Raipuram, a suitable neighbourhood for Parsees, of which we came to know on meeting some Parsee friends in Madras. The day after our arrival was a big Parsee Holiday. All the Parsees of Madras joined and held a dinner by subscription, and we, too, being asked to join in it, did not hesitate to do so.

The day was well-spent and we there had the chance of making the acquaintance of all those Parsees who gathered there at dinner. Many pleasant things were said of us by different speakers to which my son responded in adequate terms. We met such respected citizens as Mr Bhumgara, who had a large shop and Mr Clubwalla, a well-known property-holder, merchant and philanthropist. Mr Clubwalla invited me and my son to tea one day at his bungalow. His wife also was an amiable lady. They were living in English style and took delight in treating their friends hospitably. We were quite pleased with all they did for us and while parting thanked them warmly for all their kindness. They had a handsome looking son who I am sorry to say is now dead. Mr Clubwalla has built an "Agiary" (Fire-temple).

A fine drive from the Government House Gates leads to the Marina, the promenade of Madras. The Marina owes a good deal of its beauty to its surroundings. It is a favourite resort of Madras. It is always crowded in the evenings when the band plays, and much resembles the Back Bay of Bombay. Here a number of carriages and pedestrians can be seen, and the whole sight presents a fine aspect. We also used to take drives near the Custom House. It is flanked from one end to the other by some of the handsomest public buildings such as the Senate House, Law Courts, Chapank Palace, Government Presidency College, the Museum, Public Library, etc. It gives us some idea of what the Bombay Modikhana is. In the city there are splendid jewellery and other shops. The beautiful statues on the principal public roads and the buildings are also worthy of the capital of South India.

We were to proceed to the Nilgiri Hills from Bombay, but as our friend Mr Clubwalla strongly recommended us to visit Pondicherry before going to the Nilgiri Hills, we decided to go there as well. Madras has a high reputation all over India for having the biggest and best hospital in India—the General Hospital, including the Women's and Children's Hospital. The Lying-in-Hospital is another of the very best institutions that Madras can claim. We noticed that some of the roads had a magnificent avenue of banyan trees, for instance Mowbray Road leading from Royapettah to the Adyar. But generally most of the roads in the European Residential suburbs are exceedingly pretty. On passing through the public gardens we saw in front of the Secretariat a statue of Lord Cornwallis, erected in his memory for his successful campaign against Tipoo Sultan. Another splendid equestrian statue was that of Sir Thomas Munro. On the whole our stay here fully repaid our visit.

XXXVIII

Pondicherry—The Relic of an Unbuilt Empire

After a week's stay we bade adieu to our Madras friends. While going to Pondicherry we saw nothing attractive. Then we went through patches of broad green rice fields covered with water, with the reaping ploughman silently following his peaceful pursuit. In the distance we saw the blue Arcot Hills reminding us of the Deccan, but the frequent groves of palm trees bore testimony to our being very near the sea. The further we travelled the richer grew the soil.

At noon we arrived at Vellupuram junction, where we had to change carriages for Pondicherry, and after an hour's run the train drew up at a platform. Here we were surrounded by Customs Officials who took possession of our luggage and examined it with such scrutiny that not a single piece of cloth was left unturned. Soon afterwards we found ourselves passing rapidly through the main street in a "pousse-pousse." It is a sort of perambulator and one feels it as if one were wheeled down the street in the days of childhood. It is no doubt a comfortable conveyance, it makes no noise, and it is swift but safe. Horse conveyances are almost absent here and the noiseless traffic is one of the charms of the French capital. It is said about the "pousse-pousse" man that "he neither shies nor kicks nor jibs." After a short drive we found ourselves in Sooboo's Hotel which was worthy to be compared with a mansion in any European city. The fare was very modest, and we were fed far better than at any of the Indian Hotels.

Pondicherry can well be called paradise for a poor man. The projected balconies gave a picturesque aspect to the streets. The city with its architectural buildings is worthy to be called a town of the French republic. We found everything on a moderate scale, and so were the salaries of high officials. It is a pleasant little port, with a few attractive buildings. The next day we went round about the town, passing the long avenues of high grown trees. In the evening after a short rest we left the hotel and walking a few yards came to the Place-de-la-Republique where on a pedestal stands the statue of Dupleix, the great French General.

A few yards from the statue is the Government House, and on the other side there is a public bandstand where people enjoy their evening stroll, while the band discourses music. It is said that the founder of the Mahratta Empire, the famous Shiwajee, was born at Gingee, a place close to Pondicherry. We have many legendary stories of the Generals of olden time fighting hand to hand in Southern parts of India to establish the supremacy of their respective powers—the French, the Dutch, the English and the Mahrattas. It is said by an English author that Pondicherry was like a football, kicked about from the French to the Dutch, from the Dutch to the French and during the scrimmage between the French and the English.

This is a nice, quiet and cheap place for retired people to live in most comfortably. On our rambles here we met two Parsee gentlemen who were connected with a mill erected there called Rhodier Mill. They became friendly with us and treated us very kindly. Here one gets all the different wines such as champagne, claret, etc., at a very low price, so much so that people can afford to drink champagne at every meal.

After passing ten days in the French town which serves as an historical relic of an Empire in India which was destroyed before it was securely built, we proceeded to the next stage of our journey.

XXXIX

The Beautiful Nilgiris

After visiting Pondicherry, we again took train to proceed further for our trip to the Nilgiri Hills. We had to change our train at the junction of Mettapalum, where we entered a narrow and really wonderful train to go up the heights.* The hills lie at an elevation of 6,500 feet. The train is so built that our luggage had to be tied up strongly, else it would roll from one side to the other. As it had to go up quite a steep hill, it had strong pulley breaks fixed to it; but it might yet roll down backwards and cause accidents of a serious character.

Travelling up the hills we commanded exceedingly beautiful scenery as far as Coonoor on each side of the railroad, such as we had witnessed in England. The higher one went the more was one afraid of being thrown down into the deep valleys below, if anything went wrong with the train. We came across several wooden bridges on our way, and we wondered how they must have been built; in fact the whole Railway line excites our admiration at the engineering skill displayed in the construction of it.

From Coonoor the journey is made by tonga, and the drive is not very interesting, as on each side of the road one sees nothing but thick

---

*It is still possible to take this train! –*JP*

avenues of high grown trees. However, while nearing our destination, the lovely Ooty—we witnessed a sight that was really pleasing to the eyes. Coonoor is a modest town with shops scattered about here and there. But Ootacamund surpasses it greatly by its higher beauty of scenery and its more salubrious climate; and it is for this reason resorted to by most retired people, who like spending here the evening of their lives.

We were furnished by our Bombay friend with the names of some European families, who were keeping residential quarters for visitors, providing boarding as well as lodging. We were unable to see any of them immediately on our arrival there late in the night after sunset, and went straight to one of our Parsee Shop-keepers, Mr Hazari, a very old inhabitant on this hill, living with his big family. While we were making inquiries for residential quarters, he and his family would not allow us to go anywhere that evening, and extended their hospitality.

We put up at his house with his big family, and we were made quite happy and offered every assistance most cheerfully for which we were thankful to them. As the fatigue of the journey from Coonoor told in some measure upon my health, I had to keep indoors the next day, but on the following day I and my son went out with Mr Hazari to enquire about those English families whose names had been furnished to me. Fortunately, as Mr Hazari was familiar with their names, we soon found them out, and being able to come to terms with one of them, we removed the next day to the new quarters, which belonged to an English widow.

The house was located on a hill where we had a nice commanding and a fine view of the city. I liked the house, but as we were now on an elevation of 6,500 feet above the sweltering plain, I felt the place cold and windy, but this drawback was remedied by keeping the mantle always ignited [sic], so that I felt quite warm and comfortable. I and my son generally went out for a drive on the different avenues, the enchanting views of nature which we beheld were truly refreshing. Mrs Hazari and other members of her family used to go with us at times. The climate being congenial we rapidly gained in health and strength.

Eucalyptus trees are very common in Ooty, and rows of them were to be seen grown on both sides of the road. There are many artificial edifices highly to be admired, among which the palaces of the Maharajah of Mysore and the Gaekwar of Baroda are well worth visiting. There are other well-known buildings, such as the Library Assembly Rooms, Government House, etc. The race course has a nice outlook, and the band generally plays here and also at the Botanical Gardens, full of beautiful plants, shrubs and flowers. There are many good driving roads running along the ridges and going zigzag down the slopes. The gardens are gay with lovely roses and great bushes of fragrant geraniums fill the air with their delicious scent. Gardening in the Nilgiris is a pleasure, as the seeds and plants grow rapidly as if by magic. Vegetables, too, grow with great rapidity.

Many permanent European residents and enterprising Indians keep thriving gardens from which they supply the market, or as it is called "Shandy" which takes place once a week known as Shandy day, when one is expected to purchase all his or her provision of meat, poultry, vegetables, eggs, grain and other necessaries for the week, unless one wishes to pay a treble price for such articles on the other days of the week. The Shandy Bazar is one of the attractive sites of Ooty. It is a wonderful scene to behold. The products of the hill, vegetables, fruits, poultry, mutton are all there. All round are groups of buyers and sellers. Shandy day is a trial in every household as the cooks and servants spend hours there and invariably return home drunk.

There is a sect of herdsmen who are called Todas, the most interesting of all the Nilgiri Hill tribes, and they are the only aborigines of these hills. They are a striking race, being tall, athletic and of strong and sinewy limbs resembling much to Jewish origin. They appear to be good looking and some of the women are really pretty, having fine eyes, black hair and skins of ivory fairness. Their dress is peculiar consisting of a single woollen mantle wrapped round them. They live in hamlets called "Mands" which consist of two or three oval huts with a low entrance or doorway hardly two feet in height closed inside by a sliding block of wood. They crawl in and out of their huts on hands and knees. They are full of superstitions. They are an indolent race, their occupation is cattle-herding, and they live on milk, ghee and a little corn. They practice polyandry, a woman marrying all the brothers of a family.

There was Mr Cama, another Parsee shopkeeper, a merchant dealing in general stores. But the well-known, influential, wealthy and popular Parsee gentleman living here for many years on the recommendation of his Doctor with his good and noble family was Mr N. Kenny. I had known him long before in Bombay. Till now he has his business in Bombay known as Messrs Kenny & Co., dealers in jewellery, clocks and watches, and lately settled down with his family in Geneva. We had no difficulty in recognising each other, even though he looked stronger and healthier than what I had seen him in Bombay, and thus we renewed our old acquaintance when he called on me on hearing of my arrival. He has built several elegant bungalows on this charming hill, one of which he occupied and the others rented. He was a leading man on this hill-station, and much respected by Europeans and Indians alike. He was an Honorary Magistrate and a member of the Ooty Municipality. Both he and Mrs Kenny and their grown up children are of a genial nature. They held "at Home" parties every Sunday afternoon where all their Parsee friends meet together. Beautiful Lawn Tennis Courts were laid out in the midst of their beautiful garden where most of the ladies and gentlemen who knew the game enjoyed it heartily, while others delighted in strolling on the lawns and taking part in pleasant conversations. Thus the Kenny family had become a social factor among members of their own community permanently residing on or visiting this hill. Our stay lasted for nearly a month and a half, and did great benefit to our health. We were enchanted by the bracing climate and the beauty of this tableland.

XL

In Bangalore During the Royal Week

As I had no wish to leave the South without seeing Bangalore and Mysore since I had heard so much in praise of them from friends, I took leave of Ooty at the end of November with the best wishes of my Parsee and new English friends, and proceeded to Bangalore where we arrived the second day at the City Station. We went with a guide to a hotel in the City kept by a lady which we found suitable to our requirements. We had a long and pleasant drive all along the way witnessing pleasant views and attractive buildings. After staying in this hotel for a week we learned that a place was kept by a co-religionist of mine for the special use of Parsees. We soon shifted there, though we were sorry to leave the hotel, as the lady proprietor was so full of simplicity and urbanity, and the hotel itself was a comfortable abode.

Bangalore is well known for its dry climate, and it is for this reason resorted to generally by invalids. Green meadows are observable during one's drives, and the sight all around is pleasing and delightful. Living is comparatively cheap, and any amount of green vegetables and fruit can be had. Drives to the celebrated Cubbon Park and two Fort gates—the Mysore Gate and the Ulsoor Gate—are well worth taking.

In Bangalore we were very pleased to renew the friendship of our old friends Mr and Mrs Hormusji Jehangir Bhabha, for many years residents in that city. They both are extremely sociable and in their agreeable company we felt quite happy. We were often invited to tea and dinner and used to go for drives together. They both took delight in explaining to us the different interesting sights and buildings. Mr Bhabha held the very important post of Director of Public Instruction in the Mysore State and carried much influence in the Territory. Mrs Bhabha, too, was not less well known, and moved in the best English Society. Through her we had the pleasure of making the acquaintance of Mr and Mrs Armrod, who were so nice and obliging in their treatment of their friends. Mr Armrod was the Editor of a well-known Bangalore paper. They both gradually became familiar with us. On one occasion Mrs Bhabha arranged with Mrs Armrod to take us to a school concert, where we all went, and I am glad to say both my son and I enjoyed it thoroughly. Mr Bhabha was very helpful to us in many ways.

While I was here, our present King George and Queen Mary, then on a tour in India as Prince and Princess of Wales, paid a visit to Bangalore. It had been decided that the ceremony of unveiling the statue of our late beloved Empress Queen Victoria should be performed by his Royal Highness. A large mandap adorned with buntings of various colours was erected on the spot to hold the distinguished gathering invited to witness the interesting ceremony. Through the kindness of Mr Bhabha, I and my son, too, had invitations to be present. We went with Mrs Bhabha and were able to secure front seats in the mandap. We were quite close to the scene of the ceremony and so commanded a very nice view of all that transpired on the occasion, and we could closely see the beaming faces of Their Royal Highnesses. We returned home quite pleased with the splendid function which we had witnessed.

On a subsequent day we were persuaded by Mr Bhabha to visit the Kolar Gold Mines, one of the best things to be seen by a visitor to Mysore, and he gave us a letter to the Chief of one of the best mines, desiring him to show us everything worth seeing. As Mrs Bhabha promised to join us, we were all the more encouraged to go. We started from Bangalore by the early morning train and arrived at the Gold Mine Station at about eleven o'clock. To our great surprise and delight we were soon in the agreeable company of the Chief, who had come to receive us at the station. He drove us straight to the dak bungalow, which was situated on an elevation, so that we could see the different mills while seated on the verandah. The Chief took leave of us promising to return after two hours and asked us to refresh ourselves in the meanwhile. He had provided nice refreshments for us at the dak bungalow. Mrs Bhabha, too, had brought excellent provisions and had her maid-servant to attend on us. After resting ourselves for a short time we were glad to be once again in the agreeable company of the Chief, who took us to see the different departments of the mill, where gold was extracted and brought into use. We passed some hours going through the whole mill, and it struck us with wonder when we noticed the various processes that were employed to remove gold from the crude quartz ore.

Much has been written by well-known writers in praise of these gold mines, so all I can say to my readers is that if they have the means of travelling, they should visit them to witness what the human mind is capable of achieving. We returned to the station late in the evening accompanied by the Chief, and we took our way back to Bangalore by the evening train. Before the train started we all thanked the Chief heartily for the cordiality and geniality of the reception he had accorded to us. Our arrival at home was very late, and the next day when we saw Mr and Mrs Bhabha we were in no way backward in thanking them also for being mainly instrumental in making our visit so pleasant and profitable. I was glad to see my grandson here as well: he had come down to Bangalore on learning of my having proceeded to that city.

XLI

In Enlightened Mysore

At the strong persuasion of our esteemed friends Mr and Mrs Bhabha we were filled with a desire to visit Mysore, where some very interesting sights and aspects of Indian life were to be seen. We left by the night train, and arrived the next morning at the Mysore station. Their Royal Highnesses had left the city, which had not yet lost its excitement, the auspicious visit having just ended. Since Mr Bhabha had kindly addressed a letter to the Manager of a well-known hotel in Mysore owned by a Parsee gentleman who was living there with his large family, the latter was good enough to be present at the station to receive us and afterwards drove us to the hotel. While we were driving in the carriage the roads all looked gay and attractive with beautiful mandaps, buntings, flags, and various other brilliant decorations which had not yet been removed after the Royal visit, and thus we were lucky enough to behold the preparation made in Mysore for the reception of her noble guests. The Manager accommodated us in the excellent rooms engaged for us. I took a day's rest as the fatigue of the railway journey and continuous moving about had slightly told upon my energy.

The following day the Manager had arranged to take us to Seringapatam, so well-known in Indian history for its famous siege.

It was a very long drive, and on each side of the road we saw nothing but huge trees and large fields. While coming in sight of Seringapatam, we noticed countless tombs, on both sides of the road, of valiant heroes who had fought bravely in honour of the British flag during the siege, and in whose memory a beautiful pillar has been erected. When our carriage approached the halting place, we were taken through an extensive beautiful garden to a building which even from its outward appearance looked picturesque. On entering it we saw everything that enhanced its beauty. On the walls were different views of the fight the English had with Hyder Ali and Tipoo Sultan, so wonderfully painted that we could not help admiring them. It is a square, one-storeyed building, inside which there are small staircases here and there which lead one to the top, where there are small rooms with windows skilfully and tastefully constructed, and everywhere mattresses are spread. From this spot we had a beautiful all-round picturesque view, most pleasant to the eyes. It is called Tipoo's place of rendezvous.

Cool breezes were blowing which soothed us gently, and after refreshing ourselves with the repast we had brought with us, we proceeded on our march to see the Mausoleum of Hyder Ali and Tipoo Sultan, the famous Mahomedan heroes and warriors, situated in the Lal Bagh. Before entering it we passed through a big arch, on which are a number of domes where Indian musicians play music with drums on important holidays. The Mausoleum is a handsome square pavilion of marble surmounted by a dome with graceful minarets at its four angles, and surrounded by a colonnade which is supported by beautiful columns of black horn-blende. We reached by beautiful double doors inlaid with ivory to the marble tombs within wherein lie the ever-memorable warriors, Hyder Ali and Tipoo Sultan. The tombs bear inscriptions in verse recording their deaths as noble martyrs to the faith of Mahomed. Beautiful and richly-woven shawls are spread out on the tombs. At certain times of the day the "Mullah" or the priest puts floral wreaths on the tombs and recites prayers with incense burning around them. The whole aspect is very solemn indeed, and we too felt as if we were performing religious rites in the presence of the Almighty God.

When we came out we saw a beautiful monument with a dome at the top erected in memory of Lord Cornwallis, which looks splendid as it is entirely of marble. We afterwards saw the hiding place of Tipoo Sultan which struck us with amazement and wonderment for him who had built it in such marvellous and ingenious fashion. It was nearly dark when we finished our observations, so we reverted to our drive and arrived late at night at the hotel. The fatigue of the day brought us sound sleep, and we rose in the morning quite refreshed. This day we were shown the Maharajah's old and new palaces. The old one was most gorgeously decorated, and it was interesting to behold everything which it contained. The new one was in process of construction and not quite finished when we visited it. It was full of artistic work and reflected great credit upon its builder. We then took a drive round the city. The streets are nice, broad and shady, and contain many fine houses with curious terraced roofs. It gives one an impression of neatness and prosperity and the city seems busy and thriving. In the afternoon my son visited a well-known hill, the Chamundi Hill standing at a height of 3,500 feet, from which he commended the panoramic view of the city.

I put off going up such a height owing to my old age. My three days' stay at the hotel was made quite comfortable and we could not help speaking in praise of it. The Manager had a large family. He introduced us to each and every member of his family who, one and all became very friendly with us as if they were of our own domestic circle. On the fourth day we left them amidst their good wishes, and arrived at Bangalore where, after a couple of days' further stay, we had to leave our genial and warm friends, Mr and Mrs Bhabha, and several others to return to our Bombay home. It is no exaggeration for me to say that, had I not the agreeable company of such kind and agreeable friends as Mr and Mrs Bhabha, I would never have made such a long stay of more than two months in Bangalore and its environments. Mrs Bhabha and some of her relations were at the station to bid us goodbye. Our warm thanks were offered to them for all they had done to fill with pleasant impressions our visit to one of the most enlightened Native States in India and I need hardly say that our parting greetings were very hearty.

On my way to Bombay, since my step-daughter Meherbai had often wished in her letters to me that I should visit her and her only daughter, who was living with her husband, Dr C. S. Suntoke, who was at the that time medical officer at Goolburga, we halted at that place for a day, and they gave us a cordial reception. It was no doubt a happy meeting after three years. There was not much to be seen in Goolburga. However we took a short drive through the native city, and after a few hours' halt we parted amid the exchange of warm greetings. I came direct to Bombay where my eldest son and relatives were waiting at the Byculla station to receive us. My joy knew no bounds on meeting them again, and on our arrival at our own sweet home, I and my son thanked God, the Father of all mercy and kindness, for bringing us to Bombay safe and joyous, full of fresh memories of all we had seen in memorable cities of India.

XLII

My Second Voyage to England and Subsequent Tour Round the World

In the year 1906, having sold a portion of my Bombay property at a reasonably good price, I resolved to make a second voyage to England, and sailed for London in the middle of May by the S.S. *Yarra*. At Marseilles I disembarked, proceeded to London by rail, and took up my residence at "Batliboi House," 16, Trebovir Road, Earl's Court—a newly opened Parsee house kept by an old acquaintance, a most desirable haven for a stranger in a foreign land, as it brought me into immediate touch with my own countrymen and countrywomen, even though most of them were young students.

What gave me most delight on this occasion was to meet in London one of my best and oldest friends, Mrs Ahlers, whom I had not seen for twenty-eight years; also India's foremost politician, Mr Dadabhoy Naorojee, who knew me and my family from infancy. The presence of so many young students was not, however, exactly to my taste, and at the suggestion of Mr Dadabhoy who was residing at Balham with his granddaughters and grandsons, I removed to that more suburban—and therefore, quieter—part of the Metropolis. Here I stayed for three months, and Mr Dadabhoy—the Grand Old Man of India as he is called—despite his patriarchal age, astonished me by the energy and enthusiasm with which he still continued to work for the good of India and its millions of poverty-stricken and drudging people. He even contemplated entering Parliament once more, and never allowed despondency to get the better of his optimism.

My stay in England was destined to be brief, and September found me returning to Bombay for reasons partly climatic and partly domestic. Arrived, I found myself once more in the midst of my family and my friends, and acting on their advice, I now determined to part with the rest of my property comprising of land and three buildings. A newly-formed company, called the Zoroastrian Building Society made an adequate offer and I soon found myself freed from the cares and worries of managing a big estate in my old age. Meanwhile, it was agreed that the purchase-money should be paid by instalments, and as the property was being acquired for a good and charitable purpose, I readily consented. I even attended the ceremony of laying the foundation stone of the building about to be erected on part of the site of my late property. For that purpose, an auspicious day was chosen, to wit, Jamshedi Naoroz, which fell on March 21st, 1907. The longest lane has a turning, and my patience was rewarded by the purchase-money being all paid by the 15th of May the same year, and the deed of sale fully executed.

During this time I made preparations for a tour round the world, along with my two sons. My intention thus to become a globe trotter at the age of seventy-six naturally aroused not a little interest amongst my friends and well wishers in Bombay; and I received a good deal of attention also from the English and Native Bombay papers. My final step, that is to say, before setting out on my tour, was to hire a small bungalow in the compound of the property that I had just sold, for the storage of my goods and chattels, which was made easy by the good offices of the new owner.

At last, accompanied by my two sons, I set sail for Yokohama in the P&O Steamer *Delta*. This was on May 29th—Royal Oak Day, as the English call it—and when our ship reached the open sea, she made for Colombo. According to our Indian tradition, I made a "peace" offering to the sea—or shall I say to Neptune—of sugar, flowers, cocoanut, etc., and took a last long, lingering look of Bombay, with its magnificent harbour and busy wharves, and its amphitheatre of distant hills for a background—a truly sublime spectacle. Ten miles away from the Prince's Dock—our point of embarkation—we passed the Lighthouse, and there the harbour pilot handed us over to the care of the Captain of the *Delta*. We spent most of our time between meals on the promenade deck, and as we were a small but select party we contrived to fraternize to the contentment of us all. One Bori gentlemen, Salebhai Shaik Dawood-khan, bound for Bangkok, proved a very interesting companion, and indeed, we were a goodly company—all the fifteen of us, including, by the way, three Englishmen—"jolly companions every one," as the song says, not forgetting the doctor, a lively and amiable young man, and, of course, indispensable on board a ship.

On the morning of June 1st, after one or two signs that the monsoon was about to burst, we arrived safely at Colombo, the capital and chief seaport of Ceylon. Colombo is remarkable for its fine cinnamon, cloves, its drives and its world famous jewels. The handsomely appointed shops contain, amongst other things, old curios and imitation jewels, and the buildings—and especially the hotels—are, some of them, of gigantic size. There are electric trams also in the fine broad streets giving quite an air of modernity to this City of the Far East. Here, too, all outgoing steamers call, and so it is a port of call for all nations. As the interval of stay was short, I could not avail myself of the opportunity of seeing Colombo thoroughly.

In thus referring to Colombo, I must not omit to mention the Parsee cemetery there—a beautifully kept burial ground, and, in this connection I must make a brief reference also to the circular wall that surrounds all the tombs erected therein, giving the latter the appearance of a "Tower of Silence," eighteen feet high and with an iron door for entrance. It is also worthy of mention that the very unusual custom of carrying the dead in an iron carriage is here observed by the Parsees.

In the neighbourhood of Colombo there are many cocoanut plantations, and as they fringe the coasts, the drives through them are pleasant and salubrious. Before leaving Colombo for Singapore, the outward English mails were taken on board from another steamer which came direct from Marseilles, and some twenty more passengers joined us, the most important amongst them being the Chinese Ambassador and his suite, returning from London. That very modern accessory, the Gramophone, also appeared on board, and we formed quite a lively, and, in many ways, a very interesting party.

One of the diversions indulged in on the voyage was a raffle—a lottery, or sweepstake it might perhaps be called—and I was fortunate enough to draw the first prize number. Each contributed a dollar, so my win was a substantial one; and I was, of course, very pleased, though not addicted to gambling, I am happy to say. Indeed, I was far better pleased to find much admiration of my embroidery work, and, in particular, of a skull cap embroidered with gold-thread and studded with pearls. After all, the work of one's own hands—what a satisfaction there is about it, especially when it is a work of skill and a labour of love! On June 6th, that is, six days after leaving Colombo, we sighted Penang and its evergreen mountains burst refreshingly upon the vision.

What a contrast to barren, rocky Aden! Originally a penal settlement, Penang is now a health resort, with a luxuriantly tropical but salubrious climate, and a thriving commerce. Its other name is Prince of Wales Island, and the electric tram is an "institution," and a popular one. One of the sights of Penang is its waterfall, situated in the public gardens, four miles off in the midst of tropical luxuriance. The fall itself lies in the heart of ravines, and, though not large, is perennial, a reservoir supplying the town with water being close to it, evidencing the juxtaposition of the useful and the ornamental. Cocoanut tree avenues are a feature also of this part of the Peninsula and the drives to and fro are exceedingly pleasant.

There is, however, one drawback to a voyage by a mail steamer. It does not remain long at any port of call, and therefore it is better to go on a tour of this kind on a regular passenger steamer. *Experientia docet*, but I am afraid I have learnt my lesson too late this time. Singapore was our next port of call, and the voyage thither was delightful. The Straits of Malacca are narrow, and the land on both sides abuts here and there, giving the appearance of green batteries with their trees and lighthouses—a striking sight and, once seen, never forgotten.

The voyage from Penang to Singapore was short and sweet. It so happened that many proposed disembarking at Singapore, and it occurred to some of them to give a concert on board—a treat that was much appreciated. Another pleasant diversion was the taking of our photographs in a group, for which we had to thank Lieutenant Lindsay who had voyaged with us from Bombay.

On nearing Singapore we had a curious experience. The approach lies along a channel so narrow as to create a feeling that we were passing through streets or gardens. Entering the harbour, we observed that the overlooking hills almost exactly resembled our Bombay Cumballa or Malabar Hills, even to the flag-staff on the summit signalling the arrival of our steamer. Arrived, we—that is, my sons and myself—were fortunate in being chaperoned round the town by my sons' worthy friend, Mr H. P. Kaka. The city itself is of the modern commercial type, quite up-to-date, too, in its tram service. It is amongst other things the rendezvous and coaling station of the British India Squadron, and in the extent of trade done with other parts of the world it is of paramount importance.

Amongst the buildings in Singapore the Victoria Memorial Hall is worthy of mention—a thing of beauty and a joy for ever. It is so very beautiful that it enhances the attraction of the neighbourhood and the other buildings and this is no small compliment that can be paid to it. Before leaving, another old friend met my sons—I had gone on board already—Mr Taraporewalla. It was, of course, a great disappointment to me not to see him, but time and tide wait for no man and so it was a speedy goodbye to Singapore. The last goodbye was in mist and rain, but, thank God, we escaped the much-dreaded monsoon and reached Hong Kong in fair weather.

XLIII

The Sights of Hong Kong—Sir Hormusjee Mody's Hospitality

A member of the Sassoon family joined us at Singapore, and as I had known his family and relatives from early days, I learnt from him many interesting facts about the Jews in Bombay. This gentleman was on his way to Shanghai to practice at the Bar. As I intended to stay at Hong Kong a week or more, I was busy packing up, which feminine occupation considerably shortened the voyage. Here, as at Colombo, Penang and Singapore, the harbour bar is the forefront sight with its splendid haven for ships, its life, its blending of impregnable strength and picturesque beauty. Behind it rise the hills, amphitheatrical in shape, peaks sublimely lofty, protecting the town whose double name reminds us of China and the "Empire upon which the sun never sets" to wit Hong Kong and Victoria.

Taking a steam launch kindly lent by our good skipper Captain Daniel, we reached the King Edward Hotel owned by a Parsee gentleman, and I was more than gratified to find myself surrounded by fellow countrymen.

Just opposite to our hotel premises a noble Parsee family was living and they one and all treated us with great kindness. The proprietors of our hotel also supplied us with Parsee dinners as being more to our taste and liking. The head of the family living opposite to us was Mr Sorabjee Dhunjeebhoy Sethna. He was the head of Petit's Firm here doing business in Bombay yarn, and we also met the leading member of the Parsee community there, Sir (then Mr) Hormusjee N. Mody, carrying on an extensive exchange business with almost all the leading Banks of Hong Kong. The latter gentleman invited myself and my sons to take up our quarters in his palatial residence, but I preferred to remain at the hotel, though I fully appreciated all the kindness extended to me by Sir Hormusjee as well as all our Parsee friends. Beautiful specimens of Chinese artware were offered me by this amiable friend, but I had reluctantly and regretfully to decline the offer as I was touring round the world and could not see my way to carry with me even so coveted a reminiscence of my visit. Before leaving, however, I made a tour of the shops in Queen's Road.

This is the principal street, and it is one of the most magnificent thoroughfares I have ever seen. Its shops, indeed, teeming with all manner of silver, silk, ivory, lacquer and porcelain goods, cedar wood ornaments and other ornamental products of Chinese industry, are a sight which deeply impressed me and I felt that Hong Kong takes the premier place amongst the Far East appanages of the British Empire. Of course, the Chinese predominate, but there are also some 10,000 white people, and the town itself rises terrace above terrace in ever-increasing beauty and splendour, with finally a commanding view of the extensive harbour below. It reminded me of Malta which I had previously visited, and I must not omit to add that here Indian and Chinese merchants jostle each other in peaceful industrial rivalry, and the former took a lively interest in my tour round the world. As to the conveyances there are at the foot of the slope electric trams and higher up sedan chairs and that ubiquitous Eastern vehicle, the man-drawn rickshaw.

Whilst here I also visited the Victoria Park and this gave me the opportunity of seeing the "Peak district" of the town, with its fine private residences and superb view from the Peak summit about 200 feet high. At night the effect of the myriad lights from ships at anchor and of the flashes of electric searchlights, is as if one were gazing at the starry heavens with meteors bursting at intervals across the stellar space, whilst in the day time the busy traffic glows with life and animation. Steam launches dart hither and thither amongst the bulkier steam and sailing vessels, and the battleships of British build—like bull-dogs of the deep—combine to form a marine picture that beggars description. Of the incline cable tramway from base to peak it is difficult to speak in adequate praises; it is a wonder of engineering skill—one of the wonders of our mechanical age, like a score of similar wonders that add to our material comfort and facility of travel.

The spectacle of street life, too—the nearer view from the balcony and verandah of the hotel is full of interest to the visitor. So also is the view from Sir H. Mody's palatial residence—half way up the slope—where we accepted an invitation to dinner, and sat amidst wonders of the artistic and the antique in his lovely home, which was full of furniture, and choice paintings and exquisite porcelain of Chinese make. Then English ladies and gentlemen arrived, and we all spent a most enjoyable evening. As for myself it was a pleasant break in the dull monotony of my time as life had been more or less secluded since my only daughter's death. It was reminiscent, rather, of my young days, for life to me has brought strange vicissitudes and sad bereavements, and latterly I seldom attended such social gatherings in Bombay. At Sir H. Mody's that night, however, I seemed to live my young life again.

I must not omit to mention that he is one of the chief members of the Turf Club. In fact, the silver cups he has won made a rich display, but the strangest thing was, that they bore not his own name, but that of a very dear friend and benefactor, Mr Buxsee, and it was thus that Sir H. Mody desired to perpetuate his memory. I met at the banquet—for I cannot describe it by any other name—many friends and distinguished personages. With its countless electric lights, superbly served dishes and its toasts, which last elicited a speech from myself greatly to the delight of the assembled friends—it was like a scene from the Arabian Nights. I also met there a Mr Gubbay, connected with the Sassoons from Bombay, and many other friends, all of whom were full of kindness and sympathy towards me. And so the evening passed away, concluding with music and other entertainment.

On June 16th, our friend, Mr Sorabjee Sethna, persuaded us to take a trip to Macao—an old Portuguese town—the Monte Carlo of the East, with its ancient forts, gardens and grottoes, and last, not least, its Parsee burial ground situated at an elevation of about 300 feet—the sole surviving relic of Parseeism, as now no Parsees are resident there. What we saw there in all their unholy evidence were the gambling houses, frequented by Europeans—and Englishmen—and this on Sunday of all days of the week. One day sufficed to see all there was to see, but the meeting with old friends was to me a genuine delight, and, as favourable weather remained with us on our way there and back, the day was really enjoyable. Next day a *Daily Mail* interviewer sought to draw me into a political discussion, but I declined to be so drawn and he confined his interview to my views on the advantages of travel. Judge of my surprise when, in the Hong Kong *Daily Mail* of next day, my views appeared in print. These the Bombay papers reproduced in still more glowing colours. These interviewers are so fond of colouring their copy that I was compelled to point our certain discrepancies in the accounts.

Sir H. Mody was assiduous in his attentions, and my grateful thanks are due to him for his kindness. He lives there all alone—his wife and grown-up family living in Bombay, and one cannot help feeling for him that there is no one near and dear to him to cheer him in his advanced age. This reminds me that my younger son again broke down, and his state of health gave me not a little anxiety. Dr Justi, that best of physicians, attended him and convalescence followed slowly but surely.

In the meantime Mr Sethna drove us about the environs of the town—to the "Happy Valley" race course—an odd title for such an association of institutions—for the cemetery of all creeds and people is just opposite the race course. Here, as in a Christian burial ground, were monuments of all shapes and sizes, and access to it is by means of steps surmounted by parapets, as it stands on the summit of the hill. A special feature to me of this cemetery was the Parsee portion, beautifully laid out with flowers to make it look like a garden, with a fountain playing in the midst. It also gladdened, as well as comforted, me to be told that there is a fund for providing priests, and the needful floral accessories for the last ceremonies due to the departed, and the fountain itself bears the name of Sir H. Mody's wife, Bai Manakbai H. Mody, being presented by him in her name and elaborately executed in every detail, at a cost of some 7,000 dollars. Hong Kong is full of novelty and variety, and a remarkable feature of the island is the way its roads are laid out, one of them running the whole length of the Island, some eleven or twelve miles. There is also the Botanical Garden, and the magnificent aqueduct, about two miles in length. I must not omit to mention our visit to the Chinese jewellery marts, where I bought a quantity of gold and silver-ware, including bracelets, caps, table inkstands, etc.; also our visit to the palatial residence of Sir Paul Chater, a partner of my old friend, Sir H. Mody, who himself accompanied us to tea there.

Sir Paul's residence is situated halfway up the Peak. It is a wonderful structure, built of marble and granite, yet owned by the simplest of men. It is, indeed, a royal palace, both without and within, with its pillars and staircase of marble and granite, and its choice and rare collection of Chinaware—a million dollars' worth. We visited the kitchen-house, presided over by a Chinese chef, who explained to us all the many cooking contrivances, so intricately arranged as to disguise the fact that it was the culinary room of the mansion. Then we adjourned to the tea-room, and drank the cup that cheers but not inebriates out of choice China and the tea itself—it was lovely, being the purest blood of old Calboy. Sir Paul Chater begged our acceptance of a box of tea of prime quality, and told us to drink it on our voyage, as the tea provided on board is generally below par in quality, even for first class passengers.

And now the time was drawing near for us to resume our voyage. So, we paid a parting visit to Mr and Mrs Talati and to Mr Sethna's family, the former of whom have an interesting child of three versed in Chinese, and taking the unalloyed delight of tender childhood in toys and knick-knacks. Before leaving Hong Kong, it may be of interest to observe that some of the merchants here live over their own shops, as they do in England, whilst others, like Mr and Mrs Talati and Mr Sethna, occupy detached villas of English suburban type, and it often happens that the ladies, as in the case of Mrs Sethna, are a real help to their husbands.

We were due to sail on June 24th, and, as we were booking through the firm of Messrs Thos. Cook & Son we found no difficulty. The last two days—Saturday and Sunday—were divided between a last visit to our good friend, Sir H. Mody, and packing up for departure. A final *Daily Mail* interview, and the last goodbyes to our dear kind friends, who gave us parting gifts of flowers, and soon we were leaving Hong Kong. How gratifying it is to note here that the accession of our new King George V should synchronize with the event of a Knighthood being conferred on Sir H. Mody for his many philanthropic acts and public-spirited deeds in Hong Kong.

XLIV

Bound for Japan—The "Paris of the Far East"

It was a French Steamer of the Messageries Maritimes—the *Earnest Simmons*—and Captain Gerard and his officers gave us a hearty welcome, and we responded by presenting each of them with a bouquet. The boat looked superior to the *Delta*, the ship that brought us from Bombay, in its decorated saloon and music-room, etc., and so was the food. The French are born cooks, more like our Parsee cooks, and so we had everything exactly to our taste. The English, with all their good qualities have not learnt the art of cooking, and that is, I suppose, why London and the big cities have French or Swiss cooks and waiters in their restaurants, their hotels, and in some private houses too.

Our ship was bound for Japan, but Shanghai was our next port of call, and here we arrived after a pleasant voyage on June 27th. The vision of Hong Kong was still before me, with its houses perched on every available crag shoulder, and its wonderful harbour, alive with sampans, jinks, and, above all, bristling with masts "majestically stern" by reason of the presence of British battleships. Shanghai is the greatest commercial centre of China, but the harbour bar prevents the approach of the big liners, and so we had to enter it in smaller steamers.

Passing up the river Wossung, the view of the line of factories, mills, wharves and warehouses, and other buildings, is a very imposing one, and the huge fleet of jinks, lying off the native city, is, indeed impressive to behold, with the American, English, and French settlements in their respective backgrounds. The Chinese tower, of course, is the chief feature of the City, which is a huge centre of commerce with factories, mills, wharves and warehouses, abutting on both sides of the river—and like a modern metropolis, is a very hive of industry. Here we met again troops of friends—one of whom, a younger brother of Mr Sethna of Hong Kong, was alas, dangerously ill. We comforted the poor fellow all we could, so far away as he was from those near and dear to him, and his untimely death a short while afterwards filled us all with sincerest sorrow. Whilst staying in Shanghai, we visited Mr and Mrs R. V. Solina, the former being a son-in-law of a good friend of my elder son. They received us with all kindness possible, having already heard of our coming though the Bombay papers. We also saw Mr N. Tata, another friend of my elder son, the head of the Tata firm and a merchant of high standing, who had been apprised of our coming by Mr N. Sethna. Judge of my extreme delight at meeting old Parsee friends in far off Shanghai. This was a special feature in our enjoyment.

Shanghai, by the way, is called the Paris of the Far East, and this leads me to say that the wealthy Mandarin merchants come here from the interior to spend their money and enjoy the pleasures of life. The Bund and the Maloo are the two principal highways, and they stretch for miles, with shops on each side full of all sorts of fancy goods. Here, too, is a Parsee cemetery, and it is kept in very good order. The same evening on which we took our last long drive we had a real Parsee dinner at Mr and Mrs Solina's and, as we stayed for the night at their house, the breakfast was seasoned with a dish of good omen for our further voyage.

On June 28th we set sail for Japan, with but few on board, yet with everything sumptuously provided both in the matter of food and entertainment. For the first day or two we experienced a typhoon—a phenomenon common in Chinese seas—and then we reached Kobe via Nagasaki and entered the beautiful inland sea of Japan. This sea is really more like a strait, or natural canal, than a sea, being about 250 miles in length, and universally admired for its loveliness, an archipelago of surpassing loveliness, and for a background having mountains and scenic effects too glorious to describe. Then the islands and islets are a perfect study in colour and configuration. Nor must I omit rapturous mention of the creeks that abound here, with promontories of all shapes and sizes—a blending of all beauties—a gorgeous, panoramic scene, never to be forgotten, luxuriantly rich in cultivation, and dotted with houses and temples and little villages, whilst junks fly to and fro upon the waters—curiously constructed vessels which intermingle oddly with the other shipping.

Having arrived at Kobe, it was comforting to know that my elder son was not altogether unacquainted with the town. In fact, we were once again in the midst of friends, and the drive through this centre of commerce, along the Motomachi, and to the Nanko Temple, was very enjoyable. It was a brief, bright stay, an overnight call, so to speak, and the next day we heaved anchor for Yokohama.

Two of the passengers who met me on board were particularly interesting—a French gentleman and his Japanese wife. They were, indeed, a unique couple, both clever, and both of them, too, very happy in each other's company. The lady, although Japanese, could speak English and French quite fluently, and I must not omit to mention that they had with them a little baby son—such a trio of humanity I had seldom seen in my travels, and I had just the opportunity of being in their company which enabled me to enjoy my intercourse with them.

When we reached Yokohama all the city seemed to be gathered on the landing stage. And such a mixture of nationalities, too! It was a never-to-be-forgotten sight. Captain Gerard, with kindly concern for our comfort, persuaded us to stay on board all night, and a Parsee gentleman came and spoke to me, putting me at once at my ease regarding rooms at a hotel. In the meantime, however, others—Parsee silk merchants—being apprised of our somewhat lonely position, came on board, and amongst them I felt myself quite at home again. In the end Mr Sheriarjee Karanjia and Mr Pestonjee, son of Mr Cursetjee M. Bhesania, a well-known silk-mercer of Bombay, came to me, and it was decided that I should stay at the latter's residence. The Custom House officials—thanks to the above gentleman—were soon satisfied as to our *bona fides*, and now we were in the "Liverpool" of Japan, with its imposing Bund, or Sea Wall front, on the way to Mr Pestonjee's residence, where we were received by Mrs Pestonjee who, strangely enough, bore the same name as my late daughter, *viz.*, Goolbai. Their children, aged four and two respectively, spoke Japanese quite fluently. But as the English language has common currency, there is no difficulty in making oneself understood in the Anglo-Saxon tongue.

Truly, Yokohama is a cosmopolitan town, quite a European centre of the Far East, though in other respects strictly Oriental—the rickshaw is ubiquitous and its human horses are to the manner born. In the gaiety and variety of its shops it may perhaps be likened to Paris and shopping here, as in other big cities of Japan, is a favourite amusement of the tourist. The streets and shops, have, indeed, an educative character to the visitors, there being, it may be added, two chief quarters—the commercial quarter, or "the settlement," and the native quarter. All this wealth of artware, curios and manufactured goods is the growth of only half a century—so rapid has been the development of Japan. Here one sees the famous *Kanâ Kobâ*, a bazaar of all sorts of fancy stalls, artistically arranged, and full of fascination to the would-be purchaser, whilst at night the brilliantly lighted scene is so beautiful, and quaintly striking with the many types of humanity plying trade there.

The beautiful street of Benton Dori was the centre of our visit the following day, and here one is again lost in wonderment at the pictures and scenes painted on silk, the screens, the embroidery work, silk wares, lacquer work, carved ivory curios, porcelain ware, and many other productions of native art.

Mrs Apcar, originally an inhabitant of Calcutta, lives here. One of the cleverest business ladies in Yokahama, the talented widow of a talented husband, she is greatly interested in female education and is a fluent public speaker. To her I was introduced, and we soon became friends, especially as she is an intimate acquaintance of Mr Bhesania and his family. She resides on a pretty, picturesque hill, called "The Bluff," and here we all spent a very pleasant afternoon and evening, talking about India and Calcutta, and in particular, about Jewish and Armenian families—the former reminding me of my friend, the Sassoon family.

Mrs Apcar has one son and two daughters, aged fifteen and twelve; and this mention of her son leads me on to mention an auspicious event that took place during my stay in Yokahama, *viz.*, the birthday of my own son, in honour of which I gave a party, at which all my

Parsee friends were present. It was reminiscent of our days in Bombay, especially, the preparation and sending round of dishes of sweets, called *Rawa* and *Sev*, and it was a kind of finale to our doings in Yokohama; for, in the course of the following day, we set off for Tokio to see the Exhibition there.

In Hong Kong, we had been advised to take mineral baths in Japan, so our first thought, on reaching the capital, was to seek out Dr Aoyama, the eminent physician. Finding him out on calling, we made an appointment for the next day. Meanwhile, we took up our quarters at the Imperial Hotel, the most palatial residence of its kind in Tokio—a building like those you see in England and on the Continent.

Tokio has quite a look of modernity about it, with its gardens, avenues, electric lighting, and street tram lines, but it is also a city of Temples; and here, of course, are all the chief Government offices, and last not least, the Mikado's palace. Here one finds plenty of Americans and Europeans and English tourists also, with most of whom we were able to strike up an acquaintance, and had a golden opportunity of comparing notes on our travel experiences.

Our visit the next morning to Dr Aoyama was purely a formal one, and resulted in his recommending us to take the recuperative baths at Atami, but we elected to remain in Tokio; and after leaving the Doctor (to whom we spoke through an interpreter) we proceeded to the Exhibition set up in the Park, and arranged sectionally, the building being massive and impressive, and the exhibits altogether exquisite, especially the beautiful lacquer works in gold and silver—the pride and ornament of Japanese workmanship—and deservedly popular all over the world. Europeans, Chinese and Japanese constituted the bulk of the visitors, but we had the pleasure of meeting friends of our own race, Mr and Mrs B. B. Lam; and this reminds me that the Parsees, both husbands and wives, have made a departure from the old traditional habit and now visit foreign lands together.

After a tour of the Exhibition, with all its wonderful wealth of exhibits, bewilderingly magnificent, we returned to Yokohama by rail. Here we had the good fortune to be present at a time which coincided with the celebration by the Americans of the Independence Declaration Day, and our Transatlantic friends left nothing undone to make the display as imposing as possible. The ships in the harbour were illuminated, and there was a pyrotechnic performance such as it would be impossible to beat anywhere, for the Japanese and Chinese are past masters in the art. The Club Hotel, which faces the Bund or Sea wall, afforded a splendid view of the proceedings and we were the guests of the evening along with our friend, Mr Sheriarjee Karanjia; our host and hostess, made us all very much at home, reserving a special room from which to view the fireworks and the procession of boats.

Another occasion on which we saw one of these wonderful pyrotechnic displays was that of the Franco-Japanese *Entente*, though, of course, on a smaller scale than is to be seen in Tokio, the capital. This mention of the capital leads me to say that a visit to the Exhibition at Tokio was a revelation, for here we saw a wonderful blending of ancient and modern workmanship—antique models of temples and shrines—jostling side by side with the latest types of naval architecture, and goods of all description displayed in every variety of arrangement. Then too, as though to remind us of London and its Earl's Court Exhibition, there was the Big Wheel and the Merry-go-rounds, suggestive of the lighter side of life's experiences, and the truth that it takes all sorts and conditions of things to make a world.

I have made mention of Atami. This was to be our next objective. By the kind offices of our friend, Mr Sheriarjee, we were introduced to the manager of the chief hotel there, in which we were comfortably lodged during our stay. Atami's hot springs are the principal attraction, and its situation is also very charming, with hills for a background and the sea in front.

The town is reached from Yokahama *via* Kodzee, and the journey was very pleasant, Nature having spread herself out like a garden, and villages dotting themselves all along the route. The last stage of the journey, that is, after leaving Odawara, was accomplished in what is called a Trolley Car, drawn by coolies—human horses, as I have called them—and running along metre-gauge rails by the side of the sea, the road itself being cut out of the mountainside, a distance of some fifteen miles. It is all reminiscent of the hill resorts near Bombay, the road being through delightfully picturesque scenery, with views that ever change, and a height above sea level that gives a dominating effect to the whole. And the coolies! They are fine, tall, stalwart fellows, and down the sloping portion of the journey, they run at high speed, so that it needed but little exercise of imagination to fancy ourselves in a railway carriage, the cars themselves being closed but of the old-fashioned palanquin type. On the way we passed tea houses and shops, in which latter the good folks use the hand-loom, weaving silk embroideries and the like articles. On our way we had to negotiate two or three passes, boasting of unrivalled scenery. There is also the alternative route by the sea, and yet another inland route, but assuredly the ride along the shore is the most thrilling experience.

Arrived at Atami, we took up our quarters at the chief hotel, managed by Mr Higuchi, who, with his wife and children, could speak English fluently, though themselves Japanese. The hotel itself stands on a knoll in the centre of the town, and so commands a lovely panoramic view of the place. One might say of it—"It is English, quite English, you know," after the phrasing of a well-known London advertisement, and everything is in the best style, both in respect of decoration and cooking.

Atami is considered to be the best sanatorium in Japan. The famous Atami geyser is intermittently active, and during the active period—that is, every four or five hours—it emits its heating vapour; and the living stream, which runs down from the mountains above is conveyed to the hotel, and can be enjoyed by application of the water or the inhalation of the vapour that rises from it. Another remarkable feature of Atami is the Turkish bath built on a plot of earth that generates the necessary heat without any artificial aid, and here one or two baths a day can be enjoyed with impunity. As to the surrounding walks, they are delightful, and in the depths of the wood it is most refreshing to take tea in the little bungalows erected for that purpose, whilst in the hill-tops, the scenery is ever beautiful and varied, with waterfalls tumbling amidst rocky crevices, and, all around, the sweet smelling camphor trees from which the natives construct boxes, toys and trays—admirable for keeping off insects, etc. Nor must I omit to mention the "Gampi-ori," a fabric made of silk and cotton, and mixed with a special kind of paper, known as "Gapis," also a special kind of sweetmeat, called "Ame" made from limes and oranges of two kinds, hard and soft. On the beach there is bathing, and pleasure boats are provided for fishing in the bay. In short, there is every provision for the perpetuation of varied enjoyment and for rescue from monotony.

The visitors' book reveals the popularity of the town, and whilst we were there we had the felicity of meeting an Englishman from India, who was able to speak in pure Hindustani, and whose flying visit we highly enjoyed.

After a week's stay, we returned to Yokohama—this time by way of Kodzee—and took the opportunity of visiting the Exhibition on a Japanese holiday. What clever folks they are, and how exquisite is their workmanship in curios, wood-carving and painting on silk!

It had been my intention to visit the famous caves of Igoshi at Fujigama, but I relinquished the journey, because of hill difficulties, and my sons went instead. Here an annual fair takes place, and the stalls are spread out in the shape of temples, these latter being built in the memory of certain saints, and coral shells and marble curios being on sale. In the caves—the entrance to which is close to the sea and into which the sea waves roll—there are corridors of deities, hewn out of the rock, for Japan is a land of temples, and yet it is hard to believe that the cave images are the work of human hands.

Another spot of great interest is Nikko, some ninety miles off, 2,000 feet above the sea-level, and much praised by the late Sir Edwin Arnold, of "The Light of Asia" fame. Here wood-carving and the like workmanship is reduced to a fine art and Nikko has also very fine temples. It is, indeed, one of the most attractive towns in Japan, and I had quite resolved to pay it a visit; but as in all mundane affairs, man proposes and God disposes, or rather let me say that the Clerk of the Weather disposed of the matter in this case and was responsible for my inability to go—for it rained, "and the rain was never weary," so that Jupiter Pluvius compelled me to give up my intention. So making fair purchases in Yokohama and bidding a sweet goodbye all kind Parsee friends, including Mr and Mrs Desai, and my newly formed friend, Mrs Apcar, my sons and myself made our way to the good ship "Persia," lying far off in mid-stream. Our packages—the result of our many and manifold purchases of Japanese wares—had very considerably grown in bulk and caused my last day or two in Yokohama to be crowded with strenuous work.

XLV

San Francisco—Traces of the Great Earthquake

We left the harbour bar amid the fondest farewell of those of our friends who would fain accompany us to the *Persia* with gifts of lovely flowers. Thus we left evergreen Japan and all its scenic beauties.

In nine days we reached Honolulu, and we were fortunate in having on board many American ladies and gentlemen, who, like ourselves, were "globe trotting" and with whom we had voyaged on our way to Japan. At Honolulu, we had time to pay a flying visit to the town and its environs and had very enjoyable moments whilst we gazed on the thousands of cocoanut trees, the stately palms and cactuses of the island, and drank in its salubrious air. The island is part of the Hawaii group and is under the American Government. Honolulu is, in fact, a town of quite American proportions and magnificence, and has many fine buildings and a striking bronze statue of King Kamebaweba. Perhaps the chief attraction of the place is the aquarium, and certainly it is the most brilliant collection of parti-coloured fishes, being considered by no less an authority than Dr David Jordan, of Standford [sic] University, to be second to none in interest and importance.

The Bishop Museum was also a great attraction, revealing, as it does, the early life of the Hawaiians in their jungles, on the mountain tops and attired in their native dress—not to mention feathers of extinct birds, woven into crowns and jewels and armouries in glass cases. A pretty custom prevails here, that of speeding the parting guest with garlands of blossoms and sweet smelling vines, some round the neck, others round the hat or on the hair—called "leis" or regard tokens. Then taking a farewell look at Hawaii's tropical growth, its cocoanut trees, bananas, pineapples and all sorts and conditions of tropical fruit, we saw Honolulu gradually fade from view as we weighed anchor for San Francisco. We were fortunate in having amongst our fellow passengers Mr and Mrs Smith, leading citizens of America, and, in particular, Mr Frederic Dumont Smith, of Kingsley, representing Kansas in the American Congress.

After a seventeen days' voyage, we reached San Francisco (August 23rd), and entered the historic Golden Gate of California. Let me say here, incidentally, that during the voyage from Honolulu to San Francisco we were snapshotted in my Indian dress by some gentlemen of the Press, who moreover drew out, in quite a marvellous manner, encyclopaedic information regarding our Parsee faith, religion, social life, etc., including a reference also to the question of unrest amongst Indians in consequence of the deportation of Lala Lajpat Rai. On landing, our belongings were searched, and, to tell the truth, the officials were not a little puzzled by my saree costume, wondering whence we hailed, till two or three ladies came forward and explained the peculiarities of Parsee and Indian dress.

At length we reached our hotel (Jefferson's), without paying a cent to the customs, and settled down in all the comfort and luxury of a modern palace. As I shrewdly suspected the reporter on board had improved the occasion, for I found my likeness and a graphic account of myself in the newspapers—a circumstance that naturally drew upon myself and my sons much notice. By the way, on board these American liners, like the one we voyaged by, the question of tipping has become a nuisance, and even the ship's Doctor was not above suspicion. Speaking of the ship's Doctor, I am reminded of the almost despotic rule of this gentleman. For example, if he detects a passenger suffering from a contagious disease he is not allowed to disembark at his port of destination, but is taken back to the port of embarkation, which is rather rough on the poor mortal.

We did not stay long at the palatial hotel, but sought and found one of more modest pretensions, and really I liked it much better than the bustle of the former.

San Francisco had suffered from a terrible earthquake on April 18th, 1906, and a word about it may not be out of place. Traces of it were still visible and the visitation, like death, the leveller, was no respecter of persons. But, it is noteworthy that the older houses withstood the shock unharmed. Fire, however, was far more destructive than the earthquake itself, but it is comforting to think of the noble qualities of courage and self-sacrifice evoked by the widespread suffering and distress, and great praise is due to the Army and City Surgeons, and, in particular to the Navy, for the splendid work respectively done by them in binding up wounds and arresting the march of the flames. Just imagine, my reader, a devastation spread over twelve square miles, and yet, as by some magic wand, a new and more splendid San Francisco is rising from the ruins, like a phoenix from its ashes! This is what is happening in reality, and the city is once more being throned as the Queen of America's Pacific seaboard! Of course, like all American cities, the buildings are enormously high, but they are characteristic of the "big" style of doing things in the States. It was a continual surprise to us—this bigness of things—but, on the other hand, there are the parks, and they are things of beauty. Here Sunday is observed as a general holiday, and picnicking is the order of the day, with children all about in gay dresses and thousands of people perambulating these lovely parks.

We had already secured our tickets for the resumption of our journey—this time by rail—and set ourselves to spend the remaining days of our stay in seeing the lions of the place. That day (Sunday) we took a long drive through the Satro and Golden Gate Parks, where we saw, amongst other sights, the statues of past Presidents. In the afternoon, on returning from a morning drive, we had a surprise visit from the only Parsee in San Francisco, Mr Pestonjee Framjee Davar, of Messrs Lombard and Scott, Ltd, and he related to us his recent sufferings and losses through the earthquake and the subsequent fire. Yet, with that energy and enterprise so characteristic of the race, he had once more revived his fortunes, and this in a really very short space of time. He told us that in Los Angelos [sic] one of the leading firms of Bombay Parsee merchants has a shop of Indian Art ware, and two or three others have followed his example.

In the evening of that Sunday, we drove to the famous Ocean Beach, above which, standing on a Cliff at its very edge, is Cliff House, presenting a solid square to all the winds that blow, yet looking, in spite of all its wild weather experiences, as fresh as if it had been built only yesterday. Hard by are the Seal Rocks, like giant needles, the haunt of sea-lions, hundreds of which are often to be seen disporting themselves—a sight, I am told, once seen is never to be forgotten. Then further up this hill, we come to the world-famous Satro Baths (named after the donor) with their 500 bathing rooms, amphitheatre, capable of seating 4,000 persons, and having a promenade of the same capacity. To the Satro Baths there is a descent by way of a Grand Museum and a stage for spectators, and the distance from San Francisco is seven miles and along a beautiful length of road. On our way we saw the New Tavimont Hotel on the summit of Nol Hill—a palace of palaces—the abode of merchant princes, and surrounded by lovely orchards and play grounds.

On our return that night we enjoyed the company of several ladies interested in our religion, dress, educational systems, and so forth; but, in the midst of it all, we were destined to witness a great fire—a gruesome reminder of those which created such devastation after the earthquake. It was indeed a lurid sight, but was got under in a really wonderfully short time, though not before an appalling amount of destruction had been wrought—the result, chiefly, of its being a big stone house. Happily, the contiguous wooden structures escaped; else, there might have been wholesale havoc and ruin. The very word, fire, was enough to rouse the whole city and hundreds and thousands flocked to witness the conflagration, and assist, where they could, the Fire Brigade.

As for ourselves we were able, after such a spectacle, to realise the horrors of April 1906. San Francisco is built on hills and is a city of contrasts. From heights approaching 1,000 feet one can look down upon a magnificent panorama of docks, streets, edifices, and beyond the open sea. Not even Rome, Malta, Hong Kong and similar places can boast of such a view as that which the "Queen of the Pacific" affords. And what will it be when all trace of the recent visitation is obliterated defies conjecture, so absolutely inspiring is the *tout ensemble* that greets the eyes.

On returning, our friend Mr Davar offered to take us for a drive to the University of California, situated across the Bay at Berkeley; but alas! owing to the exigencies of travel and the shortness of time at our disposal, we had to forego the pleasure and turn our thoughts and preparations to the long journey on the morrow. It is a great convenience that one's heavy packages and luggage can be booked right through, and that however often one breaks the journey, they will be waiting for you at the other end. This is distinctly a comfort to the globetrotter, as is also the provision made for living and sleeping on board the express train. Before taking the Ferry Boat for the railway terminus, we visited the museum with its wonderful collection of natural products, vegetable and mineral—a convincing proof, if any were needed, of the position America holds today as a food-producer in particular, and, in general, as the premier country of the world in matters of trade.

And now, crossing by the Ferry Boat, we reached the Oakland Pier Station on the opposite shore, and so commodiously comfortable was our crossing, and so free from oscillation, that one would have imagined an electric tram or car was conveying us across. Then we took our seats in the royal train, so magnificent was it that I cannot call it by any other epithet; and soon we were on our way to Chicago. I must not omit to mention how very kind Mr Davar was to us, and how he speeded us at parting, making us forget that we were in a strange country. So too did all the ladies and gentlemen and children who came to see us off. I was lucky enough to make friends with the wife of a railway official, and she told me many interesting facts about the various places *en route*. Arrived at Sacramento, we found it full of animation, though it was late at night, and, pursuing our journey, with the moon shining in a cloudless sky, we enjoyed the unique spectacle of a mountain gradient climb and I was forcibly reminded of the Indian Railways on the ghauts. Truckee, a junction for the beautiful Lake Tahoe was far behind us, as we reached an altitude of 7,000 feet above the sea-level. Then we descended into the midst of wonderful scenery, with verdure all round and trees clinging to the mountain sides. The stations are platformless and are level with the ground.

XLVI

Niagara—The Indescribable

On the third morning at seven, Ogden, the principal junction, was reached, whence we proceeded to Omaha, after which we crossed nothing but miles and miles of barren monotonous country. It was a great relief, therefore, to reach Chicago on the fourth day after leaving San Francisco. What a busy mart this lakeside city is with its traffic and shipping! We had to cross the town in order to go forward to New York, and passengers are conveyed by a special omnibus line. Everything—buildings, parks, vehicles, even the horses—is on a huge scale. Even the waiting rooms presented the appearance of large spacious halls.

At six the same afternoon, we resumed our journey by the Michigan Central and Hudson River Railway—the Niagara Falls route—and reached Detroit. The next morning (having on the previous halt undergone the customary examination) we arrived at the Falls. Here the train stops for half an hour on the Canadian side at what is called Falls' View where the vision of the cataract bursts upon the view, with the curves of the gigantic Horseshoe Fall, magnificently conspicuous, as well as the river shining resplendent in the sun, sweeping onwards to its fall, and the Rapids below raging and roaring to their rest in the lake further on. I cannot resist quoting here a great writer, for, truth to tell, the scene that presents itself to the eye is wonderful and the pen fails to do justice to Niagara. Niagara, the Thunderer of Waters! The deep, solemn, unceasing voice! The mightiest of cataracts! Who can describe the majesty of this wonderful manifestation of Nature's power? Who can put into words the seething rush of the Rapids, or the slow, awful majestic plunge of the waters, or tell of the roar that rises out of the foam and mist below? The wonder of Niagara is for him who goes to see. It can never be told!

We, by the grace of that Almighty who is all bountiful, have realised our life-long desire to see this mighty marvel of the ages. As our American fellow-passengers told us, to realise the full effect of the Niagara Falls, you must see them from below. You must look upwards at the infinite grandeur that confronts you and must be in the midst, as it were, of the roar as the waters descend, whilst the mist blows in gusts about your head. As you look up at the vast tumbling mass of foam-edged water, with the sounds of the world all lost in the mighty tumult of Nature, your whole being is filled with wonder and awe. Impressively beautiful, too are the views of the Falls from above, for then you see the sweep and grandeur of breadth of the great cataract such as you never can see from below. Yet equally above as below are the Rapids—smooth, swift, shining above and seething below in a huge whirlpool! As I have said, the best view is obtainable by the Michigan Central Railway. The great curve of the Horseshoe Fall, and away beyond the wooded island and the American Fall, and above and below the river itself shimmers into sight as it sweeps from one lake to the other, and leaps precipitously midway amidst rainbow effects and the solemn roar of multitudinous waters—a sight never to be forgotten.

From Niagara Falls we journeyed on to Buffalo down the Mohawk Valley. How full of variety is this American scenery! Now cities flash into sight, and now it is a quiet green landscape reminiscent of Old England. At length we reached Albany, the principal town at the mouth of the Hudson River, and traversing the so-called Hudson Highlands or the Catskill Mountains region, we pass along the banks of the ever-widening river till at its mouth—called the Yappanzee—stands New York City, the largest in the New World—the Metropolis of the Western Hemisphere—with its 4,000,000 inhabitants, its wonderful buildings and famous streets.

It was in the evening of September 1st, after a five days' and five nights' continuous travel, that we reached America's commercial capital and the sight of it was indeed impressive. Apropos of New York hotels, there are two systems of hotel management in America—the "European" plan and the "American" plan—the former being preferred. That is to say, so much for bed and attendance and meals as ordered. Cabs and private conveyances are too dear, being paid by distance, but the exorbitant charges of the hack-drivers can be escaped by making use of the "express" system of sending on one's luggage. The traveller can then go to his or her destination by cab, cable, tram-car or elevated railway, and so save expense. On settling down in our hotel our next thought was of meeting possible Parsee friends, and as we had been informed previously in Bombay, several Parsee firms had been established in New York, *viz.*, those of Mr J. N. Tata, Mr Bhumgara, and Messrs Cowasji Bros. This last was represented by a brother of Mr Dadabhoy, of the London firm. Mrs Saklatwalla had also taken up her residence here with her son; she is Mr Tata's sister, and she sent us a cordial invitation.

The great artery of New York is Broadway, a long avenue, full of huge offices and shops. Then there is New York's Lombard Street, *viz.*, Wall Street, and in this part of the city are the skyscraper buildings—that of Singer's having no less than forty-eight storeys. There is the City Hall, amongst the many public buildings, "World" and "Tribune" offices, New Trinity Buildings, and last, not least, the New Custom House Building, with its statues ranged in front. In short New York is a city of big streets, big buildings and big restaurants—the last-named falling into two divisions, those for the rich and those for the poor; for most Americans take their meals away from their homes, and then it is worthy of remark that, whilst girls and women serve at the poor peoples' restaurants, only males do duty in the hotels for the well-to-do classes.

During our stay in New York we noticed how sympathetic with all things Indian the American people really are. They have given a practical proof of this by the establishment of charitable institutions under American Missions in different parts of India. Also, at the hotel, the Americans would discuss with us Indian questions. Soon after our arrival, we went to see Mrs Saklatwalla, who resided in Riverside

Avenue, some ten miles off—one of the best parts of the City. From this part, a grand view of the Hudson River is obtainable. We found our friend living alone, and we were mutually very glad to spend together a few hours. I was struck with her courage thus in leaving her own country and living in the midst of strangers all alone. Of course, there were female servant attendants upon her, and truly, she needed every care and attention, being fifty years of age. Our conversation was a short one, but it was sweetly reminiscent of old days in Bombay. Then we left her and returned by one of the three ways of travel, *viz.*, the underground or subway, overground and overhead. On the way home, we did the orthodox shopping, and visited the "William Whiteley" of New York, our Parsee dress being the object of much curiosity and attention.

Hundreds and thousands of people are always rushing about in New York, and the citizens keep very late hours—a fact that, doubtless, accounts for their shortlivedness. Then, as I have said, there is very little real home life, such as one sees, for example, in England, and the more is the pity on this account. The day after our arrival, the inevitable interviewer turned up, and we had to undergo a volley of questions as to our nationality, religion, and the purpose of our long tour; also our opinion on the people and places we had seen. The next function was a morning drive, and then Mrs Saklatwalla came to see us, the conversation meanwhile turning on the question of our visiting Boston, Washington and other cities of America. We were also advised to seek an interview with President Roosevelt, the deservedly popular head of the American Republic.

Next morning we had a visit from Mr Nusserwanji B. Panthakee, a son of a Bombay friend, now a naturalised American citizen, and he very kindly took us for a ride in what they call a "sight-seeing" car. Our tour was "tour No. 2," being round Upper New York, and including views of the palatial residences of American millionaires, the boulevards of the Central Park, the Manhattan Viaduct, with its unrivalled view of the Hudson River, the picturesque Pallisades, Columbia University buildings, Public Libraries, monuments, statues (including those of Washington and Columbus), cathedrals, churches, hospitals, clubs and last but not the least, the tomb of General Grant, at which last we stopped for a few minutes. In the Central Park there are many features of interest, including the Metropolitan Museum of Art, and Cleopatra's needle. Indeed, we had quite a surfeit of sight-seeing, buildings and nothing but buildings being the prominent feature of the round. The next morning I booked my passage in the *Celtic* for Liverpool. This vessel belongs to the White Star Line, and has a tonnage greater than that of any other of the Company's ships. She was dated to sail on September 19th. By the kind offices, and persuasion of our friends Mr Nusserwanji and Mr Bhumgara and Professor Dhalla, recently appointed as the Parsee (High Priest of Sind), we arranged to see Washington and the Jamestown Exhibition before leaving America, but had to decline their offer to chaperon us to Atlantic City. As things turned out (and through the instrumentality of Mr N. Panthakee) we changed our bookings from the *Celtic* to the *St Paul* of the American Line, bound for Southampton on the 28th of September, thus giving us a full week longer. Our next "tour" was round Lower New York, and this time the Brooklyn Bridge was our objective. Brooklyn Bridge is a 7,000 feet long suspension bridge, the centre span being 1,600 feet, height from the water 1,135 feet, and width 118 feet.

Nearly six lines of railway traverse this bridge, besides roadways and footways—and, taking it all in all, it is a remarkable monument of engineering skill. On our return from the Brooklyn side of the river, we drove through the streets lit up by thousands of powerful electric lamps. This is a city, I take it, that never knows the natural darkness of a city asleep.

XLVII

Washington and the Jamestown Exhibition

The next morning we set off by the Pennsylvanian Railway for Washington and the Jamestown Exhibition. Our route was by ferry boat across the Hudson to Jersey City, and so by rail to the political capital of the States. Philadelphia, the Capital of Pennsylvania, was one of the stations we passed—itself commanding a fine view of Penn's city and a great junction. Then we passed Baltimore, and at length reached Washington, putting up at the Burton Hotel. This edifice was built in 1780 by General Washington himself, and is situated at 226 North Capitol Street, and located delightfully on Capitol Hill. Opposite are the Capitol and Library, and the hotel where we stayed was a spacious edifice.

Next morning a drive through the city left upon me the impression that Washington was the nicest and cleanest city I had ever seen, with its broad streets and well-planted avenues. Its shape is rectangular, the Capitol and the White House being points of conveyance for the avenues, and there are the "sight-seeing" automobiles to enable the visitors to see the city at popular prices and with every comfort. It is quite a hero-worshipping city—monuments and statues being the chief attraction.

The Washington Monument, another noteworthy object, is

555 feet high, and it is surmounted by a pyramidal superstructure of aluminium. Inside are many memorial stones, and the interior is lighted throughout with electricity. The total cost was 1,300,000 dollars, and it is the highest work of masonry in the world. White House itself is a thing of beauty and of grandeur withal. George Washington laid the corner stone of this building in 1792 and lived to see it completed. It is also related that in company of his wife he walked through all the rooms a few days before his death in 1799. Hard by the White House is the National Library or Library of Congress, erected at a cost of 6,000,000 dollars, admittedly one of the most beautiful edifices in the world—a building of everything that is beautiful in architecture and art, and in point of fact, America's high-water mark of architectural achievement. When it is told that all the architects, painters and sculptors are Americans, it may be easily imagined with what feelings of pride every native of the States contemplates the National Library and all that therein is.

Once again we approach the "Hill" on which the Capitol is situated, an imposing structure of beautiful design and workmanship, and commanding a fine view of the River Potomac sweeping amphitheatrically below. The crowning glory of the Capitol is its imposing dome of fluted Corinthian columns above the central building terminating in a lantern surmounted by a statue of Freedom, 300 feet above the Esplanade. The dome is of iron, and so constructed as to expand and contract "like the folding and unfolding of a lily" with the variations of temperature. The view from the dome, reached by a winding staircase, is superb and will amply repay the toilsome ascent. On resuming our survey of the various rooms in the Capitol, the National Statuary Hall, semi-circular in shape, first claims our attention.

The Hall of Representatives located in the South Wing of the Capitol is a legislative chamber of unparalleled beauty and splendour. The Supreme Court Room and many other rooms in the building are of uniform beauty and elegance; and it is impossible to single out any particular room for special mention. My humble pen, I fear, will not aptly describe the beauty of the edifices in Washington, and as many an abler hand has already done ample justice to them, I have confined myself to only briefly referring to them in this work.

During our stay in America, one of our great visits was to Norfolk, to see the Jamestown Exhibition—or Exposition, as they call it—and we travelled or "voyaged" by the night steamer, reaching our destination the next morning. After refreshing ourselves, we went by motor car to the Exhibition—a cheap ride there and back for a dollar. Jamestown has been a settlement since 1607, and here were planted, so to speak, the first seeds of the Republican Tree. The town is situated in the Province of Virginia, and the Exhibition was being held in order to celebrate the tercentenary of permanent English settlement in America. All the States were represented in the exhibits, a distinctive feature being the military and naval drills, parades and manoeuvres. In a row facing Hampton Roads were the buildings—representing the different States and homes—halls and events, ever varying from the year 1607 to the year 1907. Held on the sea-shore and the first of its kind, it presented an ideal appearance and the industrial and historical exhibits were truly a wonderful array, every conceivable branch of the art and sciences being exemplified in the thousands of objects daily visible to the millions of visitors.

In the exhibition, I noted a stall belonging to one of my own countrymen—that of Messrs Bhumgara & Co. containing a really marvellous collection of ivories, tapestries, bronzes and other oriental wares—the first from India to be displayed in a Western Exhibition. The crowning exhibit was the reproduction of the ancient and historical Hindoo Temple of Palitana—a wonderfully carved teakwood model, representing all the gods of ancient India, and the result of many years' work by sixty-four renowned Indian Artists.

We met Mr Nusserwanjee at the Exhibition. It is due to him that we were able to have the kind services of Mr Punthakee, who took us all round the Exhibition and gave us a really enjoyable time. It is impossible to describe all that we saw in the Exhibition. Suffice it to say that the details would fill a volume. I felt sincerely grateful for the health and vigour that enabled me to see within the space of three months two such Exhibitions as the one at Tokio and the other in the States.

On leaving again for New York we caught a last farewell of the shore and Exhibition, the latter beautifully lit up with electric light. On entering New York harbour, the majestic Statue of Liberty and the great ships like floating palaces, coming in and going out, arrested our attention, and the sight of New York reminded us of its busy life and immense wealth. The next day I paid another visit to Mrs Saklatwalla—a farewell visit to a dear friend. All too quickly passed the time, and almost before I could realise that the hour of departure had arrived, we had taken up our berths on the steamship *St Paul* for Plymouth and Southampton—a voyage occupying eight days. The weather on the voyage was stormy for the greater part and calmed down only towards the close of the run and the majority of passengers had to keep to their cabins, sea-sickness prevailing. However, on nearing England, we got up a concert and reached Plymouth where we stopped to land the Mails and disembark many passengers for the Continent. Then we went on to Southampton, where we arrived at 8 p.m. and landed immediately to catch the Express for London.

XLVIII

In England Once More!

We were now on tour and away from home some five months, and varied had been our experiences. Arrived in London, we had some difficulty in settling down in suitable quarters, the Bedford Hotel in Russell Square becoming for the moment our home. Then having met by a lucky chance some Parsee friends, we found snug and suitable quarters in the vicinity of Gordon Square.

Here we heard of the serious illness of our worthy old friend Mr Dadabhoy Naoroji, and were distressed to think that the Grand Old Man of India was ordered away home at the advanced age of eighty-two, and so I sought a parting interview with him. His whereabouts I was able to ascertain (not knowing his present address) by the kind help of Mr D.P. Cama, but alas! I was doomed to the great disappointment of missing him at the last moment. My friend, Mr D. P. Cama, had informed me of his departure the very next day, and so it happened that, though I made for the Great Eastern Terminus, I found he had gone in a motor car straight from his residence to the Tilbury Docks. I saw his grandchildren, however, and presently we all took train to the Docks, but in view of the critical state of his health, none but his grandchildren were allowed to see him, and I considered it a great privilege at length to be allowed to be the one exception to the rule. Our interview was a brief one, and we all prayed for him a speedy return to normal health. He bore the journey and the voyage wonderfully, and reached Bombay once more happy to be in the midst of those near and dear to him.

The next day I paid a visit to Mrs Boyce, who is a daughter of my late personal friend Mrs R. Oomrigar. She was living with her children for their education at West Dulwich. We also had a visit from Mr R.L. Batliboi and several rising young Parsee Barristers. It so happened about this time that I needed medical aid, as did also my son, and we were advised to seek quarters at New Cross. In England rooms can be engaged per day, week or month, according to one's requirements; and so I was easily able to quit my Bloomsbury rooms for those at Jerningham Road, Telegraph Hill.

A visit to the city the following day called Sir Owen Burne to mind, and to my great sorrow I ascertained that he had recently lost his second wife. He himself was out of town, so we sent a letter of condolence. Strangely enough, and sadly enough, too, Sir Owen's first wife had died in 1878 just before my arrival in England and now the sad occurrence of the loss of his second wife took place just previous to our present visit. In the kindest manner possible, Sir Owen wrote to us from his Hampshire address, assuring of his regret at so sudden yet unavoidable an absence from London through sad bereavement. The same afternoon we went to see our good old friend Mr Dorabjee P. Cama and his good wife. Though old, being about the same age as myself, he was marvellously alert and his memory, I should say, was prodigious, for he could recount the ancient histories and folklore of the Parsees.

One of the very convenient features of London life is the accommodating transit agency work, of which Carter Paterson & Co. is a typical example. You place the legend "C.P." in your window and in a short time round comes a van, and off goes your luggage to its destination. What a saving of time and money too!

While at New Cross I received a letter from my dear friend, Mrs Ahlers, announcing her return from the Isle of Wight and promising an early visit. Lady Scott, wife of Sir J. Scott, a High Court Judge in Bombay, sent me an invitation to be present at a lecture on Indian Female Education to be given under the auspices of the National

Indian Association by Mr N. G. Welinkar, formerly a Professor at the Wilson College, Bombay; and needless to say I enjoyed it immensely, for I have myself been personally interested in promoting female education in India. Sir William Lee-Warner presided, and amongst those present were Dr Pollen, Sir Charles Lyall and Lady Scott, and many other Anglo-Indian ladies and gentlemen. Mr Welinkar, the lecturer, had been interested in founding a Poor Boys' Seminary called after India's Grand Old Man, Mr Dadabhoy Naoroji, which is built on a plot of ground owned by me, and so had endeared himself to the Parsee community, and I was glad also to hear my friend Mr P. C. Tarapore, now a Barrister-at-Law, and especially touched I was to hear him refer to my mother as the first Indian lady to send me (her child then) to the English Seminary in Bombay.

At this lecture I had the good fortune to meet the grandson of my late dear old friend, Sirdar Venayek Wasudew. After the lecture, we returned to New Cross, and as the winter days drew on, my eldest son was taken ill, and for a time his state of health was so critical that I had to call in Sir Douglas Powell, M.D., Physician to the King; but after a long and careful nursing my son convalesced, and I was able to prolong my stay in England.

Owing to my son's illness I was not able to leave my house for nearly a month. Judge, therefore, of the pleasure of a visit from such good friends like Mrs Ahlers, Mrs D. P. Cama and Mrs D. H. Cama, and many other friends of all nationalities. Mr D. P. Cama was a descendant of the first Parsee firm to open a place of business in London; and, in fact, the first to keep up the prestige of the Parsee merchant by doing so. A younger brother of my late son-in-law is also in London, and him I was also delighted to meet again along with his good wife.

While at New Cross I heard of the death of my dear friend Mrs Saklatwalla at New York. Her body was brought to London to be buried in the Parsee cemetery at Woking, and myself and two other ladies were present along with fifty Parsee gentlemen to pay our last respects to her memory.

It was now the depth of the English winter, and I spent a good deal of my time in visiting the London shops. The Secretary of the Society of Arts sent me a card of invitation to a lecture on the wild beasts of

India, and I was specially interested inasmuch as it was delivered by an old attorney of mine, Mr Gilbert, of the firm of Payne and Gilbert; and it also gave me the opportunity of meeting some Bombay friends. I had also an invitation to attend a meeting of the Parsee Social Union, where Mr Koyajee, a cultured Parsee gentleman, was asked to deliver a lecture on Persian Poetry. Unfortunately my son's sudden illness prevented me from accepting the invitation.

After the New Year came the opening ceremony of Parliament on 29th January 1908, and I had the privilege of a seat in the Royal Gallery to witness it. I went in my Parsee costume, and was fortunate enough to occupy a front row, full in the gaze of Their Majesties, I being the only Parsee lady from India present. My dress drew down upon me quite an unusual amount of attention and even evoked many questions as to my nationality, etc. By the sound of bugles, Their Majesties were announced, and entering the Throne room with all pomp and circumstance befitting the occasion, they at once became the observed of all observers—the centre of one of the most brilliant functions it has ever been my lot to witness. As Their Majesties passed to the Throne, I was near enough to be able to exchange greetings and the same pleasing experience was mine on their leaving. After the ceremony, I returned home in a motor car. The next day I saw a short sketch of mine in several London papers, and friends who were interested in my doings sent me cuttings from the Press.

Whilst in England I became a motorist, and really I found it to be the most convenient and expeditious means of getting about from point to point, and in and out of town, finally resolving to try one for transit to Bombay. On one of these motor drives, we went to the Crystal Palace, in the vicinity of which at West Dulwich lives my friend Mrs Boyce, who escorted me and my sons to Sir R. West's house, and a very pleasant evening was spent there, meeting Mrs Cooke, the wife of Surgeon-General Cooke, and her daughter, once Lady West, wife of our well-known judge of the Bombay High Court and subsequently a member of the Bombay Executive Council. I saw these ladies after thirty-four years, and it was therefore a memorable event to me. I also met Sir R. West, who is in the full vigour of health.

The time of my departure from England was now drawing near, and I had already booked my over-sea passage from Genoa, but at the last moment (the weather being very inclement) I had to cancel the arrangements, being persuaded to go direct to India by boat. In the meantime, the Marquis of Ripon, whose sympathetic nature had been so well-known, and who was the most popular Viceroy, India has ever had, granted me an interview and promised to use his influence in securing for me a presentation in person to their Majesties the King and Queen. Lord Ripon was then eighty, but he still retained much of his vigour unabated, even as when I saw him years before at Government parties in Bombay.

Whilst waiting for the return of the King from his cruise in the Baltic, I attended the annual banquet of the Parsee community on 21st March called Jamshedi Naoroz of which Association Sir M. M. Bhownagree is President. On this occasion Lord Ampthill, the late Governor of Madras and for a time Viceroy of India, next to whom I sat, and Mr H. Cox, M.P., were amongst the distinguished visitors.

On the following Sunday when I went to Mr D. P. Cama's place, I met a young son of my late cousin, Mrs K. R. Cama, who had recently married an English girl, and truth to tell was very happily married, although be it borne in mind that this is an exception to the general rule of mixed marriage. I noticed with pleasure too that the Cama family were carrying on business very successfully. The Camas were the first to establish business offices in London, and now many Parsees have followed them and are doing well.

I must not omit to mention my visit to Sir M. M. Bhownagree, son of my husband's best and oldest friend—a gentleman who has had a distinguished career both in and out of Parliament, a thoroughly representative and public-spirited member of our community. He has been settled in England for more than twenty years, and for ten years he has served India in the House of Commons with zeal and marked ability. My visit to his house was one of my red-letter events. We conversed on quite a variety of topics, and he gave me a card of invitation to an "at Home" of the National Indian Association at the Imperial Institute. The Jehangir Hall was the particular part of this wonderful building in which we met, and being itself the gift of my own cousin, such a perpetuator of the Parsee name and prestige was extremely gratifying to me.

With such a reference it seems most fitting to close this account of my wanderings with just a passing mention of my visit to the Queen's Hall, where I enjoyed the best of music and a visit to the Caxton Hall, where a meeting presided over by Sir W. Wedderburn, and addressed by Mr Keir-Hardie and members of the forward school, gave ample evidence of the sympathy of so many notable Englishmen with the Indian Empire, and all that makes for its true progress.

After attending Mr Keir-Hardie's speech at Caxton Hall, I generally passed my time in visiting my friends and going to different parks and shops of the city, and to the city in general. I had a visit from my good and worthy friend, Sir M. M. Bhownagree, who brought the delightful news of Lady Bhownagree coming over to London, at which I felt surprised and could not believe it at first, but he assured me of her coming with her grown-up son. I was extremely pleased. It was gratifying to me to see my good friends one after another in London Town, but what pleased me more was that in this advanced age my sisters are encouraged to leave their homes and travel about far and wide. Shortly after this I had an invitation to a Tea Party from my worthy old friend, Mrs Ezra, at Berkley Square, Piccadilly. It was no small pleasure to see my friend settled down in London with her grown-up daughters and sons, who were all very young when I saw them last in Calcutta. It was, indeed, a happy meeting, and our friendship, although renewed after a very long time, still remained unaltered, and before the end of a fortnight, she with her daughters honoured me with her visit at our place at King's Cross. It was, indeed one of the happiest evenings I passed.

I was staying very far from town and from my friends, who are permanent residents here, but the motor drives made everything so easy and near that I never felt lonely as constant exchanges of visits took place between us.

For some time I had given up attending gatherings, but on 7th May I attended the one held at the Duke of Westminster's Grosvenor House near Hyde Park, and found it very interesting, as I had the occasion to meet several foremost ladies of rank taking keen interest in the cause of women. On the third day after this there was a *Tableau Vivant* held at Caxton Hall in aid of the Indian Famine Fund, to which a large number of Indian ladies and gentlemen went in their own national dresses, which was a unique sight to see in London. Here I heard some good music on Indian subjects, although they were all sung in English.

Within a fortnight after seeing Lady Bhownagree, another gratifying incident I have to note here was a meeting in London with another old friend of mine, Mrs Hormusjee N. Vakil, who had come down to London from Bombay all alone on account of her son's illness. None could have believed a few years ago that ladies of my community would move about so boldly and freely as they do now. Not only are the ideas of orthodox men, but also of women, vastly changed. Now both young and aged people travel all over the wide world. I leave it to my readers to imagine with what pleasure I note on the eve of my life such marvellous changes in the mental attitude and social movements of my fellow-countrymen and fellow-countrywomen. When in the sixties and seventies my own daughter used to travel between Bombay and London all alone, what a great outcry was raised by the fathers and grandfathers of the same families whose younger generations are now following the same example. Now none of the Chabooks or Halkaroos or Mansooks would dare to comment on such public spirit on the part of my bold and enterprising sisters. The credit is due to none but my old and revered mother, Bai Meheribai, who suffered so much at the hands of the bigoted orthodoxy.

Everything appeared a little dull for a time, but at last the Franco-British Exhibition, for which I was staying in London, was opened with due pomp. It is so fresh in the memories of my readers that it is superfluous to write in detail of the gorgeous sight of the different buildings of this Exhibition and things exhibited at this great international show.

It was our peculiar good fortune to witness a succession of Exhibitions within the short time that we had spent in travelling. In the brief period of nine months we visited no less than three Grand Exhibitions, the first being in Japan, the second at Jamestown and the third being the famous Franco-British Exhibition in London. This constitutes almost a record in the matter of seeing Exhibitions.

As I was very far from town and Shepherd's Bush, where the Exhibition was opened, as well as far away from many of my friends, I resolved to change my residence. The new place which I selected was situated at Cambridge Gardens, Notting Hill. It was close to the residence of my friends Mr and Mrs D. P. Cama, as well as to the

Exhibition ground. I at once shifted from King's Cross, and had thereby the full advantage of witnessing the Exhibition. Every day there was a change of programme as to the different sorts of amusements and Olympic games, which we never liked to miss.

In the first week after my occupation here I went to see the Bazaar in aid of the Zenana Mission School, opened by H.R.H. Princess Christian, held at Morley Hall, Hanover Square, by the Hon'ble Miss Kinnaird, where a great many Royalties were also present, as it is their characteristic trait to help the cause of the poor and needy.

Three days after this, President Fallière specially came to London when there was a public reception, and it was really a grand sight to see his progress from the railway station to the French Embassy. He was enthusiastically received by the people of England. Next day, when he, in company with our King, entered the Exhibition ground, it was so thickly crowded that for a time it was difficult to move from one section to another. The spectacle was no doubt a grand one. It was a public ovation, and fully manifested the *entente cordiale* existing between the two great nations. I never found a day's rest, kind friends constantly keeping inviting me to one gathering or the other. There was an opening of the Southwark and Lambeth Free Loan Exhibition of pictures at the Borough Polytechnic Institute by the Countess of Lytton. Here I had the opportunity of making the acquaintance of the Ex-Vicerine's good-natured daughter-in-law from whom I learned that the Dowager Countess was on the Continent and not likely to return soon to London.

Every day brought with it some new amusement, and I did not fail to visit the Hungarian Exhibition at Earl's Court in the company of my good friend, Mrs D. P. Cama. Although it was on a very small scale, we still found it worth witnessing, and passed the day in the merry company of many Parsee friends who were also there.

At the time when I was about to have my lifelong desire fulfilled, I heard of the very sad death in Bombay of Sir Jamsetjee Jeejeebhoy, the fourth Baronet, which plunged the whole of my community in the deepest grief. It plunged me into a sort of perplexity, as to whether I should postpone my visit to Windsor or make it. As the death took place only two days before the grand garden party, I consulted my Parsee friends and they insisted on my attending it.

As the day for presentation to Their Majesties was drawing nigh, I was very busy with my dress for the occasion. Before a week everything was arranged by Sir Curzon Wyllie, Political A.D.C. to the Secretary of State for India. I, in company with my son, went to the India Office where he received us very kindly, and explained all about the arrangements for my reception at Windsor instead of at Buckingham Palace. In the midst of this imperial city, one thing that surprised me most was the purchase of York House at Twickenham by Mr R. J. Tata, who was lately living in London with his wife. It was originally a royal palace. I, with Mrs D. P. and H. D. Cama, was invited kindly to tea, so we took the opportunity of seeing an old royal house occupied by my Parsee friends; and what struck me most was the decoration of the Hall by Indian carved furniture in which were some of the settees and teapoys which originally belonged to me and now occupied a place in this royal house. Mr and Mrs Tata treated us very kindly. Although the drive was a long and tedious one, we found it an enjoyable occasion. It was no small pleasure to find young descendants of old orthodox families enjoying so well and free from all the old world prejudices of their forefathers.

XLIX

My Presentation to their Majesties the King and Queen

We had been in London now for about eight months and had been engaged in enjoying its sights, in which the Franco-British Exhibition, which had just then been opened, occupied a principal part. The metropolis is so vast, its interests are so many and intricate that it may be doubted whether anyone can honestly say that he "knows" London. I had no such pretensions, but confined my attention to the most interesting objects which indeed were nothing new to me in this, my third visit to London. Social functions kept crowding on me, so that time passed very rapidly without our reckoning of it.

I now set about preparing myself for the most interesting event of my tour. To be presented to our Sovereign and the Queen had been the most ardent wish of my life, and in the evening of my career it was about to be fulfilled.

The most magnificent and the most dazzling Court in the world in this twentieth century is the Court over which their Majesties the King-Emperor and Queen-Empress preside when they are in the Capital. Buckingham Palace and Windsor Castle form the theatre of the most imposing ceremonies and functions whilst the august royal personages reside in either of them. In these days Court ceremonies are real things, full of life and great formalities sufficiently imposing to give them the necessary seriousness, but without any of the stiffness which characterised the Court ceremonials of past monarchs of Great Britain. No one who has witnessed them can deny that they are worthy in their splendour of the greatest Empire that the world has ever seen.

When Court functions and presentations are in the air, the close observer is aware of an indefinable something in the atmosphere. There is a palpable stir among the great of the land when the King and the Queen come up to town with their retinue. He who has never previously seen the Court and its many ceremonials will realise that a presentation in this social temple of the Empire brings in its train a considerable amount of activity which makes itself felt over a very wide area.

The invitations are issued two or three weeks ahead, and many are the manoeuvres that are resorted to for securing admission into the charmed circle of Their Majesties' guests. I had already set on foot the machinery for my presentation, and it was my great good fortune that kind and influential friends arranged everything for me. I shall ever hold their kind efforts in grateful memory.

With a view to this ceremonial and to signalise it by something worthy of the occasion, I had long contemplated presenting to Their Majesties the King-Emperor and Queen Alexandra something fit for their acceptance. I had been working with my own hands a cap and dress trimmings, which I was ambitious enough to hope would be accepted by Their Majesties.

The cap was of black velvet decorated with miniatures of Queen Victoria, the Prince Consort, the King-Emperor, Queen Alexandra and other members of the Royal Family. Between the paintings was gold embroidery of charming design and the miniature of the King was surmounted by a crown studded with rubies and diamonds. The dress-front (trimming for a dress) and band were of beautiful design, being of stars and interlaced with gold and silver thread studded with pearls. The effect was very striking and was sure to appeal to Her Majesty's love of precious stones and embroidered work. A suitable case of carved sandalwood had been prepared for these articles and contained two portraits of myself, one taken nearly thirty years ago in 1878 and another during my present sojourn in London. Alas! how many events were crowded in that quarter of a century, but I am happy to be able to look back upon the period with equanimity and to rest confident in the belief that my life has not been an entirely wasted one.

The casket bore the following inscription:

> "To His Majesty the King-Emperor Edward VII and Her Majesty Queen-Empress Alexandra, the embroidered work of Their Majesties' Loyal and Faithful Subject."
>
> Dosebai Cowasjee Jessawalla.

Who designed the work was a question very often put to me. It went against the grain to have to answer repeatedly that both the design and the execution were mine own. Indeed, designing pretty things was a hobby of mine; and I have not only very often prepared my own dress materials but have done much designing work for others. A piece of my embroidery was exhibited in London in 1886 at the Indian and Colonial Exhibition and was awarded a prize medal.

It was a long cherished dream of mine that the articles should be tendered to Their Majesties with my own hands. That they would be accepted by them with as much graciousness as they actually did was beyond my most sanguine expectations. Presentation at Court is always a matter of no small difficulty and one involving many formalities. To be presented to one's Sovereign is a hallmark of social status and respectability, and everyone is anxious to secure the honour. Permission is always necessary, and in the present case it was not only readily granted but special features were introduced in it; several unforeseen difficulties came in the way or else the presentation would have taken place much earlier than it did.

Early in January, when the Houses of Parliament were opened by His Majesty, I happened to be one of the privileged spectators amongst the bejewelled peeresses in the Lords. The late Marquis of Ripon had very kindly interested himself in my behalf, and had procured me a card for a seat in the Peeress's gallery. Here in the midst of a galaxy of everything that was brilliant, I had the satisfaction of knowing that I was the cynosure of all beholders. My dress, which was a Parsee costume in keeping with my age, was suitable to the occasion and the august assembly, the opening of which I witnessed.

This appearance in the Peeress's gallery of the Parliament paved the way to the Presentation. Shortly after the opening ceremony of Parliament, I had an interview with Lord Ripon. In the course of the conversation, he remarked that it would not be in the fitness of things that I should go away from England without having had an audience of Their Majesties, and with his ready kindness promised to arrange the matter for me. The Hon'ble Lady Knollys was also requested to sound the Queen's wishes on the subject. Lord Ripon also asked his son (then Earl de Grey), Treasurer of the Queen's Household, to interest himself in the matter, which he did. As I hailed from India it was thought necessary, as a matter of formality, to communicate with the India Office, and Lord (then Mr) Morley was written to. Another friend, the late Sir Owen Tudor Burne, was also equally kind and helpful in the matter. He fully approved of the idea of my presentation and promised to speak to Lady Knollys and Lord Morley about it. The matter was also mentioned to the late Sir William Curzon Wyllie, who was also very sympathetic and promised to do all he could to further my wishes. It is sad to reflect that all the three gentlemen who kindly helped me in this matter are no more. A strange fatality has cut off from us within such a short interval, three men of such sterling worth who rendered me such signal service during my stay in London, and one of them, alas! done to death by the hand of an Indian. My heart goes out to poor Lady Curzon Wyllie in her irreparable bereavement, and I pray that she may have strength to bear her lot with fortitude. The subject opens up sad reflections. Let us hope that these cruel and heart-rending episodes will prove but fleeting shadows, and that the atmosphere of the future will never be clouded by such calamities.

It was at first under contemplation that I should be received by their Majesties at the Buckingham Palace. It was very thoughtful of the Royal hosts to think of saving me the journey to Windsor, and is indicative of the unvarying courtesy and consideration that actuates our gracious Sovereign and his Consort in their dealings with all subjects of high or low degree, with people of all nationalities and all countries. But as there was going to be held a garden party at Windsor on 20th June, a date not then far distant, I desired that the presentation should take place at that function as it would at the same time give me an opportunity of witnessing a pleasant function and meeting many friends. At the instance of Sir Curzon Wyllie the articles that were to be presented to their Majesties were forwarded a day ahead to Windsor to save me the trouble of taking them with me and as events proved it was fortunate that it was so. The cap and the dress materials were duly placed before their Majesties who were graciously pleased to accept them and expressed their thanks at the interview which followed the next day. As my elder son Dadabhoy was once again attacked with fever and confined to his room, I left for Windsor in my motor accompanied by my younger son Jamsetjee.

But we were not destined to reach the place without mishaps. Just as we were about three miles from Windsor, a tyre burst and we had to stop to repair the damage. Whilst we were thus detained many distinguished guests proceeding to the party passed us, several of whom very kindly offered to lend us help. But as we expected to be on our way very soon again, we thankfully declined their kind offers. But tyre troubles is [sic] the weak point of motoring and our penalty this afternoon was being three-fourths of an hour too late for the Royal party. The day opened fine, but in the course of the forenoon dark clouds rolled up ominously, suggestive of a thunderstorm. Happily, however, the clouds dispersed and delightful sunshine followed. The sun's rays were considerably modified by a cold north wind which blew out the Royal Standard from its flagstaff on the Round Tower and made the crowd crawl from the shade of the trees into the sunshine. With such ideal weather conditions it was no wonder that there was a large attendance at the party, and that the guests numbered between eight and nine thousand. Long in advance a crowd of expectant watchers was gathered outside the palace. It swarmed around all the approaches peering eagerly into every carriage as each came rolling up. The guard of honour on duty at the entrance gave the necessary military touch to the approaches of the Castle.

As we approached the Castle throngs of people who were collected on either side of the road made different surmises regarding me and my son. Some exclaimed: "Here goes an Indian Princess and her kinsman," some called us great people from Armenia. We heard many other witticisms of the kind familiar to the London Street Arab, which amused us a good deal.

Our late arrival due to the motor accident caused me no little trepidation as to our reception. But fortunately everything passed off smoothly. On reaching the entrance and showing our cards, a dignified looking officer helped me to alight from the car, and escorted us a short distance to the main part of the gathering. The delay in our arrival had, it seems, caused some dislocation in the programme, and Sir William Curzon Wyllie and the other officials responsible for the management were casting anxious glances in the direction of the entrance for our arrival. They were, however, too well-bred to let it appear either by word or sign. As soon as we had come up, and before we had time to tender apologies for the delay, we were hurried straight to the Royal tents across the great Lawn. The scene that unfolded itself when we had time to look about us was very grand and imposing. All the elite of London were there, making a great display of dress and jewellery, and the scene was one that baffles description.

Long before our arrival, the King and Queen, and members of the Royal Family had arrived on the Lawn, where they remained for nearly two hours. At the end of this time, at about seven o'clock, the Royal Party withdrew to the East Terrace, where they remained viewing the splendid scene for some time before proceeding to the Castle. The King wore a blue frock-coat and white top-hat and had a red tie and a flower in the button-hole. The Queen was wearing a costume in her favourite shade of mauve with a toque to match adorned with flowers of the same shade. The dress was of pale orchid *ninon-de-soie* charmingly embroidered. The bodice was finished with white tulle and in the light neck-ruffle gleamed beautiful pearls and diamonds.

We had been too late to witness the arrival of the King and Queen, who entered the Gardens from the Castle and found most of the guests assembled. Immediately on our arrival, we were escorted to the Queen, who was in her spacious pavilion. She received us very kindly and looked sweet and smiling in her exquisite dress resplendent with jewellery. On being presented, she shook hands with me and my son and conversed with us with great interest for some time. She told me that she very much admired my handwork and wondered at my zeal in working at such an advanced age, and when she learnt that it was always a pleasure to me to do needlework of every sort, in spite of the infirmities of old age, she was both surprised and pleased, and highly complimented me. She also gave me credit for undertaking such a long and tedious journey at my age. I suitably thanked Her Majesty for her kindness.

The most interesting part of the conversation was with reference to the cap. Her Majesty thanked me for having presented her with a beautiful cap and band and dress front. As in duty bound, I expressed my gratitude for her graciousness in accepting the same. My son had carried with him a box of flowers to be offered to Their Majesties. A magnificent garland of roses of the hue the Queen most likes was now put round the neck, and a bouquet of flowers presented to her. As I did this, I expressed my heartfelt wishes for the Queen's long life and prosperity and pronounced benedictions in the true Parsee fashion. With this the interview came to an end.

We were then led by Lady Curzon Wyllie to the shamiana, where refreshments were beautifully laid out. Lady Wyllie gave us tea with her own hands and was exceedingly kind to us. In the refreshment tent we were introduced to a number of distinguished personages, whose names my failing memory refuses to recall to my mind. From the shamiana we walked on to the Lawn, which was studded with Princes, Dukes, Chiefs, Marquises and other distinguished personages. Now and then as I passed along, some of them would very kindly introduce themselves to me. As we proceeded along the Lawn, His Majesty the King was seen coming towards us. As soon as he came near, I and my son were duly presented to His Majesty, who graciously shook hands with us. He looked in splendid health, and put on a smiling face all the time he conversed with us. We remained talking for about a quarter of an hour, during which I remarked that I had had the privilege of meeting him in Bombay in 1875 when he visited India. He looked pleased, and observed that it was many years ago, when he was quite a young man. I further assured him that we Parsees were happy under his benign rule, at which he expressed satisfaction. He also gave me great credit for courage and energy in undertaking a voyage round the world at my time of life. I bowed my thanks asked permission to present him the bouquet and garland of roses, to which he graciously consented. A benediction similar to that in the case of the Queen was pronounced by me, and His Majesty went on his way leaving us charmed with his affability.

We spent some time in mixing with the guests admiring the dispositions made for the afternoon. The gathering was a very large and brilliant one and thoroughly representative of English society.

Not only were all the best known people of rank and fashion present, but the most eminent representatives of literature, art, the drama and the church were there. India was well represented by several Princes and Chiefs, some of whom were accompanied by their ladies. No small part of the interest and spectacular effect was due to the Indian and Japanese princes in their gold turbans and coats of many colours. Their picturesque embroidered dresses with the beautiful sarees of their ladies wrought in gold and silver enhanced the general effect. The diplomatic circle was represented by Ambassadors, Ministers and staffs of the Embassies and Legations. Particularly noticeable were the King's Indian Orderlies in their fine uniforms.

We stayed at Windsor for more than two hours talking to friends and meeting different people. Amongst those whom we met were well-known Bombay friends. We saw Sir Raymond West and Lady West, Sir John and Lady Jardine and many others. Their Highnesses the Nawab Saheb and Begum Saheb of Janjira were also there, the latter in a most bewitching Oriental costume. They were on their European tour and were spending the season in London.

During the time that we remained at the party we received more than one kind message from the Queen enquiring how we were enjoying ourselves. These are amongst the traits of kindness that endear Queen Alexandra to her subjects.

We came away from the Royal Party well pleased with our reception and filled with joy and pleasure at all that we had seen, and the great kindness that we had experienced. An additional honour awaited us. Our motor having been disabled we were very courteously offered a royal carriage to go to the Windsor station. Thus was seen the curious spectacle of an octogenarian Parsee Lady and her son driving in an equipage having the royal red colour and bearing the Royal crests much to the surprise of the lookers-on.

The London press in describing the garden party made a very touching mention of my presentation and of the trifles that Their Majesties were pleased to accept from me.

L

My Return to India

As my departure from England was drawing near, many of my old and respected friends asked me and my sons to tea or At Home parties. Amongst such friends may be particularly mentioned Sir George Birdwood, who has such a high regard for the Parsee community that he has not forgotten us although it is a long time since he returned from India. He was staying at Ealing and for the pleasure of meeting Lady Birdwood and other members of the family I at once availed myself of the opportunity of going to their place though it was far away from mine. How glad he was to see us at his residence! He expressed his feelings in writing to me, and about a week before I left London he came to bid me adieu and showered all manner of good wishes for my future happiness on me and mine. It was indeed a happy meeting for both of us, as he is also on the verge of seventy-seven. On my return from Ealing I got another interesting invitation from Sir John and Lady Jardine to meet them at St Stephen's Hall, Westminster. Sir John Jardine was once a very popular Judge of the Bombay High Court and Lady Jardine, too, was a popular personage, taking a keen interest in the cause of Indian Women. It was really a happy meeting and a pleasant evening was passed in their company reminding each other of all the reminiscences of the past.

Another noteworthy incident about this time was the birthday of my worthy old friend, Mr D. P. Cama. As a true Zoroastrian he charitably distributed a substantial sum amongst the poorer classes every year. Although he had been living in this city for the last forty or fifty years, he had not forgotten the old traits of Parseeism. It is gratifying to see a member of my community giving money in charities without distinction of caste or creed. As I was near his house, which was at St Mark's Road, five minutes' walk from my place, he and his wife were always glad to have our company and Mrs Cama was indeed very kind to me and became my companion on the many occasions, when I visited different shops and also the Exhibition during the last weeks of my stay in London.

During the last few days of my stay almost all my Parsee friends as well as many of my old and new English acquaintances came to bid me goodbye. Sir Owen Burne too came down from his country seat and paid his last and memorable visit only two days before my departure. I call this a last visit because soon after my return to Bombay he died after a short illness. Sir Curzon Wyllie and Lord Ripon too died soon after I left. As I found my motor very handy and cheap in the end, I kept it till the last days of my stay in London and as I had resolved to take it to Bombay I packed it and despatched it to Bombay by a tramp boat going direct to Bombay through Messrs Thomas Cook & Son. Looking to the price I paid for it, the freight I had to give was very high, but one consolation I had was that it arrived safely at the exact time when I arrived in Bombay. As the commission was entrusted to Messrs Thomas Cook & Son, we had every facility as to the payment of freight, duty and clearing from the dock on delivery. As it was undoubtedly a luxury to drive in a motor in the city of London and its environments, I felt its absence much for a week or so. Then once more the old tramp with horse and carriage was renewed.

The Royal Party brought our stay in London to an end, and as the monsoon season was at its height in the Indian Ocean, we arranged to sail direct by sea instead of taking an overland route, but for more than a fortnight we could not get passages, as no cabins were available and it looked as if we should have to postpone our departure when Sir Owen Burne came to our rescue. As a Director of the P&O Company he had much influence and a word from him caused all difficulties to vanish and at last we succeeded in securing our passage by an Australian mail boat, S.S. *Victoria*, sailing on 31st July from Tilbury Dock, London, transferring at Aden on S.S. *Caledonia* for Bombay. As we had to sail from Tilbury Dock we had to despatch all our heavy baggage at least forty-eight hours before the sailing of the vessel, excepting the light baggage which we were allowed to take along with us. The arrangement was so efficient that not one article was missed or misplaced notwithstanding such heavy passenger traffic. One is cautioned to label and number each and every package or bundle or article, with one's name and destination, so that nothing could be miscarried or misplaced in the voyage. As for collection and shipment of baggage one has to intimate to the Company seventy-two hours before the sailing and the London Parcels Delivery Company send their cart and men to collect the baggage and convey it to be shipped on board, saving all the trouble of dragging one's luggage along with oneself.

Hearing of my returning to India, the Editor of the *Indian Magazine and Review*, Miss A. A. Smith, came to see me and had a long interview with me. She was indeed a very amiable and courteous lady of high culture and a pattern of a gentle English lady. Towards the end of my stay I had a great many calls on my time and foremost was the one to bid adieu to my dearest friend, Mrs Ahlers, who was ill at the time. I had to go to Godalming, at her fine and healthy residence called Holy Bank. It was indeed a most touching and heartfelt separation from her and her grown-up daughter and son.

The temptations to stay in London never abated, and on the evening of my last day I attended an At Home at Mrs Smith's where I saw a popular social gathering, Indian friends mixing freely with English people. Here everyone was surprised to hear that I was to leave London the next morning. We were there till late, enjoying ourselves very heartily. It has been highly gratifying to me to observe the *entente cordiale* that exists between the different Indian communities.

It was a happy morning on 31st July when we got ready to start for the last stage of my tour. There came my worthy old friend, Mr D. P. Cama and others with bouquets of flowers, and with their best wishes for a *bon voyage* we left our so-called home at Cambridge Gardens and went to the Liverpool Street Station to go to Tilbury Dock. Here again

I saw Mrs D. P. Cama with her friends and some Parsee friends of mine who came with flowers and garlands to see me off. When I left England, once again I carried with me the most pleasant remembrances of all the kindness and hospitality extended to me and my sons not only by our old friends but also by a great many of those who did not previously know us.

When we were on board the S.S. *Victoria*, we saw Mr Courtney of the London office, who left a good word for us with the ship's officers. The P&O officials, from Capt. Haddock to the Purser, I am happy to say, were kind to us and placed us in spacious cabins and treated us with great distinction on the voyage. We saw a very lively company of young and elderly passengers around us. After two o'clock our boat steamed up for our homeward voyage.

We settled down comfortably in our temporary sea-home and had a very pleasant voyage to Gibraltar, where we arrived on 4th August: the night before there was a grand concert held by the passengers. Here a great number of passengers left us, as many of them were students from different universities going to enjoy their holidays. From here, after a halt of about six hours, we proceeded towards Marseilles and arrived there after two days' voyage. Here our boat anchored for the night, as we had to pick up the passengers coming overland from London.

During our short stay of about thirty hours alongside the jetties of the dock, we engaged a car and went to the town which impresses one as a large commercial port and a magnificent city of the French Republic. It is a town full of statues and monuments and public gardens. The city is well served by electric trams running from one end to the other and its grand restaurants and other public offices and edifices give an imposing idea. The panoramic view of Marseilles from the great altitude of the sanctuary of Notre Dame de la Garde makes upon a stranger a vivid impression of this magnificent city. It has a population of more than 500,000. To enable persons to reach the height of the Cathedral Notre Dame there are lifts constructed on the principle of rope tramcars ascending the hill, and it is called Ascenseurs de Notre Dame de la Garde. We very much enjoyed our stay in the company of many other passengers.

Next morning passengers from London arrived and after their

embarkation we lifted up the anchor at about eleven o'clock and sailed towards Port Said, where we arrived on 12th August. Here we stayed for the night as we had to pick up the English mail coming from Brindisi. I have given a brief account of this port in the preceding pages, but since then many changes have taken place. Huge public buildings and Government offices as well as electric trams are laid out all over the town since I saw it last.

After the arrival of the English mail we moved further and entered the celebrated Suez Canal where the speed of the engine was slackened and we were moving in some part of the Canal at a walking pace. It took more than thirty hours to pass through the Canal, and after calling at Suez, where we did not stop as we used to do before, we steered towards Aden, where we arrived on the morning of 16th August. When we anchored, there was an uproar attending the bustling scene of transferring the mail bags and passengers' baggage on the Bombay boat waiting close by, as nearly half the number of passengers were going to India and the others to remain on the same boat proceeding to China and Australia.

As I was on the point of taking leave of the passengers who were separating from us, I was not a little surprised to see our good-natured Mr Kaikobad, second son of my late worthy neighbour of Bombay, Mr Cowasji Dinshaw, coming with his steam boat to escort us ashore. When I reached the shore the present senior member of the family, Mr Hormusji, with his good-natured wife and all the other members of the family and the whole of their staff, gave us a hearty welcome, and we were delighted to meet each other once again in their spacious mansion. Thousands of passengers who have passed and repassed to and from Aden know the name of the enterprising princely, commercial firm of Messrs Cowasji Dinshaw & Brothers. They are the first and foremost in welcoming all the Royalties and Viceroys and Governors before they set their foot on the shores of India and the other Colonies of the East. I trust it is not presumptuous on my part to say that the name and the enterprising spirit of the members of my community occupy a front rank among the merchants of the East. Who will say that it was not a happy omen, meeting with such pomp and grandeur at the end of my tour round the world?

The children of my good old neighbours had the same kind regard and love for me as before. Here in the midst of their company I and my sons passed half a day during which we did justice to a sumptuous Parsee dinner in the good old Parsee fashion. A friendly reception was not the word for it. I should say they accorded us a royal reception at the close of my tour. We took leave of our host and hostess and their children, and were escorted to the pier and in the company of Mr Kaikobad we went on board the S.S. *Caledonia* where without any difficulty we saw all our effects brought from the S.S. *Victoria* and arranged in our cabins.

As the passengers were now reduced to half the number, we found the ship like an empty boat. It was no doubt a grand and comfortable boat. Amidst the good wishes of our friends we steered to the East in the most delightful weather. Although we were crossing the Indian Ocean in the midst of the monsoon we escaped the rough weather, and in the company of jovial passengers days passed like hours. On the morning of 21st August we descried Bombay, and after an hour we entered the beautiful harbour of the East and landed on the shores of Bombay, hale and hearty after an absence of nearly fifteen months, and joined our friends and relatives with great rejoicing. We drove straight up to our old residence at Tardeo.

On entering my premises I was surprised to find a number of buildings erected on the vacant ground and as the surrounding place was reclaimed I found my quarters which I had retained during my absence unfit for habitation. I at once found a new house and shifted all my furniture, etc., and settled down at Chowpatty. On my return to Bombay I at once offered prayers to Almighty God and attended all the Fire-temples for returning home safe and sound: "All's well that ends well."

I found all my near relations and friends in perfect health and happiness. But within a fortnight after my arrival I had to deplore the loss of a great grandson of mine: he was such a favourite child in my family that I do not think I will ever forget the loss. Although he was only eight years old he looked like a boy of twelve or thirteen, and in appearance and intelligence he was more like an English boy. He was a pet of the family. His death plunged the whole family into deep mourning. What I felt most was that he died in Poona on our Parsee New Year's Day. What man proposes God disposes, was brought home to us with great force. Everything looked sad and gloomy after this bereavement. Instead of being lively and merry with my friends and near relatives on my return, I was plunged into grief unexpectedly. All were very anxious to hear about my travels and presentation, and they were all disappointed when, instead of listening to an account of our travels, they had to perform the disagreeable duty of condoling with us.

LI

Events After My Tour Round the World

Even before I came back to my dear Motherland, the popular Governor of Bombay, His Excellency Sir George Clarke, and his noble wife and daughter had already won a high place in the affections of the people of the Bombay Presidency. I was very sad, therefore, when I heard of the untimely passing away of Lady Clarke, amid the universal mourning of the entire Province in which her active sympathy had endeared her to all classes of His Majesty's subjects.

A few months after the lamentable event when Miss Clarke was once more in Bombay, I wrote to her expressing a desire to call on her. I received a reply intimating that Miss Clarke would be very glad to see me. I was pleased to receive her message, and called on her with my younger son at Government House. She gave us a cordial reception and impressed me as a highly accomplished and well-informed young lady, and a most sympathetic talker. Miss Clarke told me that she had already heard and read interesting accounts of my work, referring especially to the appreciation published by the *Indian Magazine and Review* of August 1908 during my last stay in London. She was also good enough to invite me to come and have tea with her the following day at the Princess Ladies' Gymkhana. I expressed my gratitude for her kind thought in inviting me, but had at the same time to regret my inability to meet her wishes, as owing to my weak health I could not feel equal to the task of attending social gatherings. She even offered to get me out of my carriage on a chair to help me in going into the Gymkhana, for which manifestation of sympathy I felt sincerely thankful. Unfortunately, however, my health did not permit of my attending the function.

Hardly had ten weeks elapsed since my interview when the sudden demise of Miss Clarke cast even a deeper gloom than the death of her mother, for she had been spared to us for a longer time than Lady Clarke, during which she had lived and worked amongst us in a manner which may well be followed by other ladies placed in similar positions offering so much power and opportunity for the discharge of little acts of kindness and of sympathy. It is a matter of great satisfaction that God had healed the wounds of our universally respected Governor in His own divine way, and the present Lady Clarke is already establishing herself in the hearts of the people amongst whom she has chosen to cast her social lot. But the saddest event which it is my solemn duty to record in these humble pages is the demise of our late revered Sovereign, King-Emperor Edward VII, universally loved and mourned by millions and millions of men and women inhabiting His Majesty's glorious worldwide Empire.

It was only a few months before his unspeakably sorrowful loss that I had the unique honour, privilege and pleasure of being presented to our gracious Sovereign and his noble Consort, to whom the hearts of countless loyal subjects go forth in spontaneous sympathy. Immediately on learning the sad intelligence of the sudden passing away of our great and good monarch, I cabled to London the following message of condolence to Her Majesty:

> From Mrs Dosebai Cowasjee Jessawalla, Cumballa Hill, Bombay,
> To the Private Secretary to Her Majesty Queen Alexandra, London.
>
> Loyal heartfelt condolence from octogenarian Parsee Lady graciously received at Windsor in 1908. Bewail my lot to bemourn loss of Sovereign.

My humble expression of loyal sympathy on the mournful occasion was acknowledged in the following official reply:

No. 3844.

From H. G. Stokes, Esq., Deputy Secretary to the Government of India,
To Mrs Dosebai Cowasjee Jessawalla, Cumballa Hill, Bombay.

SIMLA, 7th July 1910.

Home Department (Public)

Madam,

I am directed to inform you that the Government of India have received intimation of the receipt of your telegram to the Secretary of State and to express the sincere thanks of the Government of India for the expressions of sympathy and condolence which you have been good enough to convey upon the occasion of the lamented death of His late Majesty the King Emperor of India.

I have the honour to be,
Madam,
Your Most Obedient Servant,
(Sd.) H. G. STOKES,
Deputy Secretary to the Government of India.

It only remains for me to note another regretful event in the recent passing away in England of my worthy friend, Mr Dorabjee Pestonjee Cama, to whose sympathetic regard for me and public-spirited appreciation of my social services to my community, these pages have borne grateful testimony, as well as to his truly Catholic charities, so characteristic of the Parsee type that is unfortunately now passing away. May God enable my dear friend, Mrs Cama, to bear the loss, which hundreds of admirers of her respected husband earnestly share with her, and may the soul of so good, so quiet, and so worthy a Parsee representative rest in divine peace!

LII

Closing Reflections

Here I conclude the story of my life, leaving the indulgent reader to judge for himself or herself what has been accomplished during the half-century and over that I have engaged myself in the field of women's education and of social progress. To enable the generation of the present day to realise the condition that was prevalent at the time I entered that noble arena amidst the vortex of controversy and opposition, I give the following extract from the issue of an old Indian journal, *The Bombay Courier,* dated 19th August 1842:

"*The United Service Gazette* of Tuesday stated that a young Parsee lady has been placed as a pupil in Mrs Ward's seminary, but that the Editor was unable, owing to the lateness of the hour at which the intelligence reached him, to state the father's name; and adds with great truth: 'The *Courier* will rejoice at it when he knows it.' We assure our contemporary that we do sincerely and unaffectedly rejoice at it. We consider the man, whose mind is sufficiently enlarged to admit of his taking the initiative in breaking down the prejudices of country and of caste, in so good a cause, not only deserving of our humble applause, but of the approbation which he is sure to obtain of the whole civilised world.

There was a time, a period of European History when a premium was offered to ignorance—when reading and writing were left to clerks and considered badges of vulgarity by the Sovereign and his Feudal Chiefs—when the proud peers would only make their marks, or impress their signature with a stamp. But this was in the time of barbarians, when the human intellect lay fettered—when bodily strength and dexterity in the use of arms constituted almost the sole pretentions of a gentleman. Happily, knowledge superseded ignorance and a brighter day has dawned on the intellectual horizon. *Ex Oriente lux*. In the East arose the sun of human enlightenment, it travelled Westward, and confers that power which consists in knowledge. We of the West are bound, therefore, and feel the obligation to return to its Eastern source, as far as lies in our power, the blessings of enlightenment. The dissemination of knowledge over the whole earth is a paramount object with the philanthropist of every clime.

The Parsees, of all the inhabitants of this portion of the globe, ought peculiarly to appreciate and prize the cultivation of the mental faculties, for to their education is to be attributed in a great degree, if not altogether, their wealth, their liberality, and their acknowledged influence. They know this and they prove their knowledge by the pains they take, and the expenses they incur, in the education of their male children. Why they have so long neglected their female offspring, can only be accounted for by their blind subserviency to the usage they found established in a country which afforded them protection. The fear of ridicule, the censure of the common herd, the dislike to innovation have deterred many of even the masterminds of our own country from departing from the established usages of their fatherland, and it required the exercise of the most transcendent moral courage to break the bonds of prejudice and senseless reverence for time-hallowed and established usage.

In considering the sacrifice which this Parsee gentleman has made of early prejudice, we do not regard it as an occurrence of ephemeral interest, but as a type and forerunner of superior intellectual advancement amongst the class to which he belongs; and we hail it as a happy omen of what may be accomplished even in our own day.

It will not be disputed that the happiness of life principally depends upon the enjoyments of our home—that the enjoyments of home principally depend upon that sex, in this country hitherto debased and degraded by the profoundest ignorance—that a woman's powers of pleasing mainly depend upon her capabilities to participate in feeling and in objects common to both her husband and herself—that man of education can have but little community of sentiment with women whose knowledge is confined to the acquirements fitting them merely for the household drudgery of superior domestic slaves. The experience of the world teaches us, that from such an ill-assorted association, nothing but disgust must eventually ensue and mutual estrangement is too commonly the result.

This in Eastern nations evinces itself, in a toleration of plurality of wives, and concubinage. When the freshness of youth and beauty have faded, the woman has lost the only charm that once attracted, and in the absence of the beauties of the mind, she has no resource but to conform to her lot, and become in her husband's house the principal domestic. From such a fate, from such a degradation, from such a prostitution of the ends and objects of marriage the liberal minded Parsee bids fair to rescue his child. We heartily wish him life and health, to reap the reward of his devotion to his daughter's true interests. This is a theme so grateful to us to descant upon, that we could write upon it by the mile as Coroner Wakeley writes verses, but until the name of the Parsee reaches us, with a confirmation of the fact, we think it would be premature to say more, than that we fully expect his name will be handed down to posterity, as a benefactor of the human race, on the same page with that of Sir Jamsetjee Jeejeebhoy—different traits of the same liberality of sentiment, and nobility of mind, are exhibited in the conduct of both—they are a step in advance of the age they live in—and will be proudly recorded in the living page of England's History."

The *Courier*, however, has erred in one respect which it is most essential to rectify. It mentions that I was educated by my father. This is a mistake, as at the time I was being educated, my father was not living but had died four years previously. Thus the mother alone was my sole guardian, and as such evinced great care and solicitude in looking after me. It was a very courageous step that she took in placing me in Mrs Ward's Seminary at the tender age of ten. In this wise the plaudits belong to my late revered mother Bai Meheribai only, and in justice to her memory I have rectified that error of the *Courier* even at such a remote date as seventy years after the event.

In the evening of my life it is gratifying to notice that Mr M. M. Murzban, Bar-at-Law, a Parsee author of remarkable ability, who is translating Mademoiselle Menant's French work *Les Parsis* into English, points out that at page 339 of that history, Miss Menant in a footnote observes as follows: "It is but fair to note here the efforts of Mrs C. J. Jessawalla (Bai Dosebai, wife of Cowasjee Jehangir Jessawalla), actively co-operated in the work of Manekjee Cursetjee, on behalf of English education for Parsi girls."

I have emphatically to contradict the statement of Miss Menant inasmuch as I had never had anything to do with Mr Manekjee or any member of his family. I have always held my own course irrespective of any of them.

On this point I should like to refer my readers to the correspondence which was published on the subject in the *Bombay Gazette* as far back as 1887 soon after the death of Mr Manekjee Cursetjee, wherein the correspondent said that no small credit was due to Bai Meheribai for championing the cause of women's education. He has referred in detail to the difficulties she encountered at the hands of her co-religionists. The correspondent in good faith pointed out that Mr Manekjee was not the gentleman who took the lead, but the germ was first laid into the soil by the hand of a woman (Bai Meheribai) who had the courage and foresight to take the initiative. The writer who supports the cause of Manekjee candidly admits that he (Mr Manekjee) had at a considerably subsequent period engaged the services of a governess but did not send his daughters to the school conducted in those days by ladies like Mrs Ward.

I have no desire to enter into discussion on this point as it is too well-known to the public, especially those of the old generation, as to who the originator of this movement was. But since people ignorant of the actual state of things have come forward authoritatively to throw into obscurity the claim of my revered mother, I have thought fit as a loyal and dutiful daughter to stand on her side and place the historical facts publicly on record. The perusal of this humble work will convince my readers how matters stood in the early days with regard to women's education. Just a week before I started on my tour round the world, a short sketch of my life was published in *The Times of India* in May 1907 and several well-known, leading Gujarati papers. These accounts were also published in several leading papers of London, and none has dared to refute one iota of those long and truthful accounts. I have to thank Mr Murzban for inserting the whole of the article in *The Times of India*, in his translation. It clearly indicates that Miss Menant was probably misinformed or else the note under discussion would not have appeared.

Thus comes to an end the story of my humble yet eventful life. In spite of the various difficulties that intervened, I have at last been able to place it before the world; and it only remains for me to thank the Almighty God for having spared me to see the desire of my life accomplished, and to express a confident hope that the coming generations of women in my beloved Motherland will emulate whatever of good and noble and beautiful they may gather in these pages.

In Memoriam

The work, containing the autobiography of our dearly beloved mother, was almost entirely set in type when she was called away from this life on 11th January 1911. His Will be done. It only behoves us to declare that the eloquent testimony which the Press has universally borne, both in the East and the West, to the pioneer movements which distinguished her eventful career, has even deepened our moral conviction regarding the public value of her "story of progress and reform—of the victory of self-sacrificing courage over narrow-minded opposition—of the march of advancement in the face of obloquy—of the final triumph of that which is noble and virtuous and beautiful in human life."

We, therefore, publish this book in obedience to the solemn filial duty which we owe to her, whose physical presence is not more amongst us, but who still lives in the ideals she had entertained and sought to visualise throughout the years her protection and guidance was ceaselessly offered to us. We hope, as she did, that the coming generations of women in our great Motherland will emulate "whatever of good and noble and beautiful they may gather in these pages."

When the history of India comes to be written in future times, it will bear witness that she owed her progress in the nineteenth and twentieth centuries, not only to her gifted sons, but also to her heroic daughters.

Dadabhoy Cowasjee Jessawalla
Jamsetjee Cowasjee Jessawalla

Cumballa Hill, Bombay.